AF256371

StartupBench

Beginning the Journey into Entrepreneurship

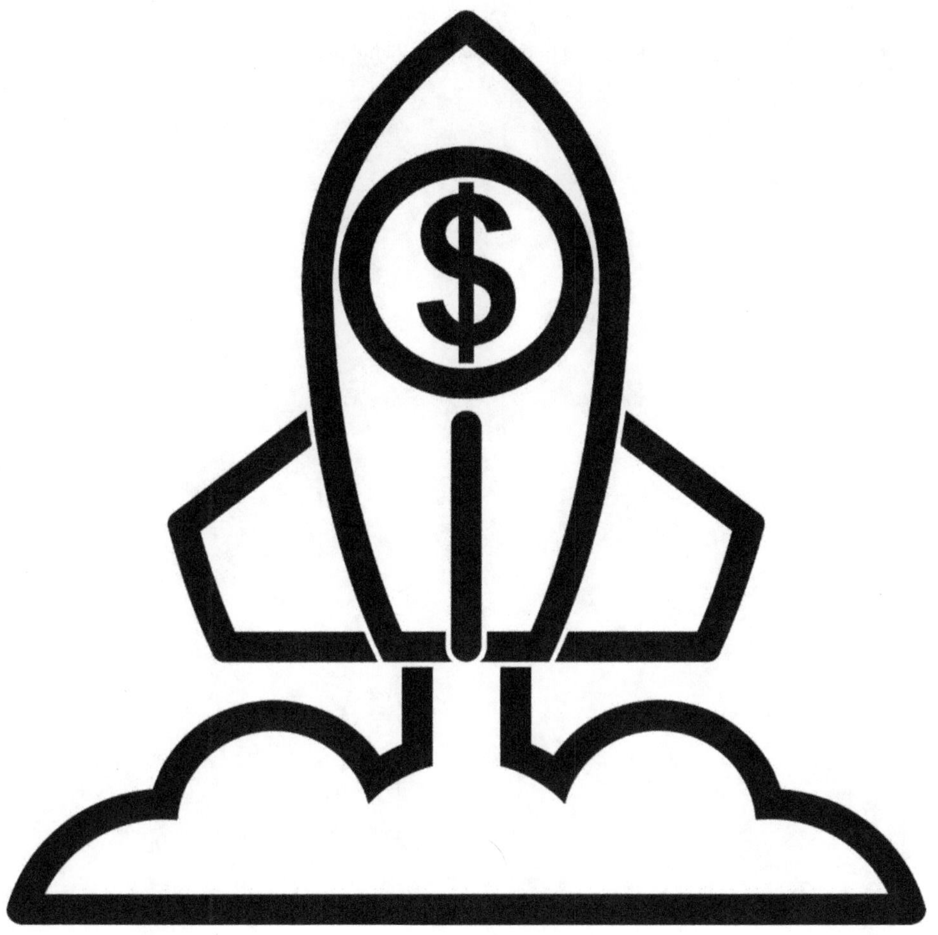

Phillip Selleh

CBA Press
6440 Sky Pointe Dr #140-550
Las Vegas, Nevada 89131

CBA Press
6440 Sky Pointe Dr #140-550
Las Vegas, Nevada 89131
www.cbapress.com

StartupBench: Beginning the Journey into Entrepreneurship / Phillip Selleh. — 1st ed.
ISBN-13: 978-1-7338309-6-6

Dedication

This book is dedicated to the many service members I met at Walter Reed, who wanted to start their own businesses after giving their lives for this country by serving in the military—without them, I would never have found the inspiration to write this book. I thank retired Lieutenant General David Fridovich, who provided me with leadership, guidance, and inspiration throughout challenging times in my military career, and who also provided me with valuable advice and mentorship in aiding the disabled veteran community. I thank Dr. Rory Cooper, the founding director and VA Senior Research Career Scientist of the Human Engineering Laboratories, as he inspired me to apply my skills and abilities to assist the veteran community by helping them achieve their life dreams. I also acknowledge my family and friends, who supported me during my injuries, hospitalization, and time away serving the military.

May this book help anyone beginning their journey into entrepreneurship.

Table of Contents

Introduction

Starting a successful business is a viable option for *anyone* with the ambition, motivation, and diligence to take educated and well-planned steps into entrepreneurship. Starting a business can be an incredibly powerful and rewarding experience. In fact, becoming an entrepreneur is a common aspiration, and this feat has already been accomplished and proven possible by many people like you. Whether you have a fantastic business concept or are hoping to become your own boss, know that with the right tools you *can* achieve this dream.

Unlike a typical job, which limits your creative freedom, potential promotions, and maximum pay, owning a business opens up a world of purpose and new opportunities. For example, you could run a lucrative business that becomes a lasting and well-known brand. You could opt into a franchising opportunity and thereby free more time for your family and loved ones. You could even start a company that becomes the next Apple, resulting in a wealthy, comfortable, and enviable lifestyle.

Be prepared, starting a business can also be challenging. Nothing worth having comes easy, and starting a business is no exception. At times, obstacles such as losing a steady paycheck or finding start-up capital can seem insurmountable, especially to aspiring entrepreneurs who are starting their businesses for the first time. Every individual seeking business ownership must appropriately prepare for these challenges, as they can halt even the most experienced entrepreneurs if overlooked. Let us explore three examples of individuals who succumbed to major hurdles faced by most entrepreneurs:

***

Example #1: Jenny

Jenny is a corporate attorney, but she has always dreamed of starting her own practice. She likes the idea of controlling her own hours, growing her own company, and possibly even trading a regular paycheck for much bigger returns. As she thinks about starting her own practice, she becomes excited by the possibility of growing her career.

However, when Jenny begins to explore specific details of starting her own practice, she realizes she would be facing stiff competition. There are dozens of practices in her city, Atlanta, and many of these existing practices specialize in copyright law. The more Jenny examines the competition, the more anxious and doubtful she becomes about her abilities to start a successful practice. She starts to convince herself that if there are already dozens of practices in her area, she will not be able to find clients in the first few years of starting her business. She imagines terrifying scenarios in which she makes no money, the practice fails, and she is forced to move back into her parents' house.

As a result of all her doubts, Jenny decides to postpone her dreams of starting her own practice. She figures she can put her dreams "on the back burner" until she moves to a new city where there is less competition for copyright law.

***

Example #2: Charlie

Charlie has always worked in the restaurant business as a waiter; however, he dreams of the day when he can start his own restaurant and become a business owner. After Charlie inherits a modest amount of money from a relative, he decides to venture into the franchising business. He researches local franchises and decides to open a Subway sandwich shop in a main plaza near where he previously worked.

Right away, Charlie realizes he does not have sufficient capital to keep his franchise running. There are bills to pay, employees to hire, and stock to keep. In addition to these challenges, Charlie realizes he has not mentally or emotionally prepared himself for the responsibilities of being a business owner. He finds it hard to make important decisions, and he realizes the stress of running his own business is causing his home life to suffer. He finds himself longing for the days when he waited tables and did not have to worry about having enough money to pay for bills, inventory, and employees.

***

Example #3: Shannon

Shannon has always been interested in working with the government, and she has been especially focused on initiating and maintaining social programs within her neighborhood. When she receives a government grant to help launch a new antipoverty initiative in a nearby city, she is delighted to be brought on board.

Though Shannon has always considered herself to be a dedicated employee, she finds it difficult to transfer her nine-to-five experience to the world of government contracting. She finds that much of her work needs to be self-driven, rather than directed by a manager. In addition to this change, Shannon finds there are many intangible problems that she did not mentally or emotionally prepare herself for. Her lack of a government phone number or email address inhibits her ability to complete her work. She is also frustrated that, now, as a civil servant, she does the same job as she did previously, but she is held to a higher degree of responsibility and standards.

Shannon becomes so frustrated by the unexpected challenges of becoming a government contractor that she returns to her previous corporate job after only one year of government work.

***

Owning a successful business can lead to greater wealth and life satisfaction, and requires hard work, patience, and an ability to deal with stress in a healthy and productive manner. Allow the three examples above to demonstrate that starting a business also requires a great deal of physical, mental, and emotional preparation and planning. The individuals in the previous examples missed their entrepreneurial dreams because they were not fully prepared for many of the challenges that come closely associated with starting a business.

Jenny did not properly research her competition to determine whether or not the market was large enough for another practice that specialized in copyright law. Instead, she let her intimidation get the best of her, causing her to potentially miss out on a lucrative customer base that needed another practice.

Charlie did not mentally or emotionally prepare for the toils of becoming a franchise owner. He was not prepared for the stresses and decisions involved in managing employees, nor was he ready to invest necessary time in his business. Additionally, Charlie did not have enough capital to support his franchise through the difficult first few years.

Shannon was not fully prepared for the mental and emotional frustrations of becoming a government contractor. She was not prepared for the amount of time she would have to devote to her new role, or for how she would always be on call, unlike a civil employee. By continuing to compare herself to other employees—rather than comparing herself to other contractors—she became dissatisfied with her experience.

As you begin your journey into self-employment, we want to provide you with a solid understanding of what potential challenges you might face, and what the tools and techniques you can use to overcome them.

Throughout the contents of this book, we will also encounter the stories of 8 service-disabled veteran entrepreneurs who have succeeded in their start-up businesses. These men and women successfully applied the concepts contained in the following chapters to their own business ventures, which span a variety of industries, products, and services. In this book, you'll find the wisdom and experiences of Victoria Buggs, Joshua Earsley, Desma Brooks, Jonathan Mart, Justin Charnell, Jeanette Dempsey, Raul Lopez, and Anita

Williams. We'll also hear from experts in the field: William Elmore, Joseph Molina, Michelle Keshel, and Jody Friend.

When you have prepared yourself for any obstacles you might face while starting your business, you can take a proactive stance in protecting your business and guaranteeing its prosperity. By understanding your potential challenges, you can minimize any risks to your business's development and instead allow it to thrive.

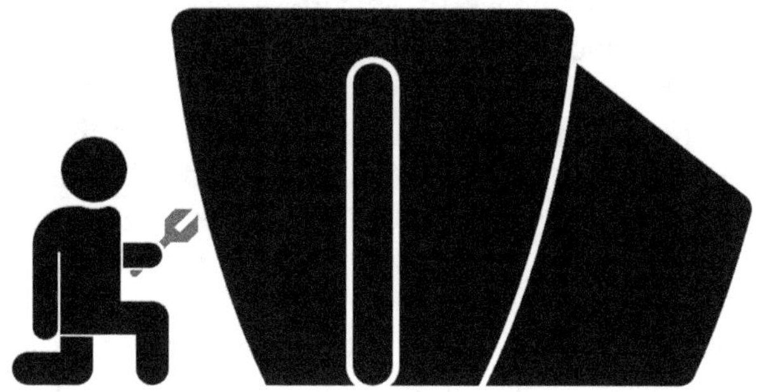

In this book, you can expect to learn the tools and techniques that will help you proactively protect your business. From identifying opportunities to conducting market research and protecting your business with legal representation, you will learn some of the most critical elements of starting a successful business. Each chapter will be filled with relevant information and necessary steps for setting the foundation of a successful start-up. You will learn the following:

- ✔ Why entrepreneurship can take many forms.

- ✔ Why industry research is one of the first steps you should take—and how to conduct it.

- ✔ How to identify your products and services.

- ✔ How to find the consumer markets that need your products and services.

- ✔ How to find the best legal structure for your business.

- ✔ Why risk and business insurance are critical to your start-up.

- ✔ How to find the best lawyers and accountants to protect your business.

- ✔ How to manage the finances of your business.

- ✔ How to secure capital and take out well-researched, informed business loans.

- ✔ How to implement basic human resources within your business.

Finally, all these lessons will culminate in a step-by-step guide for creating your own formal business plan, a key asset to any start-up business. In the final chapter, you will learn the following:

✔ How to create a business plan, including the business concept, marketplace evaluation, and details of your financials for potential investors.

This book aims to teach entrepreneurs the most common steps and challenges associated with starting a business. While not all chapters or techniques will be relevant to every reader, focus on the steps that can be utilized within your own entrepreneurial experience. Now that we have outlined what you can expect from this book, let us examine the three hallmarks of a successful business.

Know the Three Factors of Business Success

Many individuals believe that a great product or service idea will ensure success in starting a new business. Although this may play a critical role, even the greatest idea cannot save a new business from failure if the entrepreneur has not focused on the following three factors:

1. **Operational Excellence:** This factor is important for start-up businesses, and it will probably be the aspect that you focus on most throughout the beginning stages of your business. Without your company's operations under control, you might find it very difficult to focus on the remaining two factors. Think about this in terms of human needs: without food and water, we cannot focus on making new friends or learning something new.

   Operational excellence refers to the company's capacity to deliver high-quality products at a reasonable price. It also reflects the company's ability to make it easy for customers to purchase its products and services. In order to achieve operational excellence, business owners must design the business processes (the processes used to create and deliver the product or service) to be simplified, controlled, and standardized. This way, they can produce and deliver as many products and services as possible without needing to continually make major decisions or frequently conduct review sessions throughout the course of the process. We will review how to design and implement business processes in Chapter 3 of this book.

   In addition to the above criteria, operational excellence also requires that the company delivers a hassle-free customer experience. If the customer needs to complete difficult tasks to purchase your product, then your business may not fulfill this important criterion. We will discuss how to embrace operational excellence in your start-up throughout the course of this book as well.

2. **Product Leadership:** This factor refers to your company's ability to create exceptional products and services. Emphasizing product leadership within your new business means that you can fulfill the needs of your customers while establishing yourself as an industry expert. Product leadership requires that you examine your competition's products and services to discover how you can improve your product without incorporating your competitor's work.

   Product leadership also refers to your ability to foster innovation and market research within your company by implanting the following conditions:

   ✔ A business structure that encourages employees to take risks, and that easily adjusts itself for any entrepreneurial ideas or redirections that may be required.

   ✔ Management systems that reward your employees for innovations and product success.

   ✔ A workplace culture that encourages employee innovation and creative thinking.

   As this book is dedicated to the beginning stages of starting a business, we will not elaborate excessively on the nuances of creating an encouraging and creative workplace culture. However, aspiring entrepreneurs should realize that setting a foundation for a successful business with the techniques in this book can ease the process of creating an encouraging workplace filled with creative and innovative employees.

3. **Customer Intimacy:** This is the final facet of a successful business, and it is critical to embrace if you want to stay in operation for years to come. Successful entrepreneurs often live by this mantra: "Customers are the lifeblood of your business." If your customers are happy and satisfied with your products and services, you can expect to run a successful business. However, if your customers are unhappy with your products or the customer experience you offer them, you may find it is much more challenging to keep your business afloat.

   Businesses that are obsessed with solving the main problems, desires, and needs of their customers are the businesses that thrive. Focusing on the wants and needs of your customers may feel difficult in the initial stages of starting a business—especially when you are dealing with operational challenges—but it is critical to lay the foundation for customer intimacy from the start. To accomplish this, entrepreneurs must embrace the following criteria:

   ✔ A business structure that empowers customers and the employees who work with them.

✔ Management systems and processes that create results for clients.

✔ A workplace culture that encourages the development of thriving relationships within its customer base, rather than general solutions focused on making more money.

These criteria may not be entirely covered within the scope of this book. However, like with product leadership, the foundation for excellent customer service should be built on market research, customer segmentation, and business processes, all of which will be explored throughout this book.

Starting a successful business means ensuring that your operations are running correctly, researching your market as well as your competition to verify that your products are superior to others, and consistently offering customers an exceptional experience. Throughout the course of this book, you will learn the techniques that can help you ensure that your future business is able to meet the three factors that lead to a successful business.

Know Your Entrepreneurial Interests

In addition to the three factors that lead to a successful business outlined above, an entrepreneur must also align opportunities with his or her interests. Only then can the entrepreneur create a successful business for himself or herself.

If you see a business opportunity and seize it without having a real interest in it, you are likely to be unsuccessful in the long term. If instead you take the time to recognize your interests and strengths, then seize business opportunities based on these interests and strengths, you are much more likely to find long-term business success. The six major areas of interest include the following areas, defined in greater detail below: realistic interests, investigative interests, artistic interests, social interests, enterprising interests, and conventional interests.

- **Realistic Interests:** Entrepreneurs with realistic interests prefer activities that include practical, hands-on problems and solutions. These people enjoy outside work, such as dealing with plants, animals, and real-world materials like wood, tools, and machinery.

- **Investigative Interests:** Entrepreneurs with investigative interests prefer activities that center on thinking, problem-solving, ideas, and questioning, rather than physical activity. These people enjoy searching for facts and answers, and solving problems mentally, rather than persuading or leading other people to decisions.

- **Artistic Interests:** Entrepreneurs with artistic interests enjoy activities that involve designs, forms, and patterns. These people enjoy self-expression in all their work, and they prefer to work in settings without strict set of guidelines or rules to abide by.

- **Social Interests:** Entrepreneurs with social interests prefer activities that involve assisting others and promoting both learning and personal development. These activities could include teaching, providing advice, helping, or otherwise being of service to people. In essence, people with social interest prefer communicating with others, rather than working with objects or machines.

- **Enterprising Interests:** Entrepreneurs with enterprising interests enjoy activities that deal with starting and carrying out projects, especially business ventures. These people enjoy taking risks for profit, as well as persuading and leading people to making decisions. These people tend to prefer action over thought.

- **Conventional Interests:** Conversely, entrepreneurs with conventional interests prefer activities that follow set rules, guidelines, procedures, and routines, with clear boundaries set by authority. These people enjoy working with "black and white" data and prefer detail, rather than creative ideas. These people prefer to work in settings with specific predetermined standards, rather than settings where they might be forced to make independent judgements.

Each of the six major interests listed above can be important to operating a successful business. However, you may find that your own interests align more with a select few qualities rather than others. Note any natural preferences, as they may guide you to make important business decisions in the future.

Consider Supplements to This Book

Additional information pertaining to starting a business can be found through the Center for Business Acceleration (CBA) accessible at centerforbusinessacceleration.com. Our curricula are designed to help business owners grow their sales, enhance their processes, and develop their skills and abilities, as well as those of their employees. To establish the most complete and well-rounded business, we strongly recommend these courses, as they delve more fully into aspects of a business that can only be glimpsed in the medium of a book.

We researched hundreds of entrepreneurs, conducted a measurement-based analysis, and discovered that those who completed their business plans, as well as our courses, found improvement in several important business qualities, including the following:

- **Improved realistic interest scores:** People with realistic interests enjoy work activities that include practical hands-on problems and solutions, and they typically prefer to engage in these activities by oneself. This characteristic is an excellent quality for a potential business owner to possess, as he or she will be solving a variety of practical problems and making important decisions independently.

- **Improved investigative interest scores:** People with investigative interests enjoy searching for facts, solving intellectual problems, and working with thoughts and ideas. This characteristic aids business owners immensely, as they will be analyzing data on their businesses and making critical decisions for their companies.

- **Improved artistic interest scores:** People with artistic interests think in forms, designs, and patterns, and tend to enjoy expressing themselves through their work and setting their own rules and schedules. In our LeadersBench courses, available through the Center of Business Acceleration, we discuss the importance of pattern recognition for business leaders, which may explain how some business owners were found to be more artistic after completing our courses. This characteristic is highly conducive to business ownership, as owners will be required to express themselves and sense productive or disruptive patterns of behavior, workplace functions, and business needs.

- **Improved conventional interest scores:** People with conventional interests enjoy work that follows predetermined procedures and routines. These people prefer working with data and detail with precise standards. This characteristic supports new business owners, as organization, attention to detail, and clear delineation of authority are highly beneficial to a start-up business.

Each one of the qualities listed above can be improved with consistent and focused practice. Consider supplementing this book with additional training and educational materials available from the Center for Business Acceleration.

Owning a business can be an exciting and incredibly fulfilling experience. Use this book to learn critical methods for seizing viable a business opportunity and transforming your ideas into as successful and lucrative business.

As you read this book, believe in your own abilities to start a successful business. Remember, this process has been completed many times before, and you have no reason to surrender your dreams. Maintain your hope, give yourself a chance, and know that many resources—including this book—are available to guide and assist you through your personal journey into start-up entrepreneurship.

CHAPTER 1

How to Identify Your Viable Business Opportunity

"Opportunity is missed by most people because it is dressed in overalls and looks like work."

-Thomas Edison[1]

Popular conceptions of business opportunities might resemble an inventor's experience: An entrepreneur suddenly has a fantastic idea (the "light bulb" moment), gets a patent on a product, and takes out more than a few loans to start a local store. Think about your own conception of starting a business: how much does it align with the quote that opened this chapter?

While there are still entrepreneurs who follow this tried-and-true method of starting a new business, the advent of new technologies—including the Internet—has significantly shifted how modern entrepreneurs start their own businesses. Today, it seems as though anyone can become a consultant simply by starting his or her own website and getting a tax code for the business. This makes entrepreneurship even more exciting than it was in previous generations, because it is now much easier for individuals to start their own businesses that focus on their hobbies, passions, and interests.

One expert on the changing ethos of small-business ownership is William Elmore, who has been deeply involved in the business world for almost forty years. Today, Elmore is the proud owner of a small business called M2BA. Located in the St. Louis, Missouri area, M2BA has three associates around the country, in addition to the wide network of Elmore's connections from prior positions. "I'm at retirement age, so I'm not working incredibly hard," Elmore says. "With M2BA—and this is one of the values of being self-employed—I get to choose who my customers are. I'm not paid in every instance, but if I like your motives, I'm going to support you. If at the same time I can generate some cash flow to help my small business, I'm going to do that."

If cash is not the reason for Elmore's latest business venture, then what is? There is currently, he says, "an explosion of interest and growth in the world of self-employment across America for veterans." Having been the top federal

---

[1] "Thomas A. Edison Quotes," BrainyQuote, accessed November 1, 2018, https://www.brainyquote.com/quotes/thomas_a_edison_104931.

employee working in this arena for more than a decade, Elmore is making sure that America builds its economic community in the private sector. Elmore explains, "My interest is helping do that, through universities, other businesses, through state and federal government, but primarily in the American economic marketplace. How do we grow our ability to support ourselves, to support our families, to support our community, and ultimately to make our country better? That's what I'm focused on."

Engaging with the world of business ownership for the first time is often difficult, acknowledges Elmore. There are a thousand things for the new owner to know, and not many of them are learned in the military. Elmore acknowledges: "When you come home, you're already behind the curve in terms of your nonveteran peers. All the services available—the Small Business Administration, the Department of Veterans Affairs, the Department of Labor, small business development centers—all of those help accelerate critical lessons necessary for you to succeed in self-employment. When you make that first decision to enter self-employment or business ownership, you're risking your family's economic future. If you don't have their support, that complicates it even more."

Elmore's advice for anyone newly interested in entrepreneurship is to take advantage of the help available: "Go somewhere and see if you can find some free help to help you understand and overcome the lessons you're going to learn as you start to purchase or build your own business. There are great benefits to starting your own business, and many veterans do quite well with their own businesses. But again, there are a thousand and one things to learn—what kind of accounting system do you set up, what's your legal entity going to look like, do you want to incorporate or be a sole proprietor, is there a market that you want to do, can you manage the business side in addition to producing the product side—all of those things are important and become critical as you succeed and grow. There are thousands of people across America that want to help veterans do well in this arena; it's just a matter of finding them and asking them."

Especially helpful are local entities, such as local Small Business Administration (SBA) district offices, which usually know what resources are available to support local businesses. The SBA's sixty-eight locations around the country contain people who are paid to help you succeed, and that is an excellent starting point.

In addition to the prospects offered by these resources and the help offered by the SBA, there are many other aids for new business owners. With the rise of the Internet, telecommuting, and other technologies, there are so many business opportunities that can provide individuals with a wealth of entrepreneurial experiences. Let us preview with three examples of the business opportunities that will be explored in this chapter:

***

Example #1: Robert

Robert has always dreamed of starting his own business; however, he has found very few opportunities to apply his entrepreneurial desires. He is not interested in starting his own restaurant, and he does not want to start a store. He does not consider himself to be an inventor with a new product that will sell rapidly or in large quantities. In fact, Robert has never invented anything in his life—but he nonetheless dreams of becoming a business owner.

After working for one year at an accounting firm as an office assistant, Robert is ready to leave the corporate "nine-to-five" world and start his own business. He considers himself to be a strong business writer, so he is curious to discover whether he can use these writing skills to start a business.

Robert researches online to determine if his skills could lead to a new business opportunity. After reading a few articles and discovering several websites that advertise for business-writing consultants, Robert realizes that he could go into business for himself as a business writer. He finds that many entrepreneurs do not have the time to write business plans and letters, and that they are willing to outsource this work.

Robert also realizes that he could transform his freelance writing into a copywriting firm. He determines that once his client load becomes too great for him to handle on his own, he could hire additional business writers to accommodate more clients and earn more profit. Robert concludes that this could be an excellent way for him to turn one of his greatest passions into his own business without requiring a great deal of capital to start.

***

Example #2: Delilah

Delilah has always been interested in starting her own restaurant, but she feels hesitant about pursuing this goal alone. She wants to work in the food industry, and she wants to use a restaurant model that is practically guaranteed to be successful. When her favorite fast-food restaurant indicates that it has new franchising opportunities available, she decides to investigate this business opportunity further.

After meeting with the local office for the fast-food chain, Delilah realizes that she will need a certain amount of capital to buy into the franchise. She talks over the business opportunity with her family members, who are more than happy to support her with this venture. After taking out a loan from the bank, Delilah buys into the franchise and opens up a new location near her home.

Delilah imagines that her franchising opportunity can become lucrative, as she has opened a location adjacent to a busy commuter road. She believes if this attempt is successful, she will be able to invest in additional franchises, resulting in a wealthy and lucrative business for her and her family.

***

Example #3: Sarah

Sarah is a landscaper who wants to branch out with her own landscaping business. However, she has noted that the competition is particularly fierce in her neighborhood, so there would not be an additional market for her landscaping services. When Sarah mentions this to a friend of hers, the friend recommends that she seek out government contracts, as government organizations often hire landscapers to maintain their lawns and landscapes.

Sarah investigates the government contracting opportunity and discovers she indeed would be able to bid on available landscaping jobs. She knows that government contractors must adhere to strict rules and regulations, so she ensures that she meets all criteria before applying for jobs. She then visits the federal website that contains all the available job postings, selects her state, and bids for landscaping jobs in her nearby area.

When she is successful with many of her bids, she realizes that she would, in fact, be able to make a living by landscaping for government buildings and memorial landscapes. Thanks to a few online bids, Sarah now owns a landscaping business that specializes in government contracts.

***

As these three examples demonstrate, a new business does not always start with a firm product idea and a great deal of cash flow. In fact, many entrepreneurs discover that a business opportunity exists in a talent, passion, or hobby they have possessed all their lives. The challenge is to find an opportunity that can transform those talents, passions, and hobbies into a viable business opportunity.

Even if you have a defined area of interest, finding your market niche is not an easy path. Victoria Buggs, MPH, RN, BSN is the owner of Center for Health Educators and Safety Specialists, LLC (CHESS). CHESS is a premier training center specializing in emergency safety training. Their customers include healthcare professionals, childcare providers, and laypersons. CHESS offers certifications from four nationally recognized agencies: the American Heart Association, the American Safety and Health Institute, the American Red Cross, and the National Safety Council.

"In October of 2014, I decided to drop my [military] retirement paperwork," says Buggs. "While waiting for a decision, I began to ponder what I would do as a military retiree. I had over 20 years of Human Resources experience, I worked several part-time jobs, and I had 4 academic degrees, so

I knew I was marketable. However, I was not 100% sure I wanted to work for anyone." Upon this realization, Buggs began to explore self-employment.

In order to determine what her offerings should be, Buggs spent time carefully analyzing her environment and market: "I've taken the opportunity to participate in several seminars, free groups, SBA, etc. This group consistently helps me when I get in a jam. Locally, the Economic Development Agency has provided so much valuable information that has allowed me to become a vendor for the county public school system, connected me with resourceful people, and invited me to sit on panels to learn as well as assist others on their entrepreneur journey." You will learn how to conduct your own market analysis as you work through the following chapters of this book.

In this chapter, you can expect to learn about the three main types of business opportunities that exist for beginning entrepreneurs: independent business, franchising opportunities, and government contracting. Each of these opportunities comes with a specific set of challenges, advantages, and special considerations. Be sure to carefully examine each business opportunity to discern if it fits your needs and aspirations. If you are still unsure about which business opportunity is right for you, the last section of this chapter will help you decide how to select your ideal entrepreneurial opportunity.

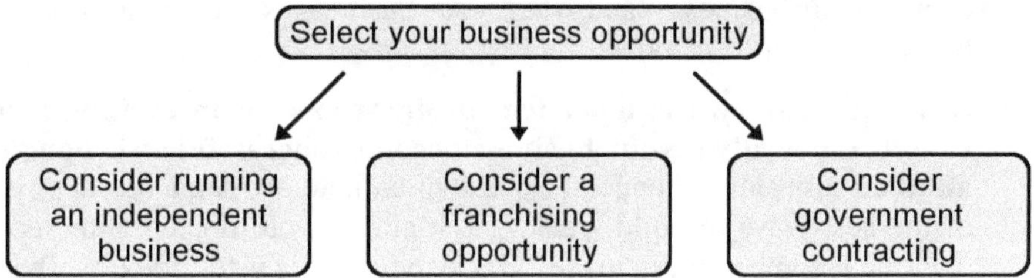

Consider Running an Independent Business

If you like the idea of being in complete control of a business—with every decision ultimately left to you—then consider running your own independent business. While franchising opportunities and government contracting come with their own restrictions and regulations, running an independent business leaves choices entirely in your hands. The ability to make her own decisions was a deciding factor in Victoria Buggs' career change. "I didn't want to work for anybody else," she says. "At 38 years old, I knew I was not ready to sit down. Becoming a business owner allowed me to do things on my own time until I figured it out."

Running an independent business is ideal for entrepreneurs who have a strong idea of what they like to do and how they want to do it. From opening a mom-and-pop restaurant to starting a business that specializes in creating iPhone apps, an independent business allows you to specialize in anything you want, so long as you can find a market for it. Below are more advantages associated with starting your own business:

- **Running your own independent business can be an extremely rewarding experience.** No matter how you define that reward—whether it is venturing into the unknown or turning a dream into reality—starting an independent business can leave you feeling fulfilled. While there will be very stressful times running your business, starting up can give you the kind of rewards that come from surmounting a challenging experience. "My life has been impacted a lot. For the better!" says Buggs, echoing a common sentiment among business owners. She has experienced the rewards of being her own boss already: "I have been able to truly find my niche, collaborate with others, and obtain local contracts within my community."

- **Starting your own independent business means that you are seated firmly "in the boss's seat."** If you have spent your entire life managed by someone else, this can be a freeing and empowering experience. When you are able to control your own hours, decisions, and consequences, you truly control your business—and when your business is successful, it is solely because of you.

- **Running your own independent business can be an exciting income source, especially if your business becomes successful or is bought by another company.** Financial experts often note owning a business is one of the best ways to build wealth, as it allows you to exert some control over the income you can make. Think about it this way: if you work in the nine-to-five world, you can only earn a certain amount of income based on your paycheck. If you start your own independent business, your income is tied more closely to the success of your company. If you "play your cards right" and grow your entrepreneurial venture into a successful company, your income could be life changing.

- **Operating your own independent business allows you to set your own working hours.** This is often why stay-at-home parents start independent businesses online, as it allows them the flexibility that is not typically available in the corporate world.

- **Starting an independent business gives you the fulfilling feeling of having your ideas materialize into the real world.** This is probably one of the biggest appeals of starting your own business, as it gives you the gratifying knowledge that your ideas are out there changing lives. Seeing others' business ideas gave Buggs the inspiration she needed to get started: "While doing research on entrepreneurship I ran across a weekend conference and organization called Veteran Women Igniting the Spirit of Entrepreneurship. I attended this three-day conference and felt empowered. I went home and pondered on what I can do to leverage all the knowledge and experience that I had to become an entrepreneur and today, here I am." As the owner of the Center for Health Educators and Safety Specialists, Buggs inspires others with her own story.

✔ **Running a successful independent business can provide you with a sense of security.** For example, if you start a business and it grows into a successful company, you could sell the company as part of your retirement plan.

Now that we have examined the impressive benefits of starting an independent business, let us examine its drawbacks:

✗ **Starting a new independent business involves a large amount of financial risk, especially in the beginning stages.** If you do not have enough money to start your business (known as undercapitalization), your business will very likely fail. If you overcapitalize—or have too much money to start with—your investors may own a larger portion of your company.

✗ **Running an independent business involves a significant time investment.** Operating your own independent business will inevitably involve long working hours, especially in the beginning stages of your venture. This could mean you will need to forgo the idea of clocking out of work by 6:00 p.m., as your business may require a hefty number of hours worked to sustain itself. If you have not prepared yourself (or your family) for this change in scheduling, you may become overly stressed and anxious about the amount of time you are working.

✗ **Starting an independent business can mean your income will not be as predictable as a steady paycheck.** Business owners often refer to this phenomenon as the feast-or-famine cycle: some weeks may be lucrative, while others hardly see any income at all. If you do not save your money to prepare for those "famine stages," you may find it difficult to pay your business bills, as well as your personal ones.

✗ **Running an independent business may require you to manage a great number of tasks and responsibilities, particularly in the first few years, when the number of employees you have may be limited.** You may not enjoy the experience of being a bookkeeper, accountant, administrator, and IT specialist all in one; however, if you push these tasks to the side, you risk undermining the operations of your business.

Running an independent business certainly comes with its share of advantages and disadvantages. However, many readers may find the idea of running their own business attractive because it gives them freedom, challenges, and responsibility that are not often available at other jobs. Starting your own independent business may mean you personally bear a greater amount of risk, but it also means that any success is entirely yours as well—and for many, the prospect of success is an exhilarating feeling worth pursuing.

Some entrepreneurs might already have an idea for a product or service that allows them to start their own independent business. Other readers might be interested in starting their own independent business but still be unsure as to what they can offer the world. Industry research will be key for the former group, and will be discussed in Chapter 2. For the latter group, you will want to research start-up-business ideas that take into account your hobbies and interests. You can make a list of these hobbies and begin from there, using the Internet to search for businesses, markets, products, and services that are related to your interests.

Transform Your Hobby into a Business

Unfortunately, not every hobby will have moneymaking potential. In order for a hobby to be considered a potential business, it must encompass the following factors:

- **The hobby must involve a product or service that is in high demand by the market.** For example, someone who wants to transform his or her hobby of writing into freelance copywriting will be far more financially successful than someone who wants to sell homemade knitting. In Chapter 2, we will focus on how you can conduct industry research to determine whether your product or service is in high demand.

- **The hobby must have the potential to generate more profits than raw resource costs.** A hobby is not financially worth turning into a business if the resources continually drain the money you are earning. While this can be fine—and even expected—for the first few months to a year of your new business, any hobby that costs more than it makes over the long term should be rejected as a business venture. Later chapters will discuss how to analyze both the short-term and long-term potential for your new business.

- **The hobby must have the potential to grow into a successful business.** Ask yourself if you can imagine your hobby as a new business in the next one to two years. If you cannot visualize yourself growing your hobby into a company, then it is probably worth finding another idea for a business. If you do see that kind of potential, then the hobby may be a worthwhile investment of resources and time.

If your hobby encompasses all three of the above factors, brainstorm exactly what steps you will need to take to transform your hobby into a bona fide independent business. Ask yourself the following questions to determine how successful the hobby might be as a business:

- Who would be your market? How would you reach out to that market?

- Would you remain exclusively in a local market, or would you want to sell your products or service online? If so, are you prepared to invest time and resources into learning the how to run an online business?

- Are you aware of how much time you will need to invest to get your side business started?

- How much time each week can you devote to your business?

- Is this something that you could see yourself doing in one, two, or five years' time?

- What are you prepared to do to make this happen right now? In a month? In a year?

The more seriously and thoughtfully you answer the questions listed above, the more successful you will be in this venture. Remember, not all hobbies will transform into profitable business ideas—and it is your responsibility to ensure that you are investing in a project that will eventually return profits.

Transform Your Skills into a Service

You may find a huge market demand for your skills. For example, if you are great at plumbing or interior design, or if you have a fantastic way with words, you may be able to exchange these skills for profit. For the administrative assistant who could take on work as an online assistant or the graphic designer who could make a living freelancing, the problem is not identifying the marketable talent—the problem is finding the market in the first place.

Victoria Buggs knew she had marketable skills but was not sure how to carve a space for herself in the healthcare industry. "I love educating, I love health, I love nursing, and I love people," she says, "My business idea had so many components at the time." While maintaining her certifications for skills she has learned, Buggs had a realization: "I did not want to keep paying for my Basic Life Saver (BLS) Card every two years for $85, so I became a CPR Instructor for American Health and Safety Institute. Once I saw their curriculum and the courses they offered besides BLS, I knew with my creativity and experience I could make more out of my business." Having narrowed down her idea, Buggs was able to transform her skills into a service.

Today, there are two facets to CHESS's training offerings: train-to-trainer, and regular certifications. Buggs acts as instructor for both, ensuring that all her students fully understand the material, whether they need a certification for their job or are looking to become instructors themselves. She also adds to the curricula developed by each agency to tailor the material to each class's needs and wants. "What I add depends on my audience," she says, "I add different exercises, knowledge-building, and strategies to ensure their comfort."

While we will discuss industry research in the Chapter 2, the primary focus of this section is finding vendors who are willing to pay you for your skills. After you find these vendors, it can be easier to take steps to grow your work into an online, home-based, or storefront business, as you already have a pool of clients who are paying you for your work.

There is an abundance of websites that can help you find vendors who may be willing to pay for your skills. Into your search engine, enter a phrase such as "freelancing websites." Read reviews of each website and to list out exactly what you are looking for from the one that you will choose to advertise your services from. Finding a website (or websites) that best fits your approach can help you immensely with your search for a market for your business.

Freelancers from around the world can find work with reputable employers on many websites. We encourage you to take a look at these sites and determine which have project boards with plentiful job opportunities and employers with lucrative projects. When you have vendors who are paying you for your skills, you can start taking the steps in this book to turn your services into a true business.

Establish an Online Presence

The Internet is still a relatively young medium, and there is still ample opportunities for a new entrepreneur who wants to know if he or she can start an independent business from home. Marketing services online is also a great option for people (like parents) who are not willing to give up their primary jobs until the new business has become successful. A home-based online business is easier to grow than other business forms, as it requires less money for start-up. However, home-based online businesses nonetheless require you to establish business value and to know exactly how to present yourself and your business.

Do not take establishing an online presence lightly and keep its importance in mind while you are doing your research. It takes time, money, and patience to find a working combination of product, selling platform, and target market. Additionally, you may need to decide exactly what you want to sell online, which can be a mission in itself. Ask yourself these questions to help narrow down what you are looking for from an online business:

- Do you know what product you want to sell? Will you create the product yourself or sell someone else's product?

- Do you have an idea how much time and money you will need to start your online business?

- Do you have technical knowledge about starting an online business (i.e., building and optimizing a website, etc.)? You can find plenty of excellent e-commerce websites online, or you can enroll in a web-hosting subscription at any highly recommended site.

- What marketing strategies will you implement to drive traffic to your website?

- Are you interested in affiliate marketing?

- Are there any online business models that you would like to follow? What have they done that has been successful? What has not been successful?

If you cannot answer the above questions, or if you have not seriously considered them, we encourage you to learn more about the responsibilities associated with starting an online business before moving forward. Whether you want an online start to a publishing business, a web page from which to sell your jewelry, your own Amazon page, or the title of the next Internet guru, starting a successful home-based online business takes knowledge and resources.

While these ideas are only the start of running your own independent business, realize they all have something in common: heavy amounts of research and preparation. Fortunately, you will find many techniques within this book that can help you determine if your independent business idea is one that stands a good chance of becoming successful.

Beware, online businesses comprise an industry where you will need to "tread carefully." It is likely that you may discover a wealth of information products about starting an online business. While there are plenty of high-quality information products available online, there are even more scam artists who want to steal your money as quickly as possible. We encourage you to research and read reviews about any vendors that you are interested in buying information products from. Great sites to visit when researching include the Federal Trade Commission and the Internet Fraud Complaint Center; use your favorite Internet browser to perform a search for their official websites. Also, a simple Internet search on the vendor will often reveal all of the information you need to make an informed decision.

Consider a Franchising Opportunity

According to the International Franchise Association, a franchise can be defined as the agreement of license between two legally independent parties, which gives:

- A person or group of people (franchisee) the right to market a product or service using the trademark or trade name of another business (franchisor).

- The franchisee the right to market a product or service using the operating methods of the franchisor.

- The franchisee the obligation to pay the franchisor fees for these rights.

- The franchisor the obligation to provide rights and support to franchisees.

Often times, opting into a franchising opportunity can make sense to an entrepreneur who wants to be involved with a successful brand without building it from the ground up. Franchising opportunities give entrepreneurs the opportunity to experience owning a business without going through the aggravation and frustration of finding start-up capital, building a business plan, and undergoing other challenging entrepreneurial experiences.

Here are a few more advantages to opting into a franchising opportunity:

- **You are associated with a well-known or well-liked brand.** This can remove much of the struggle associated with building a brand for a new company, which can consequently have a profound impact on the strength of your sales. When your customers already recognize your brand, it can be easier to start building a profit.

- **You are provided with assistance for many crucial aspects of starting a business.** For example, franchisees are usually given assistance with selecting a site, negotiating a lease, and finding builders to build the new franchise location.

- **You are provided the initial management training, which can be helpful if you do not have prior experience running a business.** Depending on the franchising opportunity, you may also be given continuous management training.

- **You may be provided financial assistance when starting up the franchise.** This can be a significant advantage to opting for a franchising opportunity, as getting start-up capital can be a challenge for traditional business owners.

- **You may have access to training and systems that can help you determine if there are any trouble spots ahead.** This may help you catch any financial risks that may occur, which can in turn help you protect the integrity of the business.

While these can be very attractive advantages—especially to entrepreneurs who may not have experience running a business—there is also a number of disadvantages to franchising, which can include the following:

✗ **You may not have as much independence in making business decisions.** A franchise must be run according to an overall franchise owner's manual, which you may find to be somewhat limiting.

✗ **You may be restricted in terms of what territories you can open up your franchise in and how you can promote it.** Franchisors often have strict rules regarding where franchises can be opened. This can be a significant obstacle, especially if a franchise operation already exists in your local area.

✗ **You may have to provide the franchisor with ongoing payments.** These payments can impede your ability to produce profits at first.

✗ **You have less control over the decision to sell your franchise business.** Many franchisors have procedures in place for selling your franchise. In addition to these restrictions, some franchisors require that they have final approval of the buyer before you can sell.

✗ **If you sign up for a certain amount of time with a franchisor, the company is not obligated to renew your contract at the end of the franchise term.** This can cause significant amount of anxiety, as you may lose your business if the franchisor decides not to renew the franchise agreement.

✗ **If you sell the franchise, you may be required to pay a hefty fee to the franchisor in order to opt out of your responsibilities.**

As the above disadvantages reveal, opting for a franchising opportunity is similar to renting a house. In this example, the house may feel like yours, and you will be responsible for maintaining the condition of the house and the bills, but ultimately your house is left in the hands of the person who owns it. In the same way, your franchise is ultimately owned by your franchisor. While this can remove much of the heavy responsibility, it can also be limiting in terms of growing as an entrepreneur. For some, it is a relief to have the structure of a business plan and operations already established. For others, however, the structure of franchising may be frustrating. As a potential business owner, you should carefully research whom you will be working for. Meet the franchise's owners if possible, and read the fine print on your franchise agreement. You do not want to overlook a restriction that would cause you to lose your enthusiasm for the business. Additionally, you will not have as much freedom in decisions about the way the business is run as you would if you were the sole owner. Therefore, you should carefully consider whether this is the right entrepreneurial opportunity for you.

No business is perfectly guaranteed. To be successful, a franchise requires dedication from each owner. Once you have decided to pursue a franchising opportunity, you should find one that meets your needs. Use the guidelines below to find a franchising opportunity that appeals to your entrepreneurial goals and aspirations:

Find a Franchising Opportunity

As with starting your own business, you will need to carefully research and select the franchising opportunity that best fits your needs, hobbies, and interests. Many franchisees approach this opportunity from the perspective of making as much money as possible; however, if you dislike your business, it will not matter how much money you make. The purpose of owning a business is to do what you love and what you are good at. If you are only interested in making money, your motivational levels may not be enough to carry you through those rough first years.

To pick your ideal franchising opportunity, find an industry that you would be happy to work in for the next decade. Ask yourself the following questions to identify these potential industries:

- What do I like to do?

- What do I know how to do?

- What am I experienced in?

- What special skills and talents do I have?

- Which industry am I the most interested in?

- Would I rather sell a product or a service?

- In an ideal world, what would I love to do?

Use your favorite Internet browser to conduct a search for websites that list franchisors. On these websites, you can often search franchising opportunities by industry type, location, or opportunities based on how much money you will need to get started.

Determine If You Can Start a Franchise

While franchising may ease the process of starting your own business, you will still need to invest some money into the franchise. Even if the franchisor supplies you with financial assistance, you may need start-up money to cover the following costs:

- Location design

- Construction

- Equipment

- Furniture

- Insurance

- Labor

- Opening advertisements

- Salaries

- Utilities

- Rent

- Loan interests

While the above items will not be applicable to all franchising opportunities, it is important to note that if you do not have the necessary capital to buy into the franchise, you may find it difficult to get started. We will discuss how to analyze your financials in Chapter 7 of this book.

Know Your Market

If you have the money for a franchising opportunity and it is in an industry you love, you may think you have all you need to get started. However, if you do not perform market research, you may miss valuable information. For example, when researching your market, you may find that there are not enough customers to support your business.

Market research is a critical element to running a successful business, whether the business is one that you have franchised or started from the ground up. We will discuss industry research in detail in Chapter 2 of this book. For now, consider the following questions that will provide a framework for your later market research:

- How many customers are in your area?

- What need does your product or service satisfy?

- Who are the biggest competitors in your area?

- How will your product or service be unique among what your competitors are offering?

- What marketing niche will you be appealing to?

Whether or not you know how to answer these questions, keep them in mind as we move forward into Chapter 2.

Consider Government Contracting

Government contracting is a unique business opportunity you may be interested in, particularly if you are an experienced entrepreneur with your own small business. A government contractor can be defined as someone who provides goods or services to the government under contract. Government contracting is a lucrative industry, with the federal government spending more than $400 billion per year on government contractors.

Beware, becoming a government contractor involves taking several steps that may preclude you from this industry. Government contracting is regulated by strict rules, and not all entrepreneurs will qualify to become government contractors. If you are hired to be a government contractor, you may find that you need to follow industry-size standards as outlined by the United States Small Business Administration. This will be explored in greater detail in the Chapter 9 of this book, which addresses human resources.

According to the Small Business Administration, a small business can be defined in terms of the average number of employees that the business has over the past twelve months or the average annual receipts over the past three years. In addition to these requirements, the SBA considers the following when defining a small business:[2]

- The business is organized for profit.

- The business is located within the United States.

- The business operates primarily in the United States or makes a significant contribution to the country through payment of taxes or use of American products, materials, and/or labor.

- The business is independently owned and operated.

- The business is not dominant in its field on a national basis.

In addition to the above requirements, the small business can be defined as a sole proprietorship, partnership, corporation, or any other legal form. We

---

[2] "Size standards," U.S. Small Business Administration, accessed November 1, 2018, http://www.sba.gov/content/am-i-small-business-concern.

will discuss these legal structures in Chapter 4 of this book.

The Small Business Administration (SBA) is specific about the size of government contractors; therefore, before you start bidding for jobs, you will need to gain your North American Industry Classification System (NAICS) code. To do this, go to the NAICS section for the Bureau of Census, which can be found online. Once you are there, you should identify the NAICS code that best describes the activities of your business. Once you have done this, you can identify your industry's size standard using the Table of Small Business Size Standards, which is provided to you on the SBA website. To help you further identify whether you qualify as a small business according to government standards, you can visit the Size Standards Tool website (also linked to the SBA website), where you will be asked to enter your industry code and business size to get your result.

Before we move on to the advantages and disadvantages of becoming a government contractor, realize that the date you bid for federal contracts can play a critical role in how successful you are. According to the Small Business Administration, on the date of your bid, you cannot exceed the small-business size standard that the procuring agency's contracting officer is specifying for the contract. Therefore, pay careful attention to what the job description says, as it can determine which opportunities you may apply for. As long as you meet the size standard for that contract, you can qualify as a small business.

For more information about industry size standards, contact the SBA. Their website and physical address are both available online, and a simple Internet search will direct you to them within moments.

Now that you know what a government contractor is and some of the restrictions placed on becoming one, let us analyze the advantages of becoming a government contractor:

- ✔ **Government contracting opportunities are probably available in your industry.** The government spends over $460 billion dollars on contracting, which means government contractors stand to make a considerable amount of money with each fiscal year.

- ✔ **Contractors are always in demand, as the government relies on these workers to provide vital goods and services.** In fact, the Department of Defense outsources 50 percent of its needs to contractors. The Department of Energy and the National Aeronautics and Space Administration almost wholly rely on contractors, with 70 percent and 80 percent of spending directed toward contractors, respectively.

- ✔ **Contracting can help diversify the income you bring in and can be a much steadier source of income than other clients and opportunities.** The private sector is much more likely to be impacted by economic factors than the government sector, which makes contracting a more stable option for small-business entrepreneurs.

- ✔ **The government is looking for a wide range of products and services, which increases the likelihood that you will be able to sell to the government.** Additionally, finding these government opportunities can be relatively simple, as it can all be done online.

Now that we have considered the advantages of becoming a government contractor, let us also explore the disadvantages of this type of business:

- ✘ **The government determines the rules and regulations that you must abide by in order to be a government contractor.** This can often be confusing, as you may need to navigate the "red tape" of government obligations in order to make sense of the rules and regulations attached to the contract. If you are found to be noncompliant with these rules—even through ignorance—your contract may be immediately revoked.

- ✘ **Submitting bids for government contracting can be difficult, as there is a great deal of "red tape" involved.** Many contractors have even been disqualified simply because they did not have the correct margin sizes in their proposal documents. Attempting to follow all the rules and regulations imposed on your contracts may be cumbersome and fraught with unintentional errors.

- ✘ **If you consider yourself to be a subpar networker, you will need to amass critical networking skills quickly.** Networking is crucial to getting government contracts. If you are not comfortable establishing relationships with government workers, you might not be successful at acquiring coveted government contracts.

- ✘ **Securing a government contract can take a significant amount of time.** Some experts claim that you should prepare for waiting at least eight months before you acquire your first government contract. In those eight months, you may need to submit hundreds of bids and network with a great deal of government officials before you finally achieve a contract.

As with starting your own business or opting for a franchise opportunity, government contracting can come with its own significant challenges and frustrations. Government contracting is not a get-rich-quick opportunity, so it should not be treated as such. Regardless, the stability and general lucrative nature of government contracting makes this an ideal option for entrepreneurs who are willing to put in the necessary time and work.

Register Yourself as a Government Contractor

Now that we have outlined the advantages and disadvantages of becoming a government contractor, let us define the steps you need to take in order to become registered as a contractor. Once this is in place, we can begin exploring which of these three entrepreneurial opportunities is right for you. According to the Small Business Administration, you need to take the following steps to register for government contracting:[3]

1. **Obtain a D-U-N-S Number.** This is a Dun & Bradstreet number, which is a nine-digit identification number for the location of your business. This assignment is free for all business owners and is a requirement if you want to register with the federal government for contracts, grants, and other financial assistance. To obtain a Dun & Bradstreet number, visit the United States government's website.

2. **Register with the System of Award Management.** Once you have obtained your D-U-N-S Number, register with the federal government's System of Award Management (SAM), which is the database the government uses for vendors who wish to earn government contracts. You also need to be registered with SAM to set up a basic agreement, basic ordering agreement, or blanket purchase agreement. Using this system will allow you to register your business size and socioeconomic status, as well as complete necessary clauses and certifications. Once you have completed these requirements, government agencies and contractors will be able to search for your business based on your size, ability, location, ownership, experience, and more.

3. **Find the NAICS Code for Your Company.** As mentioned earlier in this subsection, the North American Industry Classification System (NAICS) provides the government with information regarding your economic sector, industry, and country of business. To identify your NAICS code, return to the beginning of the subsection on government contracting for a detailed explanation.

4. **Obtain Performance Evaluations from Previous Customers.** If you want to increase your chances of acquiring government contracts, enlist your company on the United States General Services Administration Schedule (GSA). To do this, you should obtain an Open Ratings, Inc., Past Performance Evaluation, which is another Dun & Bradstreet evaluation. This is an independent audit of customer references and provides the government with a rating based on the statistical analysis of various performance data and survey responses. This evaluation may be obtained online with ease.

---

[3] "Basic requirements," U.S. Small Business Administration, accessed November 1, 2018, http://www.sba.gov/content/register-government-contracting.

According to the Small Business Administration, you will need the following items to register as a government contractor:[4]

- Your NAICS codes

- Your Data Universal Numbering System (DUNS)

- Your Federal Tax Identification Number (TIN or EIN)

- Your Standard Industrial Classification (SIC) codes

- Your Product Service codes (optional but useful)

- Your Federal Supply Classification codes (optional but useful)

All of the above are crucial steps in planning your government contracting business. If you are still confused about the process of becoming a government contractor, we recommend visiting the Small Business Administration website. Here, you can find useful links and information about the process of becoming a government contractor, in addition to a database of opportunities for landing contracts.

Consider SBA Program Eligibility

The Small Business Administration certifies businesses who are eligible for additional contract considerations under the Small Business Act. Regarding this program, the SBA website states the following:[5]

"To help provide a level playing field for small businesses owned by socially and economically disadvantaged people or entities, the government limits competition for certain contracts to businesses that participate in the 8(a) Business Development program. Disadvantaged businesses in the 8(a) program can:

- *Compete for set-aside and sole-source contracts in the program*

- *Get a Business Opportunity Specialist to help navigate federal contracting*

- *Form joint ventures with established businesses through the SBA's mentor-protégé program*

---

[4] "Basic requirements," U.S. Small Business Administration, accessed November 1, 2018, http://www.sba.gov/content/register-government-contracting.
[5] "8(a) Business Development program," U.S. Small Business Administration, accessed November 1, 2018, https://www.sba.gov/federal-contracting/contracting-assistance-programs/8a-business-development-program.

- *Receive management and technical assistance, including business training, counseling, marketing assistance, and high-level executive development*

"You can compete for contract awards under multiple socio-economic programs, as they apply."

This coverage extends only to socially and economically disadvantaged citizens of the United States, or those who have been lawfully admitted permanent United States residency. The United States Federal Government defines socially and economically disadvantaged individuals under the Small Business Act (15 USC 637) as follows:[6]

"Socially disadvantaged individuals are those individuals who have been subjected to racial or ethnic prejudice or cultural bias within American society because of their identities as members of groups and without regard to their individual qualities."

"Economically disadvantaged individuals are socially disadvantaged individuals whose ability to compete in the free enterprise system has been impaired due to diminished capital and credit opportunities as compared to others in the same or similar line of business who are not socially disadvantaged."

"The following groups of individuals are deemed to be socially disadvantaged:

- *Black Americans*

- *Hispanic Americans*

- *Native Americans*

- *Asian Pacific Americans*

- *Subcontinent Asian Americans*

"Individuals not members of one of the listed designated groups may establish social disadvantage based on personal experiences of substantial and chronic social disadvantage in American society, not in other countries, which is the result of a distinguishing feature (i.e., race, ethnic origin, gender, physical disability) that has contributed to the social disadvantage."

---

[6] "8(a) Business Development (BD) Program Suitability Tool Statements," U.S. Small Business Administration, accessed November 1, 2018, http://web.sba.gov/sbtn/sbat/8aAssessmentTool.html

Women are presumed to be included under this act due to the social, and therefore, economic disadvantages women frequently encounter. Other individuals that are not specifically mentioned or identified in the act may be still considered on a case-by-case basis.

If you believe you may be eligible, contact SBA directly regarding your business' certification. This consideration is particularly relevant if you are planning to start a Federal contracting business.

Identify the Right Business Opportunity for You

No matter which business opportunity you want to take advantage of, diving into your own entrepreneurial venture requires a great deal of courage. Still, there are differences between simply starting a business and growing a business into a successful company. Keeping a business up and running requires a great deal of patience, perseverance, and tenacity to keep going when you encounter difficulties. To determine if you are ready for the long and sometimes rocky road of owning a business, ask yourself the following three critical questions:

1. **What Type of Business Owner Do I Plan to Be?** Of course you plan on being a successful business owner, but before you become an entrepreneur, it helps to assess how much you already know about your intended business. In general, there are two types of business owners, who can be identified as follows:

   - **Business owners who know what they want to do.** These are the people who focus on their plans, know what to do, and plan exact steps to start their businesses. These business owners have probably already experienced starting their own companies, and they are familiar with the process.

   - **Business owners who do not have a definite idea of what they want to do.** These are the entrepreneurs who may have the education or skills to venture into their own business but may not be clear on what they want to accomplish. As a reader, you may fall into this category. Our example Victoria Buggs did, too. Starting out without a definite idea is not a problem, but it is important for you to pay attention to the business opportunities available to you, as well as to merge your passions and interests with the right opportunities.

2. **Do I Have the Skills I Need?** You must determine whether or not your current skillset is aligned with your entrepreneurial goals. The most

successful business owners are those who understand their strengths and are able to compensate for their weaknesses. These strengths do not need to apply directly to their businesses, though this can make it easier to be business owners.

Understanding your strengths and weaknesses can also help you gain a better understanding of yourself as a business owner. To help identify your skills, strengths, and weaknesses, consider the following steps:

- [ ] **Ask a family member or friend to outline the positive attributes they ascribe to you.** Write down these characteristics, as well as what they reveal about your potential strengths as a business owner.

- [ ] **Ask the same family member or friend what he or she would consider to be some of your weaker characteristics.** This process is not intended to cause you to doubt yourself as a business owner; rather, it will help you to understand the challenges that you need to overcome in order to become a better business owner.

- [ ] **Assess how you have handled responsibility in the past.** If you often give in to procrastination or find it difficult to manage yourself, it is vital that you acknowledge these trends. As a business owner, you must be able to manage your own time and complete tasks without hesitating. If you find you do not have the most stellar history of responsibility and self-management, consider working on these crucial skills to ensure that you are ready for the workload that comes associated with being a business owner.

3. **Do I Understand the Responsibility of Ownership?** While owning a business comes with the potential for major rewards—like financial incentives and professional fulfillment—there is no denying there are considerable personal risks.

    For example, if the business fails, you could end up owing a great deal of money to banks and other lenders that provided you with initial capital. You should also prepare to play the roles of every employee in your business in the first stages. You will not only need to be the business owner, but you will also be the mail clerk, the administrative assistant, the record keeper, and more. As your business grows, you can give these roles to relevant employees; however, be mentally and physically prepared to handle a great deal of work when you first start your business. Over her first five years, Buggs poured her time and talent into the Center for Health Educators and Safety Specialists. "I work over 40 hours a week to ensure that my business is successful," she says. For five years, she wore every hat in her business. Two years ago, she was finally able to hire a virtual assistant. "When I look back," she reminisces, "I have grown so much in five years, and it did not feel like I rushed. The stars aligned and I put in the hard work."

Consider the following actions for mentally preparing yourself for business ownership:

☐ **Gather your family members together and let them know that you are considering starting a business.** It is likely that your spouse or partner already knows, but it is important to keep any children informed of your goals. This can prepare them for the upcoming changes in lifestyle, as well as provide them with a healthy example of work and entrepreneurship.

☐ **Be open for discussion if your family tries to share their concerns with you.** For example, if your partner worries that you will not be home to help with the household, listen to what he or she is saying. Once he or she is finished sharing the concern, ask what you can do to work out a compromise. Remember, not only is your life being affected, but the lives of your family members are being affected as well. Set boundaries so that the new business does not take 100 percent of your time, as this can help your family give you the support you need during the first few years.

☐ **Let your family know you plan on protecting your time with them, then follow through on this promise.** Treat family time as you would an important meeting with a CEO. If work occasionally needs to take more time, be sure to let your family know that you will be working late. However, do not let this happen too often, as part of being a successful and fulfilled entrepreneur involves valuing your personal life as much as your professional life.

It is important to stress that being an entrepreneur will involve some significant changes to your life, particularly if you have never started your own business before. Hours may be long, your stress levels may be up, and your take-home pay might vary from week to week. However, if you mentally and emotionally prepare yourself for being an entrepreneur, you may find that it is a rewarding experience that allows you to flex your leadership muscles. "Ask yourself the hard questions," says Buggs, "is this what you really want to do, regardless of how hard it seems—no customer interaction, low funds?" Entrepreneurs are not born; they are made via careful preparation and research. Rely on the resources and support you have. "Always seek counsel," advises Buggs, "there is someone waiting to help you."

If you have not yet decided upon a direction, you are not alone—many business owners start with merely an idea that they want to work under their own authority and take charge of their schedules. In the next chapter you will learn just how critical industry research can be to the success of your start-up. Industry research can reveal whether you have stumbled across a great idea for a product, or if there is no market for your potential new business at all.

Review Chapter 1

Now that you have completed Chapter 1, reflect on its content and how you will identify your viable business opportunity. As you review this chapter, consider the following questions:

☐ What type of business are you considering starting? Remember this is an important decision that will shape the remainder of your entrepreneurial journey.

☐ Have you considered the advantages and disadvantages of each type of business? Could you transform your hobby into a business venture, would you be more successful within the structure, or is government contracting the best fit for you?

☐ What kind of presence will your business have? Will your business be primarily online, or will you have a physical presence as well?

We recommend re-reading the final section of this chapter, as this section contains critical considerations for new or potential business owners. If you are satisfied with your understanding of how you will identify your viable business opportunity, resume reading with Chapter 2.

How to Conduct Thorough Industry Research

"Research is formalized curiosity. It is poking and prying with a purpose."
-Zora Neale Hurston[7]

Many entrepreneurs believe that if they have an excellent idea, they will naturally encounter business success. While a great idea for a product or service can certainly help propel a new business to success, it is still important to consider what markets are available for your product or service. You need to determine whether customers are going to buy your products, how much they will pay for them, and whether any other competitors will make it difficult for you to start a new business.

Unless there are a wealth of customers and somewhat minimal competition within your industry, you may struggle to get your business running. Let us explore two entrepreneurs who discovered the drawbacks of not conducting industry research:

***

Example #1: Kate

Kate is an entrepreneur who believes she can create a software application that helps small-business owners determine customer buying patterns quickly and easily. She is highly enthusiastic about this idea because she believes this software could be used by businesses that might not have the money to invest in marketing research and customer segmentation. Whenever she talks to friends and family members about her idea, they all seem to agree that it sounds like a fantastic basis for a start-up. Due to this positive response, Kate decides to "dive headfirst" into starting a business based on her software application.

Kate invests a considerable amount of her own capital into creating this software. Once she has it running, she decides to market the software through websites and social-media platforms to save money. However, when Kate starts to build websites and landing pages to sell her software application, she discovers several freeware applications that resemble her own products—and

---

[7] "Zora Neale Hurston Quotes," BrainyQuote, accessed November 1, 2018, https://www.brainyquote.com/quotes/zora_neale_hurston_132635.

they are being offered at no cost. Kate finds herself in a dilemma: she needs to market her product to a customer base that is already able to get a version of her product for free.

She concludes that she needs to completely change her marketing tactics by demonstrating how her software is superior to the freeware that is already available. However, she loses valuable time altering her marketing strategy and she struggles to generate the sales that can make up for the marketing expenses she incurs. After a year of marketing her software, Kate might be forced to give up on this business dream.

***

Example #2: Thomas
Thomas wants to start his own home-based business selling information products. As Thomas formerly worked in the IT industry, he believes that he can make a great deal of money by writing books on how readers can solve some of their most common IT problems. His idea is largely spurred on by the success of Mr. Excel, who made a fortune writing books and leading webinars on how to master Excel spreadsheets.

Despite having expertise and a business model to follow, Thomas finds it difficult to market to customers. These customers often have specific IT problems that are difficult for him to address in his book, as he is writing a general manual. Additionally, Thomas discovers that many of the biggest troubleshooting issues people have can be answered for free on forums, other websites, and manufacturer manuals.

After a few months of struggling to sell his books to customers, Thomas decides that the project is no longer worth the money or effort it requires. As a result, he deactivates his website accounts and considers this a failed venture.

***

In the two examples above, many of the problems arose as a result of failing to conduct the proper industry research. Due to this oversight, both Kate and Thomas are shocked to discover that despite their excellent business ideas, they either cannot find the proper customer pool, or they face strong competition. In Kate's case, she discovers one of the worst problems: something very similar to her product is already being given offered for free.

Now that we have explored some examples that illustrate how avoiding industry research can damage the potential success of a business, let us examine why research is important, how to do it, and how to determine who your biggest competitors are.

Know the Importance of Industry Research

Regardless of how great you think your business idea is, you should always wait to implement your business ideas until after you have conducted thorough industry research. Taking this step can help you determine a number of factors with critical roles in the success of your business, including the following:

- ✔ **Industry research can aid in determining if there is a market for your product and what kind of market it might be.** There are different types of markets that can greatly influence what your bottom line might be, how often your customers may buy from you, and whether your business can anticipate long-term versus short-term success. We will discuss how to determine these markets in a later section of this chapter.

- ✔ **Industry research can reveal your biggest competitors.** If you want to become successful in your particular industry, you need to know who your competitors are, how successful they are, and why their customers shop with them. Industry research can also help you determine if there is room for your product, which can play a huge role in how profitable you may become. For example, if your industry is oversaturated, you may find it difficult to make a name for yourself. You may also find it difficult to raise awareness of your products via marketing, especially if you are in competition with successful businesses that already have millions to spend on their marketing and advertising budgets.

- ✔ **Industry research reveals how long your business might be viable.** While a business might become successful when it is first established, not all markets are able to sustain a business. For example, if you have a product that can only be used once by a customer, you may need to spend a considerable amount of money acquiring new customers to maintain your bottom line.

- ✔ **Industry research helps you minimize the risks you encounter as you begin your business.** When you understand what your current competition is, who your customers are, and what they want to buy, you can help design your business processes to ensure that you're making appropriate decisions.

  Additionally, industry research can help you identify any potential problems that might arise from your products. As you are developing your business, you can gauge customer reactions and adjust your products according to your market's opinions and buying behaviors.

- ✔ **Industry research allows you to recognize your current position in the market.** When you first begin to grow your business, you must know your position in relation to your biggest competitors. This can be crucial for helping you make decisions related to growing your business.

✔ **Industry research can help you clarify your brand's message.** When you understand what your competitors are offering prospective customers, you can tweak your message so that it offers your customers something different. By taking this step, you can stand out from the crowd and offer your customers a unique buying experience.

As these benefits have revealed, industry research can help you determine how your business can be positioned, how many customers are willing to buy from you, and whether the market is already oversaturated with businesses like yours. It can help you make critical decisions that can help your company grow and flourish over the years.

Joshua Earsley, owner of Semper Fi Catering, specializes in California smokehouse barbecue. "I always knew that I wanted to do something with food," he explains, "I wanted to prepare it, I wanted to serve it to people. And my favorite type of cuisine has always been good old fashioned American barbecue—smoked meat, rich sides, really tasty desserts." Market research helped him realize that the market for his products was underserved in his area: "In terms of Southern California, I've never experienced anything like this. It's just not available out here. It was clear to me I needed to do something out here to open people's eyes to what real, authentic barbecue is supposed to be like."

Earsley had an idea and researched his market to ensure its viability before starting. If you know what products you will offer, industry research helps you carve out your niche and establish your business. However, there are many business owners who are not sure how to begin their businesses. If you are not sure what type of products or services you would like to sell, you can conduct industry research to match your skills and interests with an available market.

"When I first decided to actually stop talking about it and said, 'I'm going forward with it. I'm going to do something I love on my own terms,' I wasn't considering was everything else that goes behind it," explains Earsley. "It's not just about doing something you love. The reality is that the part I love doing is probably twenty percent of the job. I'm not able to prepare the food until I sell it. I can't make sales without prospects, [I] can't get any prospects going unless I market effectively, [and I] can't have a solid marketing strategy without a solid business plan. I need target demographics, and the likelihood of the people in my area actually purchasing my catering services." Building on the strong foundation of market research, Earsley can focus on doing what he loves. We will discover the process of conducting good research in the next few sections of this chapter.

Conduct Industry Research

As an entrepreneur, you should understand where to save money when it counts. While understanding your industry is a critical element for determining the success of your business, you might not have the capital required to engage in in-depth marketing research. This is why it is advised that you utilize low-cost industry research techniques to gather an accurate understanding of the potential market for your business. In this section, you will discover some of the best online industry research techniques that can help you better understand the buying power of customers in your market, as well as the amount of competition in your industry. These low-cost research efforts can be revealing, especially with regards to the longevity of your potential market.

To achieve longevity, you want to find a market with plenty of customers who will buy from you repeatedly. Many entrepreneurs have started businesses that sell products that customers only buy once; however, the most successful businesses are those that know getting the same customers to continue to buy from them is the key to success. We will discuss how to identify these markets soon.

In addition to finding a market that supports your company's long-term growth, you also want to find a market that is going to help you make a sizeable profit. You should take preventative steps against becoming involved in an unprofitable market. You do not want to learn that your niche is not worthwhile six months or even a few years in the future.

The following research methods can help you achieve a better idea of the businesses you may be competing against in your market, in addition to the profitability of said market. Follow each of the steps below to ensure that you have fully researched your market, as this can save you a lot of potential heartache and frustration along your journey.

Determine How Much Free Information Exists

One of the worst nightmares for an entrepreneur is entering a niche market with serious competition. Free information poses a potential threat to some start-up businesses. If a customer can get the same quality and ready availability of a product or service for free, he or she probably will. Though you do not always need to consider free information a nightmare, it can cut into your market, depending on the quality and availability of the offerings. This should be taken into account as any competitor who offers your product or service for a lower price than you are able.

A great example of problematic free information is a recipe cookbook. There are plenty of authors who make profit from their cookbooks—but these authors are generally big-name chefs who have five-year deals on television networks. For the average entrepreneur, making a profit on a cookbook can be a challenge for two reasons: there is an abundance of free recipes available online, and you do not have a big enough name to warrant charging a fee for your recipes. Therefore, if you wanted to sell a cookbook online, you should carefully reconsider your market options.

To find out what level of competition you will be facing for unpaid products, services, or information in your niche, take to your favorite search engine and simply type in a primary keyword in your industry. For example, if you want to start a business that focuses on training puppies, search with the words "training a puppy" or "training a difficult puppy." If your search results show that your competitors are offering free products and books on the subject, then it is best to seek another market niche. Alternatively, you may want to find ways to add to or change your product so that it is worth the fee you will be charging.

Investigate Major Online Shops and Vendors

Finding a profitable niche involves determining exactly how much money your potential clients are already spending—and the best way to do that (without spending hundreds of dollars on software) is to visit sites like Amazon, PayPal, and Clickbank to see how many products are offered in your market.

- **For Amazon, look at the number of shops in that market, not only the number of listings available in the marketplace.** If there is a great deal of shops specializing in your niche, then it is most likely a lucrative industry.

- **While most people regard PayPal as the current leader in online payment, you can also use the platform to conduct detailed research on your marketplace.** You will find a link to PayPal's shop at the bottom of its homepage; click on the link, select your industry niche, and look at the number of shops that are categorized under that niche. As with Amazon, the more shops there are, the more money customers are spending.

Look at Sponsored Listings

If you have ever conducted an online search with Google, then you have probably noticed links at the top of any search-engine query notated "Ad." Those are known as sponsored links, and they can be your greatest ally during your industry research. To get a sponsored link, a vendor pays the search engine to list his or her ad; the vendor then pays the search engine a fee based on the number of clicks the ad generates. These sponsored listings can provide a huge traffic boost to a company's website. Therefore, the more traffic the website is getting, the longer the ad will be posted online.

A quick word of warning: the following method does take a bit of time, so be sure to properly commit a few weeks to utilizing this technique.

Go to any search engine that utilizes sponsored links, such as Google, and type in your industry keyword. Once the first search page is returned, look at the listings marked "Ad" or "Sponsored."

Search | training a puppy   Q

All   Images   Shopping   More

Basic Dog Training Course
[Ad] http://www...
Learn basic dog obedience commands. Behavior modification. Behavior training system works with any breed. Veteran/Military discount. Call for free trial offer.

One-on-One K9 Consulting
[Ad] http://www...
Professional Dog Trainer with 25 years of experience. Expert in animal behaviors. Best classes. Offers in-home and one-on-one training. Call now for $25 discount.

2 Week Boarding & Training
[Ad] http://www...
Premier overnight dog care and training services. Dog training with expert staff. Any age dogs. Puppies learn basic and advanced leash obedience, and socialization.

Ask yourself the following questions:

- What are those sponsored listings offering?

- Who are the vendors posting the links?

- What information is revealed to you when you click through the link?

Make note of these sponsors, and then put aside your market research temporarily. The next day, type in the *exact same keyword* and make note of the sponsored links. Ask yourself these new questions:

- Are the ads the same ones from yesterday?

- Have completely new ads taken their places?

Record your findings, and then repeat this process the each day, conducting this research over the course of two weeks, all while using the *exact same* industry keyword as from the first day you performed this technique.

After two weeks of research, look at what your research has revealed. Either one of two things is likely to have happened: the sponsored links remained relatively unchanged, or the listings were more volatile and unpredictable. In a lucrative market, the sponsored links will remain unchanged, as these businesses are making plenty of money from their customers to justify the expense of advertising. If the links frequently changed, that is a big indicator that online vendors are not making as much of a profit from the industry as they would like, as those ads can be relatively expensive investments to make.

Look at a Search Engine's Natural Listings

Take to your favorite search engine again and type in your industry's primary keyword. Instead of looking at the sponsored listings like in the previous method, look at the results that appear in the center of the page. These are known as the search engine's natural listings, and these can tell you a great deal about your potential market niche—but only if you know what to look for.

Look through the top ten results returned for your industry keyword. Ask yourself the following questions to analyze what you are looking at:

- What are these websites focused on?

- Do they give away free information?

- Do the websites offer a range of products in your niche?

- Do these websites have plenty of ad space (in other words, space exclusively rented out to online advertisers)?

- How professional do these sites look?

These questions will give you clues as to what to prepare for when it comes to market profitability and competition. If it seems like your top ten competitors are making plenty of money, then chances are you will as well. On the other hand, if the search engine's natural listings reveal that your competitors are practically giving away free information, then you might reconsider your business idea, as it is possible there is not much money to be made in this particular niche.

Peruse an Industry Forum

Explore the forums and blogs that are devoted to your industry. You can find these by entering a simple search engine query. Pay close attention to what the commentators are discussing. Ask yourself the following questions to gain as much information as possible about your potential market:

- Is there hype about your intended market?

- Are there any big names that are mentioned repeatedly?

- Does anyone talk about the price of industry-related products as being too low or too high?

- Is your industry being talked about at all? That is an important caveat to consider: if there is no hype around your industry, then it might be difficult to make money in this particular market.

When researching your market, do not underestimate the power of these forums and blogs; these are your customers directly revealing their hopes, dreams, and expectations to you. This is another benefit of these industry-research techniques: you do not need to conduct expensive consumer research in order to figure out what they need from you and your business.

Conduct Direct Research

Joseph Molina, Executive Director and CEO for the Veterans Chamber of Commerce, is an expert in business start-up and financing. He emphasizes the importance of industry research to your financial success. Through years of business consulting, Molina has found that a lot of business owners have an idea of what they would like to do, but they do not have a very specific or concise idea of what product or service they are going to offer. Molina says, "They have a general idea, for the most part, but they lack that clarity as to what type of benefit they offer a consumer, and believe it or not, that's probably the greatest obstacle that small businesses have when they want to start up. [...] There is an overview of overall industry research that should take place and that should happen through trade associations. They have databases and information that you can access." Molina recommends a visit to your local library, which should help you to obtain a list of books to direct you. In his words, "I recommend that you go to someone whose job is to research, like a librarian. Look for information like how many people are in this business and how much this industry is making—all of that is in reports. Once you find a trade association, they might have a local chapter that you can access, or you can go online to their website. You may have to contact them to get information about the ups and downs of that industry. That will give you a sense of whether this type of business is growing, or if this is an industry that is having problems."

However, this is only the first, most general step. Molina continues, "The second part is actually going to do direct research. The first step in direct research is called market research intelligence. You have to go to the competition. You go into an open store and look into those locations to gather information on their parking lot, accessibility, lighting, the look and feel of the storefront, the look and feel of the environment within the store, the type of employees they have and whether or not they have uniforms, what happens when people walk in, what is the customer service like, etc. Then, look into newspapers and such, and see how these stores market themselves. Get a sense of how many people are in the stores. If they're empty, you want to seriously reconsider that type of business." One benefit to direct research is that it gives you a picture of your competition and your immediate market.

"Finally," explains Molina, "there's online research. You want to go to the competitor's website and see what kind of format they use, what colors are on their template, how they communicate with the customers. Do they have a Facebook page? A LinkedIn page?" After collecting this information, Molina says, a business owner can begin to imitate the successful patterns of his competition. "Imitate first, innovate later. Imitate before you come up with your own creative things—that is your starting point for the business. Doing research tells us where our competitors are strong and where their weaknesses are, so that you can fill in the gaps and excel."

Consider Utilizing Paid Industry Research Services

Consider supplement your industry research by utilizing paid industry research services. Be aware, you may prefer to acquire sufficient information about your industry by simply using the techniques described above, as the above alternatives will save your valuable start-up finances for more rare and vital resources. Some additional online industry research services, which may charge fees to access their information, include the following:

- **Dun & Bradstreet:** This provides free statistical data on specific industries.

- **BizStats:** This also provides statistical data on specific industries.

- **Hoovers Online:** Use the "Companies and Industries" tab to learn more about your specific industry, as well as your potential competition.

- **MarketResearch:** This retailer provides private market reports; there is a fee associated with ordering these reports.

Now that we have disclosed some great research methods that you can use on your own to determine the viability of your potential market, you may now have a great deal of information about your market. Once you have this information in hand, you must next determine if this market can help sustain long-term business growth.

Understanding the Demand for Your Business

In a previous section, we mentioned that the ideal market for a start-up business is one that has great potential for longevity—one in which you will not have to struggle to find a consumer base. With this in mind, let us explore the three market types that are available and how you can identify whether or not they can help your business make enough money for long-term growth.

The Short-Life/Short-Life Market

Customers in a short-life/short-life market have a short-term problem, and are looking for a short-term solution. Unfortunately, there is very little money to be made with the customers in this pool. These customers will only need to buy a product from you once in order to solve that short-term problem.

These types of markets are best for those who enjoy dabbling in start-up websites and niches. However, if you are new to the entrepreneurial world, this might not be for you. It might be worthwhile to invest your time and efforts into a market that will pay you back and be more sustainable.

A great example of a short-life/short-life product is anything electronic. Let us examine the Kindle, for example. When the Kindle was released, there was a huge line of people waiting to purchase this product, and when they finally got their hands on it, they did not need to purchase from a Kindle vendor any longer. Unless their Kindles malfunction or they would like to upgrade to another version, there is very little chance that these customers will return anytime soon to make another purchase, as their main problem (not having a Kindle) has already been solved.

The Short-Life/Long-Life Market

Though this is not the ideal market to start up in, this is a market that has made plenty of entrepreneurial millionaires—and for good reason. Although the customers in this niche will have their problems solved after one purchase, there will always be customers interested in purchasing within this niche.

The major challenge about the short-life/long-life market is that it can be difficult to market to new customers. After all, in order to keep making a sizable income, you need to ensure that your websites and marketing materials are reaching new potential customers who have not heard of you before. That can take plenty of time, not to mention a great deal of capital invested in your marketing ventures.

Generally speaking, all facets of the health industry (save for weight loss) provide great examples of the short-life/long-life market, particularly when it comes to nutritional supplements and medication. For example, suppose your business specializes in a type of product that reduces of acne. If your product works, then once a customer purchases the product, his or her acne (in other words, their short-term problem) will be eliminated.

However, there will *always* be a demand for anti-blemish products, so even if you cannot hold one customer, you can be assured that there will be plenty more entering "through the revolving door." This market is a long-term one because there will always be people who need your type of product.

The Long-Life/Long-Life Market

Here is the kind of market that many entrepreneurs should become familiar with, as it is one of the few niche markets that seamlessly blends together the possibility for long-term customer relationships and the best market longevity. A great example of the long-life/long-life market includes hobbies and interests like writing, knitting, losing weight, fashion, marketing, and the like.

Let us examine the weight loss niche. Normally we would recommend against going into this market, as it can be very competitive; however, for ease of comprehension, let us use this as an example. While you may think that weight loss would be classified as a short-life/long-life market, remember that people do not stop using diet and exercise advice as soon as they reach their goal weights.

By selling a product for long-term weight loss—say, a maintenance program that helps customers maintain their weight loss over the long-term—it is easier to develop an ongoing relationship with old customers *in addition* to adding new customers to your clientele base. A long-life/long-life market allows you to build a strong clientele base, in which you can foster lucrative client relationships, market to new customers without much effort, and build up a business empire, all with relatively few products.

While we have carefully analyzed each of the three niches that you might come across, it is important to determine what category your potential business might fall under. Your category will essentially depend on your prospective customers' experiences of your business.

Let us suppose you wanted to sell an online program on training dogs. Now, you know there are plenty of customers who need to have their precious new puppies trained—and as long as people keep buying man's best friend, you might assume that you can stay in business.

However, this might be a false assumption. A dog-training program falls into what we would call a short-life/long-life market. Your customers have a short-term problem: they need their dogs trained. If your product works, then they will not need to buy from you anymore. So long as another customer with a disobedient dog is ready to "walk through the door" and make a purchase, it is easy to lose touch with that customer who has already bought from you.

According to direct-marketing research, a client who has already purchased from you will be three times more likely than a new customer to buy from you again. Retaining your previous clients means undergoing less marketing effort to make the same amount of money.

To determine what category accurately described your potential business, ask yourself the following questions. Your answers will reveal if you have stumbled across a profit-grabbing long-life/long-life market niche. Get out a pen and paper, and track your answers to the following questions:

- Is my product renewable? Will my clients have to return to me again and again to buy more?

- Can I develop a product range for this niche, or will I have to focus on one product?

- Can I charge a membership fee for this product/service? Can it be a monthly or annually recurring fee?

- Is this highly specialized information that can only be sold once, or is there an opportunity to develop this into a larger brand?

Once you have analyzed your answers, carefully determine if you have a business niche worth pursuing. If this is the first time you are starting a business, we recommend that you pursue a long-life/long-life market. Wait until you have gained more experience, and take the entrepreneurial "training wheels are off," before you start pursuing more aggressive short-life/long-life and short-life/short-life markets.

Before we close this chapter, let us address a question that might be perplexing some readers. While this chapter has assumed that some readers may already have a distinct idea of what business they would like to start, other readers might not yet have a clear direction. For those who know what you want to start your business in, market research is relatively straightforward. But if you do not have an area of expertise or simply are not sure what market you want to specialize in, it can certainly be challenging.

Do not panic if you are in the latter category; this is often a common experience for people who know they want to start a business but are not yet sure what they should specialize in. We have developed a series of questions that can help you narrow down your ideal business niche. Ready your pen and paper, and answer the following questions to discover what potential business ideas you might find the most appealing:

- **What am I interested in?** Being an entrepreneur is no fun if you are specializing in something that does not interest you whatsoever, even if you do earn a sizeable profit from it.

- **What are my experiences and interests?** Do you consider yourself a strong stamp collector? Do you know what it takes to train for a 10k or even a marathon race? Are you the most organized person, even in the midst of domestic chaos? Do not overlook a single experience or interest in your search for the perfect market—it just might lead to a fantastic business idea.

- **What accomplishments am I most proud of?** Did you lose fifty pounds by eating well and working out? Did you earn a terrific score on a notoriously tough standardized test? These accomplishments might reveal you to be an expert that potential customers are willing to listen to.

- **What do I want to learn about?** You do not need to be an expert at a certain hobby or interest to become a master at a certain niche or industry; as long as you are willing to learn about an interest, you can become an expert at it. It will take you slightly longer to start your business, but the rewards can be worth the extra time.

Now that we have analyzed some of the basics of conducting industry research, let us explore an example of how an entrepreneur might discover a lucrative skill that can be quickly leveraged into a successful business opportunity.

***

Example: Sue
Sue had always been told that becoming a writer was just a very distant dream. Even in high school, her guidance counselor gently directed her to another career of choice. "If you want to be a writer," the counselor said, "then you need to be prepared for major disappointment. What about working in the publishing industry? Or better still, what about becoming an English teacher?"

Sue continued to hear suggestions like these through college. That is why, when she graduated from college with a bachelor's degree in English, she settled for an administrative-assistant job.

But then Sue lost her job, and she needed to find a way to make consistent money quickly. Tired of applying for administrative-assistant jobs, she decided to strike out on her own and find a way to turn her writing skills into a lucrative new employment opportunity. After applying for countless editing and publishing jobs, she decided to become an online freelance writer.

After a few years of establishing her writing business and building a steady list of clients, Sue wanted to find a way to produce a new kind of income stream: one that was automatic, passive, and would allow her to take some time off without worrying about money. She decided to start her own online business.

The first obstacle Sue encountered was a big one. How could she start an online business without a line of products or a discernible talent? She did not know how to sell anything, she was not a health and wellness expert, and she did not know a thing about affiliate marketing. The more Sue researched marketing niches, the more panicked she became about her likelihood of starting a profitable online business.

Sue had an intriguing thought. She realized that in the days before she had become a freelance writer, she had searched online for writing opportunities, advice from other writers, and websites that could show how to make money writing. Sue realized that if she had struggled to find writing opportunities, others just like her were now doing the same. After conducting marketing research, she learned that there was a wealth of people who wanted to launch writing careers without waiting to get published.

This market research demonstrated a viable opportunity. Sue would start a home-based business that specialized in showing would-be writers how to do exactly what she had done: become an online freelance writer.

***

As the above example demonstrates, your first step does not need to be a clear idea of what you want to start a business in. After taking stock of your skills and expertise, you may discover a marketable talent that can help establish a platform for starting a business.

Throughout the course of this chapter, you may have discovered that a potential business might not have the kind of market you were hoping for. If this is the case, do not be upset about this missed opportunity. Instead, be thankful that you discovered this before investing your time, effort, and capital into a business opportunity that was likely to fail. Keep searching for a business idea that satisfies your industry research. When you find one, you will be much more confident that you can start a business that will be successful.

As he grows his business, Earsley continues his market research to determine Semper Fi Catering's potential: "Within the next five years, I want to corner ten to thirteen percent of the catering market in my area. In the next five years, I may do some competitions and may open up a bigger space. Maybe provide takeout services, maybe bottle barbecue sauce to sell." Knowing your market well, as Earsley does, can reveal areas for potential expansion and increase your revenue.

Earsley's advice to new entrepreneurs re-states the importance of understanding your market before investing in your business. "My advice to someone strongly considering this is to make sure you really understand what you're getting into before investing tens of thousands of dollars," he says. "Do your research, look into it. Read books, read articles, ask questions to professionals, talk to people in the line of business that you're interested in. Find owners and ask them, 'What do you think I need?' or 'What did you need to get started?' before jumping into it blind. That's how a lot of companies go under. They're really excited about something and then jump in. Even if they have a great product, if nobody knows about it, it's not going to happen."

Review Chapter 2

Now that you have completed Chapter 2, reflect on its content and how you will conduct thorough industry research. As you review this chapter, consider the following questions:

- ☐ Do you understand the importance of industry research? Can you identify ways this background information will aid in the foundation of your business?

- ☐ Do you know where and how to conduct industry research? Can you competently utilize online resources available to you?

- ☐ Upon conducting your industry research, what did you learn about your industry that you did not know before?

- ☐ What is the demand for your business? Do you understand the type of market and consumer base you are seeking?

If you are satisfied with your understanding of how you will conduct thorough industry research, resume reading with Chapter 3.

How to Identify Your Needed Products and Services

"Business is not just doing deals; business is having great products, doing great engineering, and providing tremendous service to customers."
-Ross Perot[8]

In order for your start-up business to be successful, it will need to be capable of consistently producing and offering a product or service that fulfills the wants and needs of your potential customers. Unfortunately identifying and designing the creation process for desired products and services can be a challenging task for some entrepreneurs. Let us explore one example that illustrates common obstacles many entrepreneurs may face:

***

Example: Jeff

Jeff wants to create a new type of logistics software that tracks shipment deliveries for small-business owners. Jeff envisions this type of software can help business owners provide their customers with real-time shipment information, which can improve the delivery process. After conducting industry research, Jeff is excited to realize that there is significant potential for this software to be a big hit with customers.

However, before Jeff can begin selling his software to his prospective customers, he needs to develop a process that can help him create versions of his software as quickly and as accurately as possible. Additionally, Jeff wants to ensure that his product completely matches his customers' emotional needs. He knows that if his product cannot satisfy his customers, his business is will be unsuccessful. With this in mind, Jeff decides to implement the following actions:

- ✔ Jeff worries that his software product will not match his customers' needs, as he does not have enough information to determine their buying behavior. He decides to research his competitors' average customers, as

---

[8] "Ross Perot Quotes," BrainyQuote, accessed November 1, 2018, https://www.brainyquote.com/quotes/ross_perot_159902.

he believes that he can apply this knowledge to his own business. He also decides to have a brainstorming session with his less involved "silent" business partner, who invested a substantial amount of capital into Jeff's business. During the brainstorming session, they think about why their customers need their product, how the customers are going to use it, and what emotional need it should fulfill.

✔ Jeff does not have much information available regarding how his operations should be designed. He asks professional colleagues and industry peers what business processes they use to create their software. His colleagues inform him the best way to create a high-quality software product efficiently is to develop an operational process that minimizes risks and does not cost too much of his money and resources.

✔ While Jeff is planning on doing the majority of product design himself, he knows he will need to interact with other designers to create and launch the product. He worries that he may have a hard time communicating the requirements of his customers to the designers, as the designers will need to use more technical language. In order to overcome this obstacle, Jeff joins in several meetings with his designers to discuss how the software needs to function. He also schedules several milestone dates that allow him to periodically review the product designers' progress. This way, if his designers are off track in creating a viable product for his customers, he can make necessary revisions without falling behind on this schedule.

After taking these actions, Jeff feels confident that his software product will meet the needs of his customers. He is also delighted to realize he now has an operational process in place that he can continue to use as his business grows. He is relieved by knowing when he starts hiring employees, this process will become practically automatic. This process allows him to focus on other aspects of growing his business without constantly micromanaging the product's operational process.

***

In the example above, Jeff is faced with several dilemmas that are common to entrepreneurs, which include the following:

■ He needs to create a product that will meet the needs of his potential customers, but he does not have enough information about his customers to determine what these wants and needs are.

■ He needs to create an operational process that will aid the creation of his product, but is not sure where to start.

■ He needs to find a way to translate his customers' requirements to his designers, who might need more technical information to design the product.

As an entrepreneur, you will likely encounter these difficulties yourself. Each can seem like a chicken-and-egg scenario: it is difficult for you to design a product without learning more about your customers, but you cannot determine customer information without releasing a product for them to buy. This can be a frustrating experience for entrepreneurs, as it can make them feel stuck with no apparent decision in sight.

Fortunately, this chapter is dedicated to helping you conduct market research in order to create the best customer-pleasing product possible. A variety of methods will be explored, including those that can be implemented without your own customer data.

In addition to these valuable techniques, you can expect to learn how to create a business process that will allow you to create a product or service. The operational process can be a critical part of your business success, as it can automate the product-design experience.

Finally, you will discover how to communicate customer requirements to product designers. This can be a vital part of designing a successful product, as you need that product to be functional in addition to meeting the wants and needs of your customers.

Match Your Product to Your Customers

Product design may be a critical component of starting a successful business, but even the most innovative design will fail if it does not match customer requirements, the wants and needs that your customers have. Your products need to fulfill these wants and needs as efficiently as possible.

Part of running a successful start-up business involves understanding precisely what your customers need from your organization. The more in tune you are with your customers, the greater the likelihood that you can develop high-quality products that strengthen your company's brand.

At 3rd Time's a Farm, Desma Brooks works directly with her customers to determine their needs and wants. At startup, her community-supported agriculture (CSA) grew the easiest or most cost-effective produce: "First off, it was what I knew—to grow tomatoes, green beans, peppers, everything I knew that I would want in my garden. Then I went to groups like the Farmer Veteran Coalition to listen to other farmers talk about what did they grow, what didn't work for them." Brooks also found some products that didn't work. "I rolled back watermelon because they seed so heavy," she says, "it takes so long to recover that ground. I also don't do pumpkin because while they were fun, and I got a lot of farm traffic with those, the Amish in my area grow more pumpkin than anybody in the world could ever carve." If those products didn't work for her, what did? She found that her customers' feedback and guidance was the most valuable determiner of what produce she should focus on, and what other methods she could use to increase her revenue. "It really helps when [customers] give me their input. A lot of the older couples are just happy that they don't have to grow their own, and it shows up at their house. They're like, 'Oh, my goodness, that was so great!'"

Negative feedback can be helpful, too. "I grew turnips my first year and I had a lot of people ask, 'What is that?' So I [started giving] them a three by five index card for everything I sold and how to prepare it. Like rhubarb: some people had never seen rhubarb, so I gave them a couple of recipes (pie or strawberry shortcake). If they have any questions, most of the time they just text me." Brooks keeps track of each customers' requests, so she can personalize their subscription. "I make a mark on that person's label," she explains, noting which produce they liked and disliked.

Developing customer requirements can also aid in identifying issues that are only implicitly stated by your customers. Your customers may not explicitly state what they need from your products, but they still have opinions about how your products should function. Brooks reads her customers' reactions to understand what produce they might be interested in. "Salad greens, most everybody is just surprised that you can grow them here. And with all the romaine lettuce issues, most people would prefer to have mine than anything that came out of a grocery store. Those are the kinds of things I look at," she explains, "It really makes a difference for how much work I have to do." Prepare to brainstorm with your other business leaders or relevant professional peers, as this will likely make it possible for you to identify the customers' needs that are not explicitly communicated to your business. This focus is necessary no matter what product or service you offer, and it allows you to connect better with your customers' exact wants and needs.

Before you can begin applying customer requirements to your product or service design, conduct more in-depth research about your market to learn exactly what your potential customers might want and need. Learn how to use customer-segmentation methodologies, which can help you identify customer wants and needs, buying behaviors, and attitudes regarding your products. This process can help you better understand your market and design or develop products and services that precisely match its needs. In this section, we will explore low-cost customer-segmentation methodologies to better analyze your target market for the purpose of product design.

> **Determine Customer Requirements**
> to identify a needed product or service.
> Use customer segmentation.
> Use RFM analysis.
> Use clustering strategies.
> Conduct market research.

↓

> **Design Your Product or Sevice**
> to match your customer requirements.
> Use technical language.
> Determine required resources.
> Identify the "look."
> Set minimum functional benchmarks.
> Test.

↓

> **Create Your Business Process**
> to consistently create quality products or services.
> Determine needs.
> Determine objectives.
> Analyze each step.
> Establish oversight.

Know the Importance of Customer Segmentation

Customer segmentation is nothing new—in fact, since the rapid growth of the Internet, many companies have devoted teams of researchers to developing complicated analytical models that showcase customer behaviors and benefits. As a new entrepreneur, you may not have the luxury of assigning this task to teams of surveyors and statisticians. Also, capital might be somewhat limited for you at this stage, which means you need to be careful about how your money is spent.

Grocery stores are abundant and may seem to have the produce market covered, but Brooks has found her niche in two areas: customers with special dietary needs and customers who prefer having their produce delivered. "I'm the only one in this county who offers the CSA with delivery," she explains, regarding the second group. "A lot of my customers are older, and they don't want to get out early on a Saturday morning to go to the market or they've got grandkids that they're cooking for, they don't want to go. The younger ones, I have a couple of vegetarians who are just tickled to pieces to get fresh stuff. I just have to deliver them good products and communicate well, and it pretty much does itself." In addition to vegetarians, Brooks has several customers with even more specific dietary needs: "I've got a couple of celiac patients. I have one lady that pays her whole CSA just for beef, because she has celiac disease and when she has a flare up, the only thing that she can process is the beef." She keeps these customers coming back by tailoring her offerings each season to their wants and needs.

Fortunately, the reasoning behind customer segmentation is not at all complicated. In fact, it only requires a basic grasp of marketing knowledge to realize why it is so critical to a new business's success. As an entrepreneur, you must focus on customers with the greatest potential for profit. The fastest way for you to identify these customers is to divide your customers into groups, or segments. Members of a segment should meet the following three criteria:

☐ They are identifiable by common characteristics, like age, location, or buying behaviors.

☐ They are profitable (in other words, you are not spending more money than what they are paying).

☐ They are constantly growing.

To develop your own customer-segmentation methodologies and learn more about your market, focus on the following behaviors and characteristics:

- Age

- Lifestyle (What is the average salary of your customers? The average personal net worth? What industries do your customers work in, etc.?)

- Attitudes toward money

- Purchase behavior (How often have they purchased your products? How often do they purchase your competitors' products? What's the total net profit of each customer?)

- Geographical location

- Psychographic segmentation (otherwise known as behavioral segmentation)

We recommend you keep your customer segments as small as possible. This can help you master the art of customer segmentation and avoid getting into overly complex research, which can be time consuming and frustrating for the average entrepreneur. Customer segmentation can help you as an entrepreneur to answer some of the most basic business questions, including the following:

- Who are my most valuable clients?

- How profitable are my customers?

- Who are my least-profitable customers?

- Why are my customers leaving?

- Why are my customers buying from me?

- What do my best customers look like?

Now that you know what customer segmentation is, let us examine why this process is important to the success of your start-up business. Investigating beyond the group psychology of your customer base will allow you to discover your customer requirements and design products precisely focused on meeting them. Without analyzing what behaviors, needs, and external characteristics make clients want to spend (or conversely, what characteristics make potential clients avoid your business), your start-up company will not be sustainable over the long term. Focusing on customers also gives you a competitive advantage that will help your business stand out from the crowd.

As discussed in this book's introduction, the following three components are critical to your business's achievement: operational excellence, product leadership, and customer intimacy. All three components are essential to the competitive success of your start-up business, but see the below for reasons why excelling in customer intimacy should be your business' main focus:

✗ Operational excellence (including technological processes that make the office run smoother) might help your business become more efficient, but this also fails as a long-term competitive strategy if your customers are not buying your excess products.

✗ While decreasing your product costs might result in short-term profits, this strategy is not sustainable long-term.

✓ **Customer intimacy can provide the long-term success that your start-up business should strive for. The best customer relationships are derived from smart customer-segmentation strategies.**

Despite its advantages, some companies do not use customer-segmentation strategies because data aggregation can be extremely difficult. Data not only must be drawn together from within the clientele base but also must be mapped to (matched with) corresponding data to enrich customer understanding.

Unless you choose the right customer-segmentation strategies, gathering and merging your clientele data can be frustrating. Luckily for you, the methodologies described in this section will help protect your valuable time while illustrating which current and potential customers are the ones who are most likely to help your start-up business grow and flourish.

Quantifying the value of your customers might seem strange. These customers will help your business grow, and it can be difficult to put an emotional price tag on that. However, you may be surprised at the number of algorithms, graphs, equations, and formulas that can be used to determine which clients offer the most value to the growth of your business. The results from these in-depth formulas can help you to adapt, tweak, or even wind down marketing approaches to your various customer segments.

Some customers are more valuable than others—and as the value of a customer increases, so too should the marketing methods and products aimed toward them. Your most valued customers, known as anchor customers, will fully reach their buying potentials with your company—thus, every effort should be made to prevent these customers from being lost. The second-most valued customers, known as value customers, are not necessarily as valuable as the previous set, but nonetheless show potential to grow and reach that level of profitability. Less valued customers, known as marginal customers, do not necessarily need special marketing attention. Finally, the least valued customers, impractical customers, cost more to maintain than they bring to the company. While many experts recommend "firing" these impractical clients, others suggest minimizing the cost of business with them in order to keep them making purchases from you.

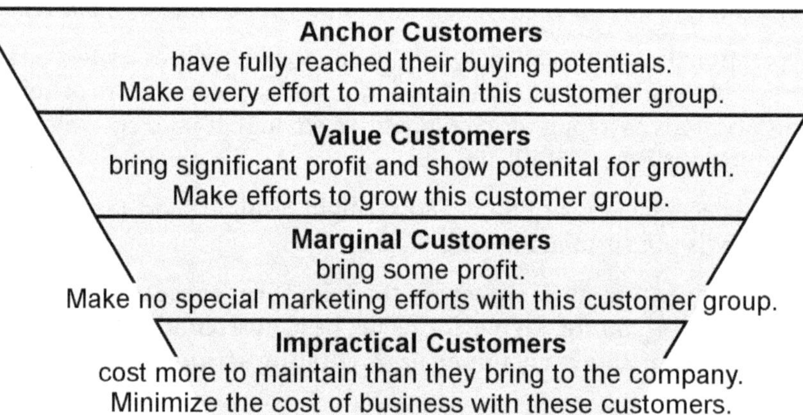

Customer segmentation might seem uncomfortably harsh and quantitative—especially in regard to managing important customer relationships—but consider these statistics and findings in a real-world example: the grocery store. Grocery stores offer many incentives for customers to do their shopping in their store. One popular incentive is the loyalty card. By simply food shopping in the same store every week, customers earn coupons, rewards, and even free shopping. Loyalty cards are a great scheme that rewards already-loyal members while turning neutral consumers into more frequent customers.

By applying this same logic to your start-up business—retaining already-valuable clients while encouraging the growth of your next customer segment—you will quickly discover that this is the most sustainable method for increasing business profits while providing your clients with highly targeted products and services. In order to develop and procure those targeted services and products, you will first need to discover the needed information for utilizing customer-segmentation methodologies.

Implement RFM Strategies

The "Recency, Frequency, Monetary Value" (RFM) analysis for customer segmentation reveals telling information about the buying patterns of your customers. RFM strategies help marketers identify how to tailor specific products and services to various client segments. Different customer groups behave differently based on the marketing and advertising that you present them with, so RFM can help you determine the most effective marketing strategies based on each customer groups' requirements.

The RFM analysis technique also identifies your most loyal and profitable customers. This customer-segmentation methodology transforms a complicated assessment into a simple quantitative number that gives you more insight into your customers.

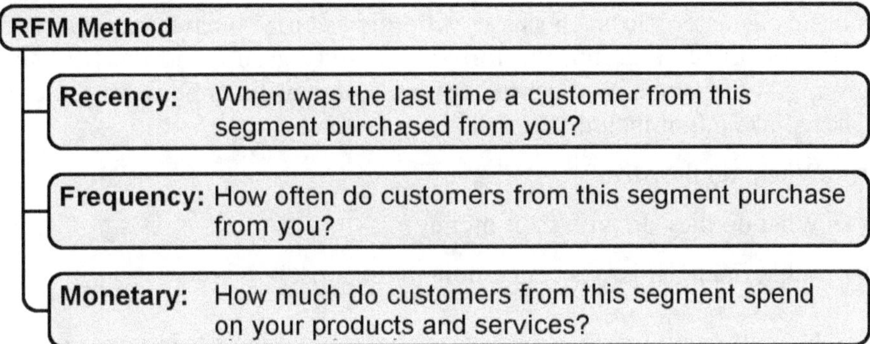

In order to gather data for your RFM analysis, you will need detailed records of your clients' transactions. Once you have this information available, ask yourself the following questions:

- How many times have they purchased a product from you?

- How many times have they followed up on a product recommendation?

- What was the value of each purchase?

This information will give you a solid understanding of who are your most financially valued customers: they are the ones who buy from you frequently and respond immediately to any marketing campaigns that you may have.

Keep detailed records of customer transactions, and always search for common links between the clients who demonstrate the most loyalty to your products and services. These common links will help you form customer segments and quickly identify future profitable customers.

Use Current and Predictive Clustering Strategies

Data clustering is another customer-segmentation methodology. There are various methods of clustering, some of which are simplistic enough—and others that are so complicated, they require advanced software to calculate. Many people confuse clustering with classification, but this methodology works from a different perspective. Instead of classifying customers based on predefined categories, you will be looking for similarities as you cluster your customers based on common characteristics.

Let us use a real-world example: suppose you are a personal-finance coach offering your clients the techniques and advice they need to make smarter decisions with their money. You have a clientele base of fifteen customers, and you would like to use that base to determine which prospects are most likely to be valuable customers (in the customer-segmentation world, this is known as creating a predictive model). First, cluster your clients according to a basic characteristic, such as age. After this step, you have three clusters: the thirty-to-forty-five group, the forty-six-to-sixty group, and the fifty-six-plus group. At this stage, you can determine common links between the clusters. These links might include the following factors:

- Where do they live?

- What do they do with their money?

- What financial issues concern them the most?

Now that you have defined what you are looking for in your clusters, let focus on the forty-six-to-sixty group and make further clusters according to their lifestyles. For this investigation, you can ask yourself the following questions:

- What is the income level of these clients?

- What are they spending their money on?

- Do they own their own homes?

- Are they saving steadily for retirement?

You will probably notice the following common links within this age group:

- They are concerned about protecting their retirement savings or 401(k).

- They are probably beginning to invest more assets and will likely respond to products that are tailored more toward smart investments.

- They have children that are in college or about to enter college.

- They are likely to have half, if not full, repayment of their homes complete.

By examining your customers' common links, you can make definitive decisions regarding how to improve their customer experiences. In the example of the financial coach, you could tailor products and services toward retirement issues, paying off mortgages, and making smart investments. This can help you experience a significant increase in your business profits.

It is best practice to use market research to discover your customers' wants and needs and to design your products so that they meet these needs. Entrepreneurs who perform needs-based analyses like those described in this chapter are more likely to own successful businesses.

Think of this kind of cluster segmentation as playing the role of a marketing detective. You can tease out revealing characteristics and commonalities from each cluster—but only if you know where to look for them. Your customer segmentation methodologies could be as simple as tracking characteristics on an Excel spreadsheet or as complex as analyzing data in high-powered software. If you are interested in the latter option, here are a few online companies that have received rave reviews for their customer-segmentation products and services:

- Survey Methods

- Mr. Dashboard

- QAS Data Plus

- Gartner, Inc.

- IDG Communications

Customer segmentation can help you carefully plan for your company's future as well as see where (and on whom) your products and services are most wisely spent. Additionally, customer segmentation can help you to identify loyal customers who you should protect at all costs, as well as potentially loyal clients who you should encourage to buy from your business.

Perform Market Research Without Customer Data

While the above customer-segmentation strategies can be helpful for businesses that have access to customer data, including sales, these might not be viable methods if you are an entrepreneur starting a business from scratch. In this case, you should meet with other business leaders in your new company or meet with relevant professionals who have experience working in your industry. They can help you determine customer requirements if you do not have sales data or if your customers are not revealing critical information to you.

In order to successfully develop and implement requirements within your work-product process, it is important for entrepreneurs to understand how to identify customer requirements. This can be a complex process, especially if your organization is limited by its size or budget and cannot gather customer surveys about your work products. Additionally, customers may not always be quick to explicitly state what they want from your products. This is another reason why business leaders should look to other industry professionals and their fellow company leaders to elicit information about customer wants and needs.

Before we explore the various techniques and methodologies that will be used to elicit needs from your fellow business leaders, let us explore how to run requirements meetings with these colleagues. By running an organized and productive requirements meeting, you and your team will be able to quickly identify your customers' wants and needs, which should help you provide your customers with the high-quality products or services they will be willing to purchase

The requirements-development meeting should have an agenda. This will provide structure and content as well as give all meeting attendees an idea of what to discuss. Be sure to provide this agenda to your meeting members prior to the meeting to give them an opportunity to prepare questions or comments. A requirements-meeting agenda should include the following items:

☐ **An introduction of the individuals who are attending the meeting.** This can be important for the members who may not have been introduced to any high-level organizational members.

☐ **The objectives of the requirements meeting.** Ensure that these participants understand what will be discussed during the meeting. This agenda should also provide you with some structure, which will keep you focused throughout the requirements meeting. Be sure to prepare an outline of the objectives and ask for any input from your colleagues before the meeting begins.

☐ **The purpose of the company's product or service.** During this part of the requirements meeting, you will want to outline to your meeting members your ideas for the product or service. You should outline how the product will be created and include information on project schedules and limitations.

☐ **The expected outcomes or benefits of the product or service.** These should include both organizational and customer benefits.

☐ **The requirements of the customers who will be receiving the product.** This should take up a good portion of your requirements meeting, as this information can help your colleagues focus on how product requirements will fulfill these customer needs. If you have any information regarding how your work product may meet the needs of your customers, introduce it at this point of the requirements meeting. If not, you can elicit customer needs by gathering information from your fellow business leaders and any relevant professionals.

☐ **The next steps your business will take.** At this point, you will want to outline how you will use valuable information to create a high-quality product or service that will fulfill the previously identified customer needs.

Throughout the requirements meeting, foster an environment where all ideas about customer requirements are welcomed. Listen to all ideas that are presented and provide helpful feedback while employing active listening skills to ensure that your meeting members feel their opinions and ideas are valued.

When identifying customer wants and needs, you may think you should survey your clientele base to determine how your work products can fulfill their needs. However, customers are not always able to articulate what they need from your organization. For example, they may not realize that they have a particular need until you introduce a product that fulfils it. Therefore, it often makes more sense to turn to your fellow business leaders and relevant professionals to determine customer requirements. Employ the following techniques to gain assistance from others in determining customer wants and needs:

☐ **Brainstorm customer requirements with family members or friends before meeting with business leaders or professional colleagues.** This can provide you with alternative solutions that you can present at the meeting in case meeting members need some assistance in coming up with potential customer requirements. For example, if your meeting members are having difficulty identifying what your primary customers require from your organization's products or services, you can lead the meeting with your alternative solutions to help them understand what your customers need.

☐ **Emphasize the importance of allowing meeting members to identify customer requirements.** Let meeting members know they are in the best position to identify these requirements and that their assistance is crucial. This can give your meeting members the encouragement they need to identify additional customer requirements.

Be sure to take the information that you gathered from your meeting and add it to your customer-requirements documentation. This documentation will detail how your products or services will fulfill your customers' requirements, which can also keep your work process focused. When translating stakeholder information into documented customer requirements, remember the following tips:

☐ **Always write requirements in the language of the customer.** This helps ensure that all focus is on the customer, including his or her wants and needs.

☐ **Avoid incorporating technical jargon into the customer-requirements documentation.** This can help ensure that any employees within your business can read your documented customer requirements without needing a translation.

☐ **Prioritize the customer requirements according to which ones your company's product or service is most likely to impact.** This will make it possible to identify a minimum quality threshold, which will be discussed momentarily.

☐ **Explain what the work product will *not* do to fulfill customer requirements.** This can be just as important as emphasizing what it will do, as it can help you proactively identify customer requirements for future versions of your work product.

☐ **Keep the documentation clear and concise.** Again, avoid clouding your findings with technical jargon, as this may cause miscommunications.

☐ **Consider keeping a section in your documentation that details non-functional customer requirements.** For example, this section could include information on how your organization's products or services will meet a customer's emotional needs, which differ from his or her functional needs.

You may find it beneficial to prioritize the customer needs that were previously identified during the requirements meeting. This can help you identify when a work product meets the primary functional needs of a customer, which can then help you adjust the product to meet any secondary needs.

After you have documented your customer requirements, you and your colleagues should establish customers' functional and quality requirements. This means that you should identify a minimum quality threshold for your products or services, which entails choosing specific customer needs that must be met before the work product can be considered acceptable.

For example, if your organization is developing a vitamin supplement that is designed to strengthen joints, developing a minimum quality threshold might involve the following acceptance criteria:

- The vitamin supplement must strengthen joints by at least 20 percent.

- The vitamin supplement must alleviate joint pain and discomfort by at least 30 percent.

- The vitamin supplement must include several minerals that aid the body in absorbing the vitamins.

These acceptance criteria may involve holding clinical trials in which subjects report their joint pain before the trial begins and again after they have been taking the vitamin supplement for six weeks.

As the above example demonstrates, documenting a minimum quality threshold and acceptance criteria helps your organization determine precisely how the work product can meet a customer's biggest needs.

Design Your Product or Service

After gathering your customer requirements, you will be in a great position to design a product that meets the needs of your target market. These customer wants and needs can also help you identify product requirements, which will determine what resources and materials must be introduced throughout the project work cycle. Incorporating customer and product requirements into the business process at appropriate times can aid your team in creating a high-quality product or service.

You must identify how your product or service can be designed to fulfill the needs of your customers. This process can involve identifying risks, work-product functions, test issues, and other attributes that need to be documented. Once these are factors are documented, you will be prepared to create a work product that meets minimum functional requirements. After these functional requirement criteria have been met, the product or service can be further refined until your customers' needs have been wholly fulfilled.

Desma Brooks has found that she is not able to fulfill every customers' requirement using only the produce she can grow, but she still accommodates them. One example is corn: "I don't grow sweet corn, because I'm not good at it. [But] a lot of people want it. If I have customers asking about sweet corn, I can call up the local lady with a farm stand who only grows that. I'll purchase monthly corn for our CSA from her, she gets a CSA share for selling to me, my customers are even happier and they'll come back next year." When she determines her customers' requirements, Brooks is able to tailor her product to them. Her dedication keeps her customers returning each season.

Let us examine how you can use the customer-requirements information you gathered in the last section to design your product or service.

Translate Requirements into Technical Language

Many of your customer requirements will be written in nontechnical terms. This is done intentionally to frame information the mindset of the customer and better express his or her requirements. However, your design team may need more technical information before they can move forward with the product-design process.

You may find it beneficial at this point to translate customer requirements into technical terms that can be used for product and product-component design. To do this, be sure to gather your product-design team together and provide them with the customer-requirements documentation. You may have a difficult time translating the nontechnical terms into something that your design team can understand, so it is best to make this a collaborative effort. Hold a meeting with your product-design team and review the customer requirements. Ensure that the design team understands what the customers need from the products or services and how the product components should meet these needs.

After the design team has this information, team members should be able to make suggestions on how to move forward from there. Be sure to document their suggestions. Ask for times when you will be able to follow up with them through the work process. To ensure that the work product is being designed to your specifications, you may find it beneficial to schedule multiple project milestones. By implementing periodic milestones, you can catch any mistakes or errors that occur before the product or service has been released to your customers.

Update the Product's Required Tools and Resources

Throughout the product-design process, you may need to identify additional requirements that derive from design decisions. For example, if your design team indicates that your work product needs to be created using new technology, you should identify the requirements associated with this technology. Apart from purchasing the new technology, these requirements may include the following:

- ☐ Obtain more funding to procure the necessary technology.

- ☐ Find professionals who can work the new technology or train those personnel who seem the most capable of using it.

- ☐ Identify when to introduce the new technology into the project's lifecycle.

- ☐ Readjust schedule milestones and deadlines as a result of the technology's introduction to the design lifecycle.

- ☐ Conduct follow-up reviews to determine if the new technology is allowing the work product to meet minimum quality threshold.

Identifying new requirements associated with design elements can allow you to adjust the product or service accordingly and minimize any risks that arise from scheduling conflicts, or lacking sufficient funding to design the product.

Identify the "Look" of the Product

Work closely with the design team to develop architectural requirements that help the work product meet customer needs. This essentially means that your design team will understand what a high-quality product will look like, in addition to how it will function. This information can provide your design team with the focus they need, as they will identify when the work product has met the minimum functional attributes that were previously identified during the customer-requirements meeting with your business colleagues.

Continually review the requirements that are essential to the design process. These reviews will identify when any changes need to be made because your design team needs new resources or materials to create the product. By staying current with requests for changes, you can ensure you have time to approve all changes and that needed resources are promptly provided to the design team.

Set a Minimum Functional Benchmark

Set a benchmark for when the product is functional enough to be delivered to your customers. You will need to use the customer requirements you identified in the previous section, as these can help you determine where to set this functional benchmark. Utilize the following steps to set your minimum functional benchmark:

1. **Determine the key mission of the product or service, and how it will help your business achieve various operational and strategic goals.** By

outlining the primary goals and missions of the product or service, you should have a better understanding of what a fully functional, high-quality product or service will be.

2. **Identify the desired functionality and quality attributes of the product or service.** This can be achieved by reviewing your customer requirements and combining them with your organizational goals. While the desired functionality and quality attributes will vary according to your products and organizational needs, these attributes will generally focus on providing your customers with a satisfying product or service experience.

Test the Product

No product design is complete without testing whether the product works in the customer's operating environment. By establishing operational concepts and scenarios, you can test to determine if the work product will satisfy its intended functional requirements. To brainstorm potential scenarios that your product or service might be used within, we recommend you utilize the following steps:

1. **Brainstorm operational concepts with the aid of any business leaders or professional colleagues.** For example, if you have created project-management software, you should generate several scenarios in which the software will be involved, like in an at-home office or a corporate environment.

2. **Define the environment where your product will operate.** The more detailed you are about the environment where the product will be used, the greater the likelihood of determining when a work product has met its functional criteria.

3. **Review these concepts with the aid of your professional colleagues to discover how your work product will operate.** If you determine the work product will not meet its functional attributes, identify additional requirements that help improve the product.

4. **Document the results of your operational concepts.** If you determine that you need alternative requirements to improve the work product, be sure to identify these requirements, how they will be introduced into the product's lifecycle, and what the expected outcomes will be.

5. **Consider testing your product with a small group of customers.** When you have a working definition of a high-quality, fully functional work product or service, you may consider testing your product or service by supplying it to a small clientele base and gathering their feedback. This testing method can be extremely useful for determining if the quality and

functionality required by your customers have been met. Additionally, this step can help you identify what changes to make if your product or service fails to live up to customer standards.

Now that we have examined how to design a product that can meet the wants and needs of your customers, we will discuss how you can create a business process that will help you produce these products time and time again. This can be critical to your success as a start-up business, as it allows you to efficiently create products without spending an exorbitant much money or time on the creation process.

Create the Business Process for Your Product

A business process can be defined as a predetermined set of actions that are continuously performed within your organization to result in a product that can be used by your customers. Regardless of what product it produces, a business process is usually crucial to the organization's success. It is vital for entrepreneurs to identify and improve business processes on a regular basis. By prioritizing this activity, you can ensure that your business process is continually operating at the best level possible. An effective business process can also enable you to focus on other aspects of running your new business without worrying about personally overseeing the production of your product.

Having a highly efficient work process can mean the difference between a failed start-up and a major success. Other benefits to incorporating a business process within your company include the following:

- **It improves your work products**. At the heart of your business process is your ability to produce high-quality work products that meet your customers' needs. Improving a business process can help you identify customer requirements and take the necessary steps toward fulfilling them.

- **It improves your company's ability to deliver products on time and within budget.** A repeatable business process makes it possible to provide products to your customers within a short time frame. This not only improves customer satisfaction and your brand's reputation, but it can also significantly increase your organization's bottom line.

- **It improves your ability to exert control over your product's budget, which is especially critical for a start-up business owner.** When a business process is inefficient or is not designed to deliver a high-quality product, your organization could lose money quickly. For example, you might spend excessively on materials and resources that create subpar products. If a business process is creating low-quality or inconsistent products, you may discover that you need to conduct product recalls. This is not only expensive to the organization, but it can also seriously affect your company's reputation. By making every part of the business process as efficient and productive as possible, you may be able to save a considerable amount of money while ensuring that your product delivers excellent quality.

✔ **It improves your ability to deliver products that meet customer wants and needs.** A business process should always be focused on providing customers with a product that allows them to achieve their ultimate wants and needs. A disorganized or poorly functioning product loses focus on the customer's needs. By designing a better business process, you can ensure your business is creating a product that fulfills customer requirements.

Now that you know the benefits of a business process—and how it can help your start-up company achieve success—let us explore the steps you can take to design and implement a business process that is perfect for your product.

Know Yourself as a Business Leader

Delivering a stellar performance as a business leader can make it possible for you to deliver a business process that is equally as successful. This knowledge can come in handy once your organization starts growing with new employees, as your positive and productive attitude can make it possible for you to lead your employees through a variety of risks and challenges. With this in mind, take a review the following advice for acknowledging and improving your business-leadership skills:

☐ **Identify your biggest weaknesses.** This can be one of the biggest challenges of knowing who you are and how you can improve. You might find it difficult to turn an analytical gaze toward yourself. It is human nature to assume that we are always delivering our best performances and that we are naturally adept at our leadership roles. However, even the most efficient and successful Fortune 500 CEO can improve his or her leadership. The key to improving is asking a colleague to provide you with insight as to who you are and what skills you bring to your start-up business.

You may find it beneficial to meet with a colleague or business peer who knows your work well. During this meeting, ask your colleague about some of your best leadership abilities and unique business skills. Be sure to document what your colleague says, as this information will be vital when developing your business process.

After you have recorded the more positive attributes, ask your colleague to detail some of the areas you need to work on. Instruct your colleague to be as honest with you as possible. This feedback can help you identify how to improve yourself and thus create a better business process.

☐ **If you want to accurately identify who you are as a business leader and entrepreneur, remind yourself of your inner strengths.** Within the professional world, it can be easy to identify your strengths. After all, you may have empirical evidence to show you what you excel at, like increased sales numbers or better customer satisfaction. Take the time to highlight the personality traits that make you who you are.

Remind yourself of times in your personal life when you have overcome major obstacles and challenges. No matter when the challenges occurred, be sure to list them all. This will give you a better understanding of the unique personality traits that you bring to your business. Examples of professional and personal obstacles might include the following:

- You graduated early with honors from a top college or university.

- You lost a considerable amount of weight through diet, exercise, and discipline.

- You were able to rise to the top of the company ladder in a considerably short period of time.

- You moved to a new city or country on your own.

These examples may not initially seem like they have much to do with improving your leadership skills, but knowing who you are involves identifying your biggest strengths and unique personality traits. Once you understand your strengths, you will be better equipped to apply your unique skills toward leading a better business process.

☐ **Have a vision of your professional future.** Entrepreneurs who understand their aspirations are often more adept at creating business processes than those who have no vision of their professional future. Perhaps you would like to expand to three new locations within four years, or perhaps you want your company to be considered a leader in your industry. Having an idea of your organization's visions and priorities can have a significant influence on how efficiently you will achieve those goals.

The same line of reasoning applies to knowing who you are and how you need to improve. If you do not have a firm idea of where you would like to be in a certain period of time, you might find it difficult to improve your leadership skills. Determine your vision and priorities before you begin creating your business process.

Know the Criteria of Successful Business Processes

Understanding the critical attributes of what makes a successful organizational process is pivotal. These attributes usually include the following eight qualities:

- **Reliability:** A reliable process can ensure you are consistently creating high-quality products that dependably meet minimum quality and functionality requirements. Be aware, if you make changes to the business process, these changes will likely result in alterations in the product's functionality or performance.

- **Usability:** A product must be usable by your customers in order to be established as a standard business process within the workplace. What's more, the product must be usable in the customer's operating environment, and he or she must be able to understand how to use the product without hassle or frustration.

  Having good usability also means the product can be used for the amount of time you have predetermined. However, the exception to this rule is if you and your employees make changes to the output and the process that produces that output.

- **Functionality:** The business process should produce a product that meets customers' functional and performance requirements. If your organization is creating a product for your customer that is difficult to use or does not meet their functional needs, the process needs to be revised.

- **Maintainability:** A business process should be able to produce a product that can be maintained by the customer without difficulty. If the customer has difficulty with the upkeep of the product in his or her operating environment, you will need to make changes to the organizational process.

- **Correctness:** An organizational process should be free from defects, risks, and other elements that could potentially affect the output's performance objectives and strategic needs. If there are any errors within the organizational process, you should implement corrective actions until the errors are resolved.

- **Portability:** The business process's end product should be easily transferred from the workplace to the end user's operating environment. If it is difficult to transfer these outputs to your customers, then the organizational process is not considered portable.

- **Testability:** Entrepreneurs might benefit from prioritizing this attribute. Your organizational process will need to prove that it has achieved its performance goals and strategic needs. If you discover that your organizational process is too difficult to test, then you should make changes to the process components until you can successfully test them.

✔ **Efficiency:** A business process should produce superior-quality products quickly and without undergoing any serious incidents or errors. If the organizational process cannot be implemented without encountering major incidents and risks, continue to revise sections of the process.

Establish the Needs of Your Process

Establishing the needs of your business-process involves identifying the major goals and strategies of your company, then using this information to create a process. As with identifying customer needs, establishing business-process needs can help you ensure that process components are designed to help the company achieve important operational and strategic goals. To discover your needs, analyze the following components:

☐ **Analyze the company's relationship with its customers.** One of your biggest organizational-process needs may involve providing high-quality work products to your customers. This can help an organization achieve many goals, including a better bottom line, a more engaged clientele base, and better brand management. Be sure to analyze the company's current relationship with its customers, as well as how you would like this relationship to change. You may wish to outline a specific focus for your relationship with your customers—for example, honesty, integrity, service, or responsiveness.

☐ **Analyze the company's financial details.** For example, you could discover that you want to improve sales by 20 percent over the next fiscal year. This means that your business-process components should be focused on creating a work product that helps your organization achieve that specific goal.

☐ **Analyze the company's operational goals.** Operational goals could include improving the technologies within the workplace, hiring new personnel, or upgrading resources and materials. The more specific you are about high-priority operational goals, the greater your likelihood of creating a business process that aids in the achievement of these operational goals.

☐ **Analyze the company's strategic goals.** Strategic goals could include expanding to a new location, building new stores, or creating multiple new product lines. These strategic goals should be prioritized by your work team, and you will want to create a business process that makes it easier for your company to implement these strategies.

Determine the Objectives of Your Business Process

Defining your process-performance objectives can help you determine what outcomes are expected when creating a high-quality work product. These outcomes can provide a benchmark for your process, as they allow your work team know when they have created a work product that meets the needs of both the organization and its customers. Examples of process-performance objectives include the following:

- **Customer-satisfaction ratings:** You could indicate that your business process needs to create a work product that achieves a certain customer-satisfaction value. This value can be accrued through online reviews, surveys, and other forms of feedback generation.

- **Time to implement:** You could require that a process be implemented within a certain period of time. This can improve process performance because it helps your team adhere to a deadline while still producing an excellent work product.

- **Incident rates:** You could indicate that an improved business process will be able to cut down on a certain number of incident rates within a specific period of time. For example, a business process will have an improved performance if it is able to cut down on incident rates, as well as close at least four incident reports within four business weeks.

- **Productivity:** You could require that a business process be able to produce a certain number of work products within a specific period of time. This can help improve a business process because it will provide you with a benchmark for how much work your employees should produce. As an example objective, you could require that process productivity be improved by at least 30 percent within the next financial quarter.

Setting these process-performance objectives will allow you to identify when a business process has improved and what work must still be completed to enhance your business's performance measures. Be sure to document all your process objectives, as this will aid in ensuring the integrity and quality of future business processes.

Analyze Each Step of the Process

A business process is essentially comprised of the individual steps you will take to produce your product. From planning and implementing the process to delivering the product to the customer, each stage should be considered part of the business process. Take the time to analyze each step and how you can make it more efficient and productive.

Determining process improvements involves identifying the various components of an organizational process and highlighting how these components are contributing to the final product. This examination should reveal if a process component should be kept in place or if it should be improved. Determining process improvements also involves gathering your designers and relevant employees together and creating multiple alternative solutions that can be used to optimize the business process.

Begin determining process improvements by arranging a meeting with your work team. This meeting will be dedicated to analyzing the business process while breaking down the process into its various tasks and activities. Depending on the business process, you may want to consider breaking it down and analyzing it according to its primary stages, as this may expedite your meeting. With the aid of your work-process team, use the following techniques to determine process improvements:

☐ **Break down the process according to its components.** This can be done by breaking it down according to activities or by milestones. You should utilize this step in a way that makes sense for you, your work team, and your product.

☐ **Examine how these process components contribute to the overall work product.** For example, if your organization is making e-commerce websites for online entrepreneurs, explore how each stage of the work process contributes to the final website. You should examine what resources are used in each stage and how they are used. Be sure to document your findings, as this documentation will be vital in later stages of the process improvement.

☐ **Ask your meeting attendees for feedback on what parts of the process are performing at less-than-optimal standards.** For example, your team members could alert you to the fact that the programming component of creating a website is difficult because the company's Internet is too slow for continual testing. Document all of their feedback, as this information will be invaluable for later stages of process improvement.

☐ **Identify the process components that involve substandard resources and materials.** There is a good chance these components could be improved, as the current resources and materials may not be contributing toward an optimal output.

☐ **Review any previous process documentation to determine some of the most common risks and errors you have encountered.** Earlier documentation of a business process could provide you with valuable insight as to what process improvements need to be made. For example, if a previous process experienced major setbacks during the testing phase, this process component may have the greatest need for your attention.

Documenting your projects and processes can provide you with the insight you need to make future improvements.

After employing the above techniques, you and your work team will better understand what stages of the process need to be improved.

Establish Oversight for the Newly Created Process

Every organizational process should be regularly monitored at scheduled intervals. Monitoring a process not only allows entrepreneurs to track its success in meeting the organization's objectives, but can also provide for opportunities to update new technologies and motivate relevant work team members.

For example, if you have a current business process that is producing exceptional work products, you should continue to analyze that process. While it may already be achieving its performance objectives, you may still discover that certain process components can be improved by new technologies or other alterations.

While process oversight and monitoring are important to your start-up's success, this stage of process improvement should not absorb a great deal of your time. Ideally, regular process monitoring should serve as a cursory activity that is designed to highlight whether or not any components could be improved so that your product becomes more successful with your customers. Consider using the following techniques to establish oversight for your new business process:

☐ **Gather your work team together to formulate a schedule for regular process monitoring.** This schedule should be firm, but it should be so frequent that it detracts from important organizational projects. Therefore, consider holding a process-monitoring review session biweekly or even monthly.

☐ **Designate a team member who can be responsible for conducting the process monitoring.** Delegating this task to a responsible employee can be especially helpful for entrepreneurs who do not have time to attend to every process-monitoring review meeting. Be sure to select a team member who can stand in for you if you cannot lead the meeting. Ensure that the team member has access to all relevant documentation, including the organization's process-performance objectives, which should be used as a benchmark for the review session. During the meeting, the work team will compare the current process against the original performance objectives.

☐ **Determine a meeting agenda that will outline the objectives of the**

review session. This predetermined agenda should make it possible for you to conduct your meeting in an efficient and highly productive manner, as you will be led to review the process components without becoming distracted from your primary objectives.

☐ **Designate someone to represent each process component, if relevant.** During the meeting, have the employee summarize how the process is performing and what issues have been encountered. This can aid in providing structure to your review meeting, as only a few team members will be asked to speak. If you discover multiple issues with a business process, reserve the end of the meeting as a time when the rest of your employees can voice their opinions and provide you with valuable feedback.

☐ **Record the findings of the review session.** If the findings reveal that a process is continuing to meet or exceed performance objectives, you can conclude the session. However, if you notice a disparity between the organization's performance objectives and the current process, be sure to note this during the process audit.

☐ **Reveal the findings of the process audit to your fellow business leaders or any investors.** These leaders may provide you with the advice and feedback you need to identify alternative solutions. For example, if you demonstrate to your business partner that a process may not continue functioning at an optimal level because you might not have enough funding, he or she may provide you with suggestions that you can utilize to minimize this risk. Your business partner may suggest cutting back funding on other projects and using this money toward process improvements instead. Your business partner may also be able to approve the use of additional funding and resources for process improvement.

It is vital for entrepreneurs to understand how designing a business process can aid in creating a successful start-up business. Process development can help your organization create a better product that fulfills your customers' wants and needs. Process development can also keep any relevant employees motivated and enthusiastic, which is essential to encouraging a productive workplace. Finally, process development can help you ensure that organizational processes are designed to help the company reach its most important strategic and operational goals.

At the start of this chapter, our example businessperson, Jeff, initially had difficulty finding a way to design, develop, and deliver his product to his prospective customers. He was unsure how to research what his customers wanted from his products, as he had very little current data to use for this research. He also had a challenging time designing a business process to create the product, as he did not know how to ensure his product met the requirements of potential customers. Let us return to the example of Jeff to assess how he addresses these issues:

***

Fortunately, Jeff is able to find a way to design and deliver a product that fulfills every customer expectation. First, he researches his potential customer market by working with business colleagues in the same industry that he wants to start his business in. These experts provide Jeff with a great deal of guidance, suggesting key customer wants and needs that help him develop an attractive product.

After researching his potential customer database, Jeff determines how to design his software product to fulfill these customer requirements. Jeff understands this is a critical part of creating a successful start-up business, as a product that fails to meet customers' wants and needs will be unsuccessful. Jeff also learns how to communicate these customer requirements to product designers, who may otherwise have had difficulty translating a customer's emotional wants and needs into a fully functional and high-quality work product.

Finally, Jeff creates a business process that allows him to practically automate the creation and delivery of his product to his customers. Jeff knows that as his company grows, he will be able to make more products in less time, as his employees will be able to implement all the steps of the business process without requiring Jeff to constantly involve himself in micromanaging the process.

***

Now that you know more about the intricacies of creating and designing a work product—as well as ensuring that it fulfills the needs of your customers—we will next examine how to structure your business. This is a very important step in the process of starting a new business, as it can influence the taxes you pay each year—not to mention if your own personal assets will be at risk if your business fails.

Review Chapter 3

Now that you have completed Chapter 3, reflect on its content and how you will identify your needed products and services. As you review this chapter, consider the following questions:

- ☐ Do you understand the market for your business venture? Have you performed the necessary research on this market?

- ☐ Do you understand your customers' wants and needs?

- ☐ Do you thoroughly understand the customer segmentation and RFM strategies that can help you identify the buying patterns of your customers?

- ☐ Do you currently have, or know how to procure, the required tools and resources for creating your product?

- ☐ Do your business processes fit all eight of the criteria of a successful business process? Do you have clear objectives and oversight for smooth and productive business processes?

- ☐ What paperwork, registrations, licenses, certifications, and other requirements will be involved in your business venture?

- ☐ Have you determined how you will transform your customer requirements into technical features of your product or service?

If you are satisfied with your understanding of how you will identify your needed products and services, resume reading with Chapter 4.

How to Appropriately Structure Your Business

"Out of clutter, find simplicity. From discord, find harmony. In the middle of difficulty, lies opportunity."

-Albert Einstein[9]

Your company's legal structure can make a significant difference in the amount you pay in taxes, what tax deductions you take, what records must be kept, and even the level of personal risk you assume should your business fail. To demonstrate this point, let us explore the following example of a business owner who was unaware of the risks associated when selecting an improper business structure, and how this mistake negatively impacted him:

***

Example: Nathan

Nathan is a small-business owner who is running his own online bookkeeping services. Nathan formerly worked for an accountant in a nearby city; however, he knew his talents could be put to better use. Wanting both to organize his own schedule and utilize his abilities fully, Nathan decided to look into starting his own business. After doing some research online, he discovered that he could apply for projects online and be paid through a website's escrow services. He was delighted at the opportunity to make money on his own. After a few months of working part time with online projects, Nathan is finally making enough money to quit his bookkeeping job.

While Nathan understands that he needs to keep track of his payment records for tax purposes, he fails to realize what a huge portion of his income will be lost to taxes. When Nathan realizes that he must pay almost half of what he has made, he is stunned. He visits an accountant to determine why he has to pay so much money, despite making the equivalent of what he made back in his previous job. The accountant informs Nathan that because he never applied for a legal structure for his business, it was therefore considered a sole proprietorship and taxed under his own social security number. His accountant

---

[9] "Quotable Quote," GoodReads, accessed November 1, 2018, https://www.goodreads.com/quotes/312724-out-of-clutter-find-simplicity-from-discord-find-harmony-in.

also informs him that unless he changes the legal entity of his business, any risks that he assumes are his own. This means that if Nathan invests any money (or if any investors or credit unions loan him money) he is personally responsible for that money, even if his business fails.

Nathan immediately makes an appointment with a business lawyer to register his company as a limited liability company (LLC). This reduces his tax code and his personal risk, although he is still required to pay the tax debt from the previous year. The financial burden is significant, and Nathan finds his tax debt is preventing him from building his business. Eventually, Nathan is forced to consider reapplying for his previous job, as he can no longer make enough money to support his family with the added burden of repaying his tax debts.

***

Often times, entrepreneurs—especially those who have never started a business before—may not realize they need to form a legal structure as quickly as possible. Perhaps they decide to wait for the business to start making profit before structuring the business, or perhaps they simply overlook this vital step because they are busy with other responsibilities associated with starting a business. Regardless of the reasons, failing to form a legal structure can have significant negative consequences for a business owner.

In the story, Nathan found it difficult to grow his business because he was burdened by the tax debt he assumed in his sole proprietorship. Although Nathan did not need the assistance of any investors, he could have found himself in even more trouble if he had taken out loans from an investor and the business had then failed to make money. By owning a sole proprietorship and making money under his social security code, Nathan was personally responsible for any financial risks that he assumed. For example, if he had asked an investor to loan him $5,000 to build a website for his bookkeeping business, Nathan would have needed to pay that money back even if his business failed. Errors like these can cause many unsuccessful entrepreneurs to go bankrupt, as they may not have the personal savings or assets to pay back lenders or otherwise make up for lost money when their businesses fail.

As the above example demonstrates, a business entrepreneur must carefully consider the legal structure of his or her company as early in the start-up as possible. Legal structure can have profound implications for the success of the company, as well as the level of personal involvement and risk that is required by the entrepreneur.

In this chapter, you can expect to learn about the various legal structures that are available to a business. You will also learn what to consider when choosing your own legal structure, as well as the impact your legal structure will have on taxation, ownership, and your legal liability.

Know the Most Common Business Structures

For new entrepreneurs, approaching the legal jargon of business structures might be an overwhelming experience. Each legal entity comes with its own advantages and disadvantages, which are outlined in confusing language that can be difficult to understand. The process of choosing legal representation to help you through this jargon may also be frustrating, as you may not have the necessary capital to invest in a high-quality business lawyer.

It might be tempting to simply read through your options and select the one that sounds like it has the best advantages. However, choosing a structure for your business should involve carefully considering both the advantages and disadvantages of each type of business structure and how each one could impact the growth of your company. You must use cautious consideration to select a business structure and legal entity that allows your company to grow, but also minimizes your tax burden and provides you with a certain amount of protection should the business fail.

Joshua Earsley, whom you met in Chapter 2, is currently operating Semper Fi Catering as an S corporation. This structure provides him personal protection as well as tax benefits. "It definitely would have been risky if I didn't decide to do this," he explains. To help you select the business structure that will work best for you, the following section will explore the various types of business structures that are available to entrepreneurs. These definitions will be clear and concise, and will explain whether or not your company is eligible according to IRS rules and regulations. Each of these structures brings its own benefits to your business; however, based on your business and your expectations for the future, each structure could also be associated with hefty disadvantages. You must know exactly what is expected of you, both personally and as a business entity, before selecting a business structure. Conducting a thorough evaluation of these business structures, as well as your own expectations for your business, will lead you to discover which business structure best fits your lifestyle, abilities, and financial situation. The most common forms of business entities in the United States are as follows:

Sole Proprietorship

Although sole proprietorship is considered a business structure, it is not considered by the government to be a formal entity and therefore has no legal structure.

A sole proprietorship can be defined as a business that allows a single person to maintain operational control and receive the profits that are associated with conducting the business. Depending on the state where the business is formed, a sole proprietorship can also be formed by married couples or domestic couples. We recommend that any couples who want to go into business together consult a business attorney familiar with state laws that pertain to sole proprietorships.

A sole proprietorship mandates that the individual owner is subject to the full liabilities of the business. For Earsley, whose business involves some risk and potential partners, a sole proprietorship was not ideal, since it involved taking on risk personally instead of allowing his business to take the risk as an entity. "[Sole proprietorship] was one that didn't provide any kind of protection to my personal assets. I wouldn't have been protected, like I would with either an LLC or an S corp," he says. If a sole proprietorship fails, the personal assets of the business owner must be used to pay back any debts and loans that the business accrued. Sole proprietorships are not considered permanent business entities, as there is a great deal of personal risk in maintaining a business that falls under this legal structure. Many business owners that start their businesses as sole proprietorships later shift to new legal entities, like LLCs or other corporate structures.

In regard to paperwork, some states require that the business owner complete a Fictitious Business Name Statement with the office of the secretary of state. This is only necessary if the person who owns the sole proprietorship is using a business name that is different from his or her personal name. For example, if your name is John Smith and your business is Synergy Company, you may be required to complete the Fictitious Business Name Statement. Again, be sure to consult with a business attorney to determine whether you must take this action, or visit your state's office of the secretary of state website to learn more.

Now that you know the basic definition of a sole proprietorship, let us will briefly outline the primary factors that determine the operation and structure of this type of legal entity:

- **Sole proprietorships are typically registered with relevant city, county, state, and federal organizations.** If the business owner is using a different name for the business, he or she should check to see if the name is already in use. Aside from acquiring a business license from the city that the company will be operated in, no other legal documents are required. If you are conducting an online business, you may also require a business license to work from within your home.

- **The sole proprietorship is wholly owned by the individual.**

- **The owner is wholly responsible for the company's legal, financial, and operational affairs.** The business owner is typically the sole signer on the company's checking account; therefore, the business owner can deposit checks made out to him or her, as well as checks made out to the company.

- **There are no requirements placed upon a sole proprietorship with regards to capitalization.**

- **The owner receives all of the profits and also suffers all of the losses.**

- **The owner assumes all liability; therefore, any applications for credit cards and business loans will be made against the business owner's personal financial information.** Should the business fail, the business owner will be required to pay back the debts, unless a Chapter 7 or Chapter 13 bankruptcy declares otherwise.

- **The owner of a sole proprietorship is taxed based on his or her social security number.** The company's profits are listed as personal earnings and the owner can deduct relevant personal expenses for the company. The business owner's tax debt is based upon the company's earnings; not what the owner pays himself or herself. Therefore, sole proprietorships are typically taxed at a higher rate than other business structures.

- **If the business owner wishes to terminate the business, he or she can simply cease operating the business.** If the owner was required to submit a Fictitious Business Name Statement, he or she may be required to file a certificate of withdrawal in the relevant city and county offices where the business operated. If the business sold products or services, the business owner may need to file a notice of business closure with the county and state where the company operated. Termination of a business may require the guidance of a legal representative.

The sole proprietorship may be the most common business structure in the country—and for good reason. Structuring as a sole proprietorship comes with a number of advantages, including the following:

- ✔ **There is a minimum number of formal business requirements to become a sole proprietorship.** This lack of requirements could be a significant advantage to a busy business owner who plans on formalizing the business structure at a later date.

- ✔ **No corporate tax payments must be made.**

- ✔ **The owner of a sole proprietorship maintains complete control over the decisions made within the organization.**

- ✔ **The owner can sell or transfer the business at his or her discretion.**

- ✔ **Forming a sole proprietorship requires minimal legal costs, which could be a significant advantage to cash-strapped entrepreneurs in the early stages of starting a business.**

Though these advantages can be particularly attractive, sole proprietorships also have many disadvantages that could make one wary of starting a business with this structure. These disadvantages include the following:

✕ **Investors are typically reluctant to invest in sole proprietorships.** This reluctance increase the difficulty of finding capital.

✕ **The owner of a sole proprietorship is held liable for any debts and obligations that the business incurs.**

✕ **The owner is liable for any incurred risks as a result of any actions that are performed by employees within the company.**

✕ **The owner must handle all decisions and responsibilities.** This advantage can quickly become a disadvantage if the business owner is not equipped to deal with the many needed decisions and responsibilities.

Carefully weigh the benefits of a sole proprietorship with its costs. You may discover that you are not willing to place your personal finances and assets at risk should your business incur debts and other liabilities.

General Partnership

A general partnership is an umbrella term that covers many different types of partnerships, including the following:

- Limited partnerships

- Limited liability partnerships

- Family limited partnerships

- Professional partnerships

During the following discussion of the general partnership business type, assume that all terms, conditions, and qualities presented also apply to the businesses under the above titles, as those titles fall under the umbrella term of general partnerships.

A general partnership can be defined as a business that features two or more partners. Each partner within the business is responsible for the assets and liabilities of the company. Therefore, if the company takes on debts or fails, each partner must use his or her personal assets to address these debts and other associated liabilities. This is known as joint liability, as each partner is equally responsible for any accrued debts and liabilities. For example, if a customer is injured in the company's building and sues for medical expenses, all of the partners are equally responsible in the eyes of the law.

The roles of the partners are typically determined by the type of partnership that the company has structured. For example, the primary general partner is responsible for the daily operations of the business, while the limited partner's role is usually restricted to helping the general partner by investing capital into the business. If the business is successful, the limited partner is entitled to a share of the profits based on the level of capital invested in the company. In cases of a limited partnership, the general partner typically carries the biggest financial and legal burden should the company assume liabilities and debts.

All partners are legally responsible for contracts that any other partner makes. This also applies to any legal wrongdoings or malpractices that one partner might commit. We recommend entrepreneurs have a significant level of trust and open communication when entering into business with a partner. This level of personal and legal responsibility for another partner's actions has led many to consider the general partnership one of the riskiest business structures. General partnerships are typically formed in the medical industry, as many states forbid physicians and other medical professionals from forming LLCs.

Now that you know the basic definition of a general partnership, let us briefly outline the primary factors that determine the operation and structure of this specific type of legal entity:

- **A general partnership is typically formed through a partnership agreement.** While the partnership agreement does not need to exist in writing, it is usually recommended that all partnership agreements be memorialized in the form of a contract or written communication. There is usually no jurisdictional filing requirement at the city, county, or state levels; however, you should still contact a business attorney to ensure that your legal obligations are fulfilled.

- **A management agreement typically dictates who will be responsible for managerial operations.** This agreement can also determine how profits and losses are divided.

- **A general partnership does not provide for specific rules on capitalization.**

- **A general partnership has one level of taxation. Partnerships are not tax-paying entities, although they must report their taxes.**

- **General partners are liable for the actions of their partners, even if they were ignorant of them.** A general partnership typically exposes partners to three different types of risks: which include unlimited liability for debts, unlimited liability for the actions of their partners, and unlimited liability for the risks arising from being an "unaware" general partner.

- **The death or withdrawal of a partner can terminate the legal obligations of a general partnership.**

A general partnership comes with the benefit of more flexible management and decision-making while sharing the liabilities with another person. Other advantages to structuring as a general partnership include the following:

- ✔ **The general partnership is not typically required to register with agencies and municipalities.**

- ✔ **The partners can split the profits.**

- ✔ **General partnerships typically avoid making large one-time fees.**

- ✔ **Filing an income-tax return is much easier with a general partnership, as it is considered to be a pass-through tax entity, and therefore does not pay income taxes at the corporate level.**

- ✔ **You and your partner(s) do not need to file separate tax returns.**

- ✔ **A general partnership enjoys the advantages of pooling together multiple resources, talents, and ideas.**

These attractive advantages come at a price, as a general partnership is commonly considered to be one of the most dangerous business structures for the following reasons:

- ✗ **The general partnership can be easily dissolved due to the death of a partner.**

- ✗ **All partners are legally bound to one another.** If a business partner commits illegal acts, the other business partners are legally bound to these acts and must share in the punishment. Ignorance of the other partner's actions is not considered to be a viable defense.

- ✗ **You must have a written partnership agreement.**

- ✗ **All partners are personally liable for any debts and obligations incurred by the organization.**

Due to the lack of any real safeguards in the general partnership, it is absolutely vital that you trust your partner(s). This level of trust and vulnerability may be unattractive to many entrepreneurs. If you cannot allow yourself to be so vulnerable to another person's actions, consider another business structure.

S Corporation

The S corporation (also known as a subchapter S corporation, sub S corporation, or S corp) is a type of business structure that is not required to be a traditional corporation, but is nonetheless an eligible entity. In order to register as an S corp, a business must meet all of the following Internal Revenue Service (IRS) requirements:[10]

- *Be a domestic corporation*

- *Have only allowable shareholders*

  - *May be individuals, certain trusts, and estates and*

  - *May not be partnerships, corporations or non-resident alien shareholders*

- *Have no more than 100 shareholders*

- *Have one class of stock.*

- *Not be an ineligible corporation (i.e. certain financial institutions, insurance companies, and domestic international sales corporations).*

To be considered an S corporation, the corporation must, under IRS mandate, have the shareholders sign and submit Form 2553, Election by a Small Business Corporation, which can be found online.

One of the greatest benefits of forming an S corporation is that this type of business structure allows the corporation to be taxed in a manner that is similar to a general partnership. The profits earned by the business are taxed at the level of the shareholders, not the corporation. In turn, the tax burden is less significant, which allows more profits to be reinvested into the business.

Now that you know the basic definition of what an S corporation is, let us briefly outline the primary factors that determine the operation and structure of this specific type of legal entity:

- **There are two options for preparing this business structure.** Due to the fact an S corporation is not a true corporation, a business owner can either set up a limited liability company and opt to have the LLC treated as an S corporporation for taxation purposes, or set up a traditional corporation and have the organization treated as an S corporation for taxation purposes.

  The second of the above two options may be the most beneficial for business owners who want to be viewed as a legitimate corporation. This can be useful for branding purposes, as you can use the word corporation

---

[10] "S Corporations," IRS, accessed November 1, 2018, http://www.irs.gov/Businesses/Small-Businesses-&-Self-Employed/S-Corporations.

in your marketing and advertising. Limited liability companies, on the other hand, typically use the abbreviation LLC instead of the term corporation.

To form an S corp, you must file the appropriate documents, including the articles of incorporation, at the city, county, state, and federal levels. Be sure to contact a business attorney to learn about your legal obligations when forming an S corp.

- **S corporations must have no more than one hundred shareholders.** Please refer back to the stipulations outlined by the IRS earlier in this section to determine which entities are eligible to be shareholders within an S corporation.

- **S corporations have shareholders, directors, and officers.** Management responsibilities are divided according to these titles. Generally, the officers are responsible for daily operations, while directors oversee important decisions pertaining to the company. Shareholders own the company.

- **Additional capital is typically raised by selling the company's stock.**

- **Profits are taxed to each owner at his or her personal tax rate.**

- **Termination of an S corporation can be done according to one of three options.** These options include the following: 1) voluntary revocation, 2) automatic termination if eligibility rules are not met according to the IRS, and 3) automatic termination if the organization has passive investment income in excess of 25 percent of gross receipts for three consecutive years.

S corporations are particularly attractive to business entrepreneurs because they allow the organization to receive the advantages of a corporation without becoming one. These advantages can include the following:

- **The S corporation enjoys more legal protection than general partnerships and sole proprietorships.**

- **The S corporation can benefit from better accounting protection.**

- **The S corporation can avoid corporate income taxes, which allows more profits to be invested back into the business.**

- **The S corporation has reduced costs because employment and payroll taxes are paid by the owners.**

Despite these benefits, S corporations can be associated with the following disadvantages:

✗ **Starting an S corporation requires a significant cost.** S corporations face more start-up costs than sole proprietorships and general partnerships. Fees can include accounting, tax preparation, payroll processing, and much more. It is also more difficult and more expensive to dissolve an S corporation.

✗ **S corporations can face significant banking and legal costs.** This obstacle may be prohibiting for business entrepreneurs who do not have a significant amount of capital in the beginning stages of their businesses.

✗ **S corporations face a large number of restrictions on the types of shareholders and classes of stock they can have.**

Based on these advantages and disadvantages of S corporations, you may consider legal entities that require fewer start-up costs. However, many entrepreneurs enjoy the added protection of structuring their businesses as an S corporation. This benefit was the appeal of an S corporation for Earsley, who says, "Since I'm taking all the responsibility, I'm making all the major decisions, whether it's regarding corporate formalities in accounting, sales, marketing, hiring, training, essentially all the systems. This [structure] is good—along with insurance—I'm it even though it costs more. It's peace of mind and it secures any kind of financial hit that could happen to my family, negatively." Different business structures offer different levels of protection to the owner. You will have to make your decision based on your own business and your own comfort with the inherent risks.

Limited Liability Company (LLC)

A limited liability company (commonly referred to as an LLC) provides the business owner with limited personal liability for the actions and debts incurred by the company. In addition to this major advantage, the LLC allows for much more management flexibility and pass-through taxation. While the LLC may have a different taxation code, its core structure resembles that of a general partnership entity, without the associated liabilities and responsibilities.

A limited liability company can be owned by a broad variety of entities, including a corporation, an individual person, a nondomestic company, or even another LLC. There is no restriction to how many members can own an LLC, so long as there is at least one member owning the business.

LLCs are regulated at the state level, and the requirements could change based on the state where the business is operating. Be sure to consult a business attorney to learn what obligations you must fulfill in order to qualify as an LLC in your state of operation. The IRS also mandates that certain types of businesses may not be classified as LLCs. These businesses generally include banks and insurance companies.

According to the IRS website, the LLC will be taxed as either a corporation or partnership or as part of the LLC's owner's tax return. If the LLC is owned by two or more members, the LLC will be classified as a partnership for income tax purposes, unless a Form 8832 is filed (you can find this form online). "I started out as an LLC," says Earsley, "a limited liability corporation, because I was thinking that I would have partners. But I don't need to do that now." As you can see in this section, you do not need partners to structure your business as an LLC. Some of our other example veteran business owners have chosen to use this structure.

Now that you know the basic definition of a limited liability company, let us briefly outline the primary factors that determine the operation and structure of this specific type of legal entity:

- The LLC can be formed by submitting an articles-of-organization form to your state's office of the secretary of state. The secretary of state should be provided with the purpose of the business, the principal office address, and the initial member names.

    There may be fees associated with registering as an LLC. These fees vary according to the state in which you file as an LLC, but you must be prepared for a hefty expense: fees can range from as low as $50 to as high as $1,000.

- The owners of the LLC are equally involved in the management of the company. However, a manager-management structure mandates that one owner is primarily responsible for the management of the LLC.

- The LLC should be capitalized in an amount that allows the organization to have independent funds should third-party commitments occur. Any shareholders will make good-faith efforts to provide the LLC with the funds the company needs to do business. Shareholders may opt to invest their finances in the LLC or take out loans to provide the LLC with the necessary assets to help the company become profitable.

- Members share the LLC's profit according to their investments within the company. Liability is limited. Each member of the LLC pays taxes on his or her share of the company's profits and losses.

- The LLC is automatically dissolved should any member encounter an event such as retirement, bankruptcy, or death. Should this happen, the LLC will have to be reformed with the consent of the remaining organizational members.

A limited liability company is one of the more flexible business structures, especially when compared to an S corporation. The advantages of structuring your company as an LLC can include the following:

- ✔ **You can enjoy all of the decision-making flexibility of a general partnership, while receiving the limited liability protections of an S corporation.**

- ✔ **LLCs are taxed at a lower rate, as they are considered pass-through tax entities.** LLCs are taxed based on the individual members' tax returns, not on the company's profits and losses.

- ✔ **LLCs can be affiliated with other business entities.**

While LLCs allow for more flexible management styles and lower tax rates, they bring with them a few disadvantages, which can include the following:

- ✗ **An LLC is typically required to pay an annual state operation fee, which can be a financial burden.**

- ✗ **Due to the fact LLCs are relatively new tax entities (they have only been in existence since 1996), there is not much legal precedent in place to help LLC owners who may encounter business disputes.**

Now that you know more about the advantages and disadvantages of various business entities, we will highlight a few criteria you can use to choose the appropriate business entity based on your goals and needs.

Select the Legal Entity That Fits Your Business

As every legal entity comes with its own set of advantages and disadvantages, some business owners might feel hesitant to make a decision. These fears are valid: no one can predict what situations our businesses might encounter, and no one can determine whether a business might flourish under one entity and suffer under another. Choosing a legal entity should be a decision made with careful consideration. Do not choose a legal entity because it sounds best on paper or because it will enable you to decrease your filing fees. Instead, use the following techniques to help select the legal entity that is right for your start-up business:

- ☐ **Develop your idea of how you would like your business to grow over the course of six months, one year, and five years.** If you think that your business will go through significant changes and you would like to ensure that your entity is flexible enough to keep up with those changes, you might consider opting for a sole proprietorship or an S corporation, as these allow you to restructure your business when it starts taking the shape of a more permanent company.

☐ **Assess your own risk levels and determine how much you would like to be shielded from risks and liabilities.** If you are comfortable with the idea of risking your personal assets while your business grows, you might consider a sole proprietorship. If you want to protect your personal assets or share the liabilities with another person, consider structuring your business as an S corporation, LLC, or a general proprietorship. Remember, this is a critical part of choosing the appropriate legal entity for your business. Make sure you have a solid understanding of how your assets could be affected by your business decisions.

☐ **If your goal is to minimize taxation as much as possible, consider filing as an S corporation or a limited liability company.** This helps minimize your tax burden while providing your personal assets with more protection than a sole proprietorship or general partnership.

☐ **Consider how much time you have to invest in paperwork and research.** Many business entrepreneurs prefer to start as sole proprietorships in the beginning stages, waiting to assess whether their companies will be successful before forming a more complicated S corporation or limited liability company. Just remember that a sole proprietorship cannot exist as a permanent company, so determine what legal entity you would like to become once your company makes a profit.

☐ **If you would like to bring in capital from investors before starting the daily operations of the company, consider avoiding sole proprietorships.** Investors are typically reluctant to work with sole proprietorships, as these types of companies cannot exist as permanent entities. Additionally, sole proprietorships do not have stakeholders, directors, and officers, all of whom can provide investors with a certain level of confidence that their money will be used for business purposes.

Even a general partnership can make investors cautious, as these types of entities are notorious for breaking down due to poor partnering decisions and other legal implications. Therefore, if you need capital up front, consider a legal structure that will attract investors, such as an S corporation or a limited liability company.

If you are still having trouble selecting the legal entity that is right for your organization, consider hiring a business attorney to explain the many advantages and disadvantages of each entity. There are many more specific implications involved with each entity, and a business attorney might give you the clarity you need if you are not yet ready to make a decision. This book will discuss how you can find and hire these lawyers in Chapter 6.

Let us return to the earlier example of Nathan, an online-business owner who was unaware of the amount of money he would need to pay in taxes as a sole proprietorship. If Nathan had done his research earlier, he may have discovered that he would be taxed at a higher rate because his company profits would be considered personal income. If the example had involved a lawsuit against Nathan's company, a sole proprietorship would not have offered him any protection. In fact, his personal assets (including those of his wife and children) would have been vulnerable according to the law.

By doing his research on legal structures, Nathan could have weighed the benefits between more flexibility and more protection for his personal assets. With this knowledge, he could have made the decision to move forward with his sole proprietorship or to structure his business as a limited liability company or, if he went into business with someone else, a general partnership.

In regard to structuring your business, knowledge is power. It is vital for entrepreneurs to understand the tax, financial, and risk implications that come associated with certain legal entities. As the example with Nathan demonstrates, being unaware of these implications can lead you to make a decision that costs you hefty taxes. You must also ensure that your business is protected from legal liabilities that could damage your finances.

As a start-up entrepreneur, you deserve to make well-informed and powerful decisions. After analyzing the content in this chapter, you should have a better idea of what legal structure you might consider for your own start-up business.

Review Chapter 4

Now that you have completed Chapter 4, reflect on its content and how you will appropriately structure your business. As you review this chapter, consider the following questions:

☐ Do you fully understand the differences between sole proprietorships, general partnerships, S corporations, and limited liability companies?

☐ Do you understand the tax, financial, and risk-related implications associated with each of these legal entities?

☐ Have you considered the advantages and disadvantages of each type of business structure, both generally and specifically as they relate to your business?

☐ Have you discovered which structure best provides for your business, and what that particular structure entails?

Selecting a legal structure will set one foundational element of your start-up business. If you are satisfied with your understanding of how you will appropriately structure your business, resume reading with Chapter 5.

How to Minimize Risk for Your Business

"You can never protect yourself 100%. What you do is protect yourself as much as possible and mitigate risk to an acceptable degree."
-Kevin Mitnick[11]

The previous chapter briefly mentioned the topic of risk as it pertains to your assets. There are many ways to shield yourself and your new business from financial risk. For example, William Elmore emphasizes the importance of keeping a support structure in managing start-up risk. He suggests, "If you have a day job or a full-time job providing you income while you start your business, consider starting your business part-time. Work nights. You don't have to jump both feet first—you can, as there is no one standard first step— but if you've got income, try to keep that going while you start your business."

Keeping his current income flowing is one of the ways Show Me Concrete LLC's owner, Jonathan Mart, manages risks: "I still work a full-time job," he says. "Most times I'm traveling four days a week. I'm out of town, I come home, and I immediately start doing work for the company." Show Me Concrete provides concrete finishing services to both residential and commercial clients. Their services span removal, site preparation, pouring and finishing for any type of concrete work.

Naturally, it's incredibly difficult to run a business while working a full-time job, so Mart has partnered with his brother Bryan: "We've created a pretty unique balance of how the company works. My brother's the project manager. He runs the job sites day-to-day. I work with him when I can, but I [also] manage the company behind the scenes—anything to do with accounting, invoicing, sending out estimates. He doesn't have to worry about the company as a whole, he can focus on the work at hand. There are still situations where trying to manage every detail that goes into running a company is not easy. I couldn't imagine trying to do both [roles]."

Keeping close account of every aspect of a business is exhausting. "I know a lot of previous business owners, and they said that was the biggest thing that

---

[11] "Kevin Mitnick Quotes," BrainyQuote, accessed November 1, 2018, https://www.brainyquote.com/quotes/kevin_mitnick_469447.

caused them to just be done," says Mart, "it just got to be too much. That's why we created this unique balance of who does what, so the other person can focus on their job." Being able to focus on the work at hand is critical, as you want to provide excellent products and services to your customers. The less you have to worry about, the better. Insurance policies can offer you some peace of mind, allowing you to focus on the day-to-day flow of your business.

It's best to set your business up for success, purchasing insurance before you need it. Preparation is key to a new business' success. "The best advice I can give anybody is make sure what you're doing is going to work, to the best of your knowledge," offers Mart. "Do the research, plan well in advance, don't think you're going to open a business in a month. That's just not how it works and it's a recipe for disaster. It took us months of planning before I actually pulled the trigger and started the business. […] You can increase your chances greatly if you just do the research, plan accordingly, and have all of your bases covered before you even attempt to open up shop. Being prepared is your greatest friend when owning a business, because things happen."

As a small-business owner, your company is always going to be at risk, no matter what legal entity your organization considers or how prepared you are when you start. Due to the inevitable presence of risk, you need to protect yourself and your business with risk and business insurance policies, which can provide a level of security necessary for conducting business with confidence.

The purpose of this chapter is not to frighten you; this discussion is meant to prepare you. Liabilities such as accidents and lawsuits can undermine your business efforts before they have even truly begun. Many start-up businesses fail to recover from these catastrophic events, putting a damper on the entrepreneurs' dreams through no fault of their own. Review the following example of one unlucky entrepreneur to better understand how a lack of risk and business insurance could crush a start-up's success:

***

Example: Jenna

Jenna is a business owner who decides to start a restaurant in a college town. Because the restaurant is open twenty-four hours, the enterprise is immediately a success, as local college students have the flexibility to eat at her restaurant at their convenience or meet for study groups over a late-night coffee. Jenna is confident that her restaurant will continue to be a success; however, the following accidents and incidents occur and risk undermining her business:

✗ A customer slips on a spilled drink in the middle of the tiled floor and falls. While the customer insists that he is not hurt, he later visits his doctor to ensure that his back was not permanently injured by the fall. If the customer wanted to, he could sue Jenna's company for failing to present a warning sign or clean the spill as soon as it appeared.

✗ Jenna enjoys a more relaxed and casual work atmosphere, so she does not mind the mixed apparel and shoes her employees wear. However, one of her employees wears open-toed shoes on a day she works with the fryer. This employee accidentally spills hot oil on her exposed toes and is forced to miss several days of work due to this accident. Like the customer who slipped, this employee could potentially sue Jenna for creating an unsafe work environment that exposed her to physical harm.

✗ The town in which Jenna's restaurant operates is located in California, which occasionally experiences earthquakes. When Jenna first opened the restaurant, she neglected business insurance, reasoning that the town had not experienced a sizeable earthquake in several years, and that she could always purchase business insurance in the future. However, an earthquake occurs just a few months after opening her restaurant, and Jenna's building encounters structural damage. Because Jenna did not have business insurance at the time of the earthquake, she is required to pay for needed repairs out of her own pocket.

***

As the above example demonstrates, entrepreneurs can experience situations that threaten their businesses through no fault of their own. Risk and business insurance can provide a significant level of protection that allows business owners to feel confident and secure. It also provides entrepreneurs with the peace of mind that they need to do business, without constantly worrying about what-ifs and potential disasters.

In this chapter, you will learn about the various types of risk and business insurance policies you can acquire to protect your start-up. You can also expect to learn how to determine your company's most likely risks, which can help you make smarter decisions when procuring insurance policies. Finally, you will discover how to find the most suitable insurance plan based on these risks.

Understand Risk and Business Insurance

As a small-business owner, you likely know that taking risks is a natural part of doing business. Nonetheless, it is vital to your business that you take concrete steps to minimize your risks as much as possible. Without the protection of risk insurance and business insurance, simple incidents or catastrophic disasters can outright crush your entrepreneurial dreams. Additionally, risk and business insurance can provide you with protection on a personal level, ensuring that your family's assets (like your home, car, and

101

other valuable items) will not be at risk should a customer or employee decide to sue your company over a danger that your business exposed them to.

Risk and business insurance consist of various policies that can provide your company with certain protections based on your coverage. Your level of protection will largely depend on the types of policies you enroll in and the level of coverage you opt for. As with most types of insurance coverage, business insurance is used to protect the organization (including the owner) when unexpected events happen. Having insurance coverage can ensure that you are protecting yourself and your organization from going bankrupt.

Risk and business insurance can be purchased to cover virtually every aspect of your organization. Therefore, it is critical for entrepreneurs to carefully consider the types of policies that exist and determine whether these policies are appropriate for their companies' needs. For example, if you operate a business in North Dakota, it is likely that you may forgo insurance that covers earthquakes, as the state experiences earthquakes incredibly rarely. However, Jenna's restaurant should have had this type of coverage from the very beginning, as her state has been notorious for its historical frequency of earthquakes.

Examining the different types of insurance coverage that exist can also help you make smarter purchasing decisions. As an entrepreneur, you likely do not yet have a great deal of capital, which is why it is particularly important to make smart decisions regarding your business and risk insurance. Do not be tempted to postpone this task until your company starts making profits. As the example of Jenna demonstrated, unexpected disasters could happen at any time—and you do not want to be caught without insurance if they happen in the beginning stages of starting your business.

If you believe business and risk insurance are an unnecessary expense, consider this: many policies are actually tax deductible. You can enjoy the personal and professional protection that business insurance affords while decreasing your tax burden.

Now that we have defined risk insurance and business insurance, we will next discover the different types of insurance policies that entrepreneurs might consider purchasing, which can include the following:

Liability Insurance

This is the type of insurance that most business owners will purchase, especially if the business is being operated within a physical location as opposed to an online store. For example, if a customer slips and falls on your premises, liability insurance can cover the damages of the accident. Medical bills and lawsuits that result from customer accidents can be costly, especially to a start-up business. Some liability insurance policies also cover injuries to customers that occur as a result of a product defect. Liability insurance is likely to be the first type of insurance policy you purchase.

Catastrophic-Loss Insurance

This type of insurance policy protects your company from closing or falling into debt due to an unexpected and catastrophic loss. This type of coverage typically covers loss of business assets due to fire, flood, hurricane, and other natural disasters. This insurance can be critical for businesses that want to operate again after misfortunes. For example, if you own a restaurant and it is damaged by a hurricane, this insurance policy can provide you with the funds you need to repair your business, cover your losses, pay your bills and employees, and reopen your restaurant. Without this type of insurance policy, you would be forced to either use your assets to front these costs or close the business altogether.

Litigation Insurance

Although it is impossible to prevent customers, individuals, and other entities from suing you, litigation insurance can minimize the financial damage that can occur if your business is brought to court. Business-litigation insurance can aid in covering the costs of going to court in a frivolous lawsuit, and it can also help cover part of the costs that are incurred should you lose your lawsuit.

Other Insurance

Other types of insurance policies you may consider include the following:

- Property insurance
- Worker's compensation insurance
- Insurance for company vehicles
- Key person insurance
- Life insurance
- Health insurance
- Business interruption insurance
- E-commerce interruption insurance

The type of business you operate can largely determine the type of insurance policy you buy. In addition, your investors may only work with a company that has specific types of insurance coverage, especially if your business contains expensive equipment, machinery, and manufacturing technologies. It is important to determine what insurance policies you need to purchase, which is a process that involves carefully examining the different types of risk that could materialize within your organization.

Determine Your Company's Risks

One obstacle many entrepreneurs face is the fear factor—new owners want to have a safe business. "That's totally fine, so when I talk to them, I tell them to take little steps to manage their risk," expert Joseph Molina says. In order to minimize risk, Molina recommends a very organized approach to everyday responsibilities. He advises creating a list of all the tasks and responsibilities that you know you will encounter or that keep coming up. This way, little details will not overwhelm you. After creating the list, Molina advises, "Get some assistance from someone who knows how to start a business. There's a lot of free assistance out there—going to college to take classes, and help from the SBA and others—that can help you identify what comes first. Then you can start to do things, and do them in order. Once you create that list, you can identify what needs to go first, and then you can create a realistic timeline. You're not going to start a business in one morning, and this can keep you from being frustrated." Making a detailed list of your business' responsibilities, and conducting research on them, is also the first step to determining what types of risk your business might encounter.

No one can accurately predict which disasters will happen within an organization. In fact, sometimes worrying about potential disasters might detrimentally cause an entrepreneur to retreat when he or she actually needs to push ahead. Do not stress yourself if you find that you are unsure of your company's risks. This is perfectly normal and altogether expected; unforeseen events can occur to any organization regardless of its industry or location.

With this disclaimer in mind, realize you can still gain an understanding of which risks are more likely to occur within your company. For example, if you have an online business, you probably will not need coverage for customers' accidents on your premises, as you will not have a physical store for customers to have accidents in. This knowledge can help you spend your money wisely, which is critical in the beginning stages of starting a successful business.

In this section, you can expect to learn about the most common types of risk that can materialize within an organization, which include the following:

- ✗ **Physical-Harm Risks:** This is a type of risk that presents a physical danger to you, your employees, and to the physical business itself. The most common type of physical-harm risk is construction, which can incur damage to the business's building and may even increase the risk of fire and explosions. A business owner must have a business insurance policy that covers any damages and expenses that are incurred as a result of physical-harm risks.

To help minimize physical-harm risks within your workplace, you may want to ensure all employees have access to an emergency evacuation plan, especially in the midst of construction. Outline where the emergency exits are located in the building and where employees should go if they are forced to evacuate. Make sure that emergency phone numbers are clearly posted throughout the building. You should also invest in fire alarms, smoke detectors, and a sprinkler system that can contain and lessen damage from fires that start in the building.

✗ **Locality Risks:** The physical location of your organization can play a large role in the type of locality risks you may be exposed to. For example, a business that is located in California will seek protection from damage incurred by earthquakes, while a business that is located in Florida will seek protection from damage by hurricanes. Some of the most common locality risks can involve seasonal storms (such as flash floods, monsoons, and ice storms), tornadoes, hurricanes, fires, earthquakes, and other natural disasters. Business owners should consider the most prevalent natural disasters within their operating locations and invest in their business insurance accordingly.

✗ **People Risks:** This type of risk can have a detrimental impact on the organization; therefore, it is in the business owner's best interest to protect himself or herself against it. People risks can include misappropriation of funds and property theft, which are the most common types of risks that occur in the business world. While there is not a specific type of insurance coverage that protects entirely against people, you can still protect yourself in cases of litigation and loss.

To help minimize people risks within the workplace, you may find it beneficial to install "honesty checks" throughout projects and processes. For example, you could require that two people sign off on checks, invoices, and payables, which can help ensure that no company funds are misappropriated. You can also conduct background checks to ensure that you do not place someone with a criminal background in a position where he or she can easily access checks, invoices, or other sensitive documentation.

Finally, you may find it beneficial to have health insurance policies for your employees, as this can help minimize illnesses in the workplace. Health insurance can also help any employees who are suffering from addiction and psychological illnesses. While employee health insurance might not initially seem like it can minimize people risks in the workplace, employee ailments and addictions can in fact present some of the largest risks to organizations. Business entrepreneurs may want to protect employee productivity and motivation by investing in employee health insurance policies.

✕ **Technology/Information Systems Risks:** This type of risk is experienced by businesses that almost exclusively rely on technology to get their work done. While many businesses use technologies and would experience decreased productivity if this equipment failed to work, some businesses would be entirely disrupted if their manufacturing processes or software suddenly experienced a problem. In other cases, power outages can pose a technology risk, as they may render the use of your company's technologies impossible.

Technology and IT-system risks are often brought on by catastrophic disasters. Any business insurance you have should cover you in case your company loses valuable machinery. However, to minimize this risk within the workplace, business owners may consider investing in backup generators and batteries. Business owners should also invest in a backup data-protection system, which can ensure that data lost during a power outage or system failure is not irrecoverable.

✕ **Credit Risks:** Working with customers and vendors can often expose you to credit risks, which occur when someone fails to pay back money that you loaned him or her, or when a customer fails to pay a major invoice. For example, if you provided services worth $2,000, and the customer failed to pay you, this can be a considerable loss to your company, especially in the beginning stages. Therefore, it might be worthwhile to look into your litigation coverage for business insurance, as you may find yourself having to take customers to court over unpaid invoices.

Try to minimize your vulnerability in situations where you provide your customers with invoices after delivering a product or service. Make sure that your contract is ironclad, with clearly defined delivery dates, payment dates, and penalties incurred if the customer fails to pay. You may also disclose that your company will take the customer to court if he or she fails to pay the invoice by a certain date. If you provide services or products to other businesses, see if you can conduct a credit check or research the company's BBB rating. This can give you a better understanding of the business's ability to pay your invoices.

While the above risks certainly do not cover all the risks that might exist within your business, these are some of the most common. You might find it beneficial to carefully examine the risks that exist within your company and what steps you can take to minimize these risks. Being aware of your risks can give you a stronger foundation for what type of insurance coverage you will need, which can ensure that you are spending your money wisely.

Find the Most Suitable Insurance Plans

Buying insurance for your business might seem like a complicated endeavor, but it does not have to be—especially when you already have a firm understanding of your company's risks. The following section contains steps to find the best insurance plan for your business, as well as additional tips to ensure that your business insurance is always relevant and up to date.

Assess Your Risks

In the previous section of this chapter, you learned to spot and minimize the most common types of risks in a workplace setting. While knowing the risks is crucial for preserving the operations of your company, this knowledge is also vital for ensuring that you select the right insurance coverage. For example, you can safely avoid investing too heavily in liability insurance if you own a virtual store, as opposed to a physical store that your customers will be exposed to.

When you submit an application for insurance coverage, the insurance company will assess your information to determine how great of a risk you pose. This can help them decide if they are going to underwrite you or not. If your business has a considerable amount of risk, the insurance company will charge you a higher premium, and it is likely you will also have a higher deductible.

By clarifying your sense of your company's risks, however, you can make a more confident assessment of what type of insurance payments you should be making. Compare the process of purchasing insurance with the process of buying a home: you would not submit an application without understanding your credit score. You can avoid the insurance companies that want to overcharge you, and instead, find the insurance companies that will provide you with both comprehensive policies and accurate premiums.

Explore Many Insurance Companies

Busy entrepreneurs can experience considerable temptation to get only one quote from one insurance company, especially if the quote seems reasonable. However, we recommend that you explore other insurance providers and "shop around," as you may find a competitive quote elsewhere. To minimize the amount of time you spend searching for an insurance quote, the Small Business Administration (SBA) recommends visiting the National Federation of Independent Businesses website to find insurance companies that will offer you competitive quotes based on your company's risks and coverage needs. This website can also aid in calculating your business risks and finding an insurance quote that will completely cover these risks. This website is a great tool for removing the guesswork from finding business insurance, which can be beneficial for busy entrepreneurs who need to find specialist insurance brokers.

Consider a Special Policy

The SBA also recommends that entrepreneurs consider a business owner's policy (BOP), which combines different coverage options into a single package. This option can ease any financial burdens that entrepreneurs might experience when attempting to buy multiple policies to cover different risks, as these could lead to higher premiums. The typical BOP covers property, general liability, vehicles, business interruption, and other types of coverage that most businesses need. While this combined package can simplify the insurance-buying process, you must be sure you wholly understand the coverage under your policy. You do not want to discover that you have insufficient coverage when a disaster happens.

If you have unique risks to your business, you may want to consider getting a BOP and another insurance policy that provides you coverage for the specific risk. Be sure to find a specialist insurance broker who can assist you with any unique insurance needs you might have.

Find a Reputable Agent

Find a licensed and reputable insurance broker who can get the best insurance policy for your business. A reputable agent can assist you with matching an insurance policy to your needs. You might consider researching a broker's customer history to determine how successful he or she has been in meeting the needs of other entrepreneurs. Insurance brokers are typically paid commissions based on the insurance policies they sell, so it is also in their interest for you to buy one. Do your best to find a reputable broker who cares about your insurance needs, not only his or her commission.

While researching your insurance broker, be sure he or she has been licensed by the state. According to the SBA, state governments regulate the insurance industry and licensed insurance brokers. State websites often have a directory of insurance brokers, which can ease the searching process. Avoid working with unlicensed insurance brokers at all costs.

Assess Your Coverage Annually

As your business grows, your liabilities may change from when you first estimated your company's risks. Prioritize reassessing your liabilities every year so you can determine if you need new coverage. If you find you need to change a policy or buy a new one, be sure to talk to your insurance broker for his or her advice.

Insure Your Business's Key Persons

If your business depends on the skills of one or two key staff members, ensure these people are insured in case of disability or death, as these events could close your business. To keep your business adequately protected, review your insurance policy whenever there are changes to your employee roster, as the policy may be out of date.

Risk insurance and business insurance can provide a measure of security that entrepreneurs need in order to be successful in their industries. With the protection afforded by insurance, you can avoid the worries of closing your business if a customer is injured on your premises, or of personally reconstructing if a hurricane destroys your store. Insurance is also necessary for attracting investors, as it indicates that you are serious about protecting your business (as well as its assets) with comprehensive and accurate insurance coverage.

In the beginning of this chapter, we were introduced to Jenna, a restaurant owner who experienced a number of accidents in her workplace. Without business insurance, Jenna could be forced to sacrifice the assets of her restaurant—as well as her own personal assets—to pay off debts and liabilities incurred by these unexpected events.

However, with the protection of insurance, Jenna would be able to meet each of these unexpected events with a confident and rational mindset. She would have the benefit of knowing how her business and personal assets are protected, and she would be able to create a plan of action for each event based on her insurance coverage. For example, if a customer sues her for falling in her restaurant and it is later revealed that Jenna's employees adequately warned the customer about the water beforehand, Jenna's litigation coverage would cover much of the cost of going to court.

As this chapter has demonstrated, business entrepreneurs would do well to prioritize finding business insurance as highly as the other tasks involved in starting a new company. Doing good research on your insurance may take time, but your hard work will pay off in the end. Don't be discouraged, says Jonathan Mart: "It took us about eight months of getting everything set up—brainstorming, going through every detail. As soon as you get up and running, it's going to go extremely fast. Days start to combine into other days, it just seems like one long crazy week, and things will happen that you'll be perplexed about. You won't know how to handle it, but if you have a good base set up for your business, you'll get through it. That's the best advice I can give, just to be as prepared as you possibly can." Being prepared includes minimizing your risk. Without business insurance, becoming an operational company is dangerously risky—and investors will certainly take notice of this. Make it easier for yourself, as well as the future success of your company, by finding accurate and comprehensive business insurance coverage now.

Review Chapter 5

Now that you have completed Chapter 5, reflect on its content and how you will minimize risk for your business. As you review this chapter, consider the following questions:

☐ Do you understand the types of insurance policies available to your business?

☐ Have you determined your business's most likely risks, especially considering potential physical-harm, locality, people, technology-systems, and credit risks?

☐ Have you contacted multiple insurance companies for quotes? Did you consider using the National Federation of Independent Businesses website to find insurance companies and a reputable agent?

☐ Have you considered a special policy, such as a business owner's policy?

☐ Does your coverage ensure that key persons and all risks are insured?

You should now be aware of the specific liabilities that can impact your company, as well as the insurance you will need as protection from those risks. Finding insurance for your business can be a massive relief, as your start-up is a large investment you will want to maintain secured. If you are satisfied with your understanding of how you will identify your minimize risk for your business, resume reading with Chapter 6.

How to Ensure Protection for Your Business

"If it's your dream and your life and your business, you need to be responsible for protecting it."

-Sonja Foust[12]

In the previous chapter, your learned the importance of protecting your fledgling company with comprehensive business insurance policies. However, insurance is not the only type of protection you will need to keep your business running: you will also need to find and invest in accountants and lawyers to align with your business team.

Accountants and lawyers are essential for dealing with the myriad of financial and legal obligations that you will encounter as a business entrepreneur. To help emphasize this point, let us explore the following example of an entrepreneur who avoids financial and legal problems that could have had disastrous consequences for his business.

***

Example: Matt

Business owner, Matt, specializes in creating software that helps other business owners project when their best sales will occur during the year. The software compiles data from previous sales years and provides business owners with accurate predictions of when sales will likely increase or decrease. Matt's software enables business owners to make smarter decisions with their promotions throughout the financial year.

Matt encounters success when he first launches his product. What was originally a solo venture evolves into a company of seven employees, with Matt as the CEO. He believes the company will grow by leaps and bounds, as more business owners are clamoring to buy this software.

Although Matt's company has grown significantly since its inception, he has not yet hired an in-house accountant or sought out the services of a business attorney. While he knows he needs these professionals on his team to

---

[12] Linda Lugo, "President's message," *New York State Realtor* 13, no. 4 (May/June 2016): 4, https://www.nysar.com/docs/default-source/members-pdfs/nyrs_nyrs0316_2.pdf?sfvrsn=0.

protect his company, he considers himself far too busy to pursue this endeavor. Unfortunately, his company is subjected to a lawsuit when another business owner claims that Matt stole his software idea.

With this crisis looming on the horizon, Matt realizes he needs to hire a business lawyer as soon as possible. Fortunately, a friend of Matt's recommends a business attorney who has experience working in the intellectual-copyright industry. Matt immediately contacts this attorney and asks him to represent the company in court. When the attorney agrees to take his case, Matt is relieved to have found representation so quickly. Additionally, Matt discovers he has litigation coverage included in his business insurance policy. When the case is later revealed to be unfounded, Matt is able to pay his attorney with the insurance coverage, leaving his company's profits relatively untouched. Matt is so impressed by his attorney's performance that he decides to keep him on retainer.

Tax season arrives a few months after the case is closed. Matt knows he must hire an accountant to handle the financial paperwork the company has accrued. He has done his personal taxes before, and Matt briefly considers the possibility of filing the business's taxes himself to save money on an accountant. However, the same friend who recommended the business attorney advises against Matt filing his own business's taxes. The friend gives Matt a recommendation for an accountant who can quickly file the company's taxes and also minimize its tax burden.

After the company's taxes are filed, Matt receives a notice from the IRS that his business is being audited. Matt realizes that if he had tried to file taxes himself, this audit would have taken considerable time, money, and energy to defend. By hiring an accountant, however, Matt has the protection he needs to ensure the audit is handled while he continues to focus on the business. Matt's accountant tends to the audit, which closes when the Internal Revenue Service (IRS) determines that Matt's company filed taxes correctly. Thanks to the services of this newly hired accountant, the company's taxes are barely a worry in Matt's mind.

Matt is grateful for seeking the services of an accountant and a business attorney, as he realizes that he could have found himself in serious financial and legal trouble if he decided to undertake these burdens himself.

* * *

As the above example demonstrates, Matt's company was saved from a myriad of financial and legal troubles because he recruited an accountant and an attorney to assist him with running his business. Despite Matt's company's relatively small size, Matt still found having an accountant and a lawyer on his team afforded him a significant amount of protection and confidence. In the above example, the accountant provided him with a measure of protection against an audit from the IRS, while the attorney protected him from a false lawsuit. Without these professionals, Matt may have encountered the following difficulties:

✕ **Matt would have experienced the difficulties associated with handling the IRS personally.** Audits can be stressful for a busy entrepreneur, as he or she has to collect the company's financial information, meet with IRS officials, and potentially defend the company in court. This defense process requires a significant amount of mental and physical energy that could otherwise be spent growing the interests of the company.

✕ **Matt would have left his company vulnerable to legal situations without the advice and protection of a lawyer.** It would not have mattered whether or not Matt thought the lawsuit was unfounded; if it was filed, Matt would have been forced to defend his company against the claims in court. Without the aid of a lawyer, Matt could have undermined his case and accidentally given the plaintiff some validity with his or her case.

✕ **Matt would have had to file his company's taxes himself.** There is a significant difference between filing your own taxes and filing on behalf of your company. Business taxes are intricate and complex, therefore business entrepreneurs with little or no experience in accounting should avoid filing themselves. Even if you believe you have enough accounting experience to do your company's taxes, you might reconsider. Your time is worth a considerable amount of money, and it is better spent on activities that will grow your business.

In the end, Matt made the right decisions by opting to hire financial and legal professionals to protect his business. In this chapter, you will learn how to do the same by finding accountants and lawyers who can protect your business interests. You will discover why you need professional representation, what qualifications accountants and business attorneys must have, and how to find the best professionals with minimal effort.

Know Benefits of Professional Representation

Your business needs professional representation from both an accountant and an attorney. If you are wondering why these professionals are necessary, consider this: your business is like your health. Most people eat well and exercise to keep themselves healthy and strong. They also regularly visit their doctors to assess more complicated health issues, such as illnesses. In relation to running a successful business, an accountant and an attorney are like health doctors. Regardless of how many beneficial daily habits you engage in to keep your business running smoothly, you will still need to check in with these professionals to address specialized issues. If your business "becomes sick" with financial or legal issues, an accountant and attorney can diagnose the causes of the company's troubles and provide you with solutions for improving its health.

Unfortunately, start-ups often encounter many costs before they generate a single dollar in revenue, which is why entrepreneurs can be tempted to avoid the expense of hiring an accountant and a lawyer in the beginning stages of the start-up. However, it is important not to wait until you desperately need a business lawyer or accountant to hire one. Your start-up will eventually need these services, so it is best complete the hiring process before you encounter critical situations, like an audit from the IRS or a lawsuit from an unhappy customer or competitor.

In fact, before you officially open your business, you may need the services of a business attorney or accountant to establish your legal structure. This area of knowledge is one of the many reasons the Center for Health and Safety Specialists' owner Victoria Buggs employs a business accountant. Her accountant fills in a knowledge gap for her. "They've been very informative for my business, and how to keep me safe!" she says. "For a long time, I was a sole proprietor. I became an LLC and with the goals I had in mind, my accountant told me I should probably move to an S corp. I benefited from the guidance of my accountant." You may also need a business attorney to apply for permits and licenses, review leases, develop contracts, and create contracts and invoices for your company.

With this new understanding of the importance of hiring an accountant and a business attorney, we will now examine the purposes of accountants and lawyers within your organization.

The Accountant

An accountant is otherwise known as a certified public accountant, or CPA for short. Accountants are critical resources to businesses and organizations, as they are essential for managing the finances of a company, filing taxes, and defending the organization against any audits that may arise.

Buggs has found that her complex tax situation makes an accountant a necessity for the Center for Health Educators and Safety Specialists. "I travel with different agencies to certify their companies. Basically, when I travel, I send everything to them." Earning money in different states can make taxes tricky. "My business has benefited from [the accountant's] organization," she explains. "It allows me to know when and where to pay my taxes. We do a quarterly assessment of where I am, what money I've made, what's put aside, things of that nature. Before, I would just put it in the bank and wait until the end of the year in case I had to pay somebody." With her accountant's help, Buggs feels secure in the knowledge that her business is on top of its taxes.

Certified public accountant licensure is granted to professionals who meet the requirements of the American Institute of Certified Public Accountants. Becoming a CPA is not a simple task; statistics reveal that the pass rate for the competency exam is less than 50 percent, which indicates that the exam is among the most rigorous in the country.

In order to become a CPA, the potential candidate must have at least a bachelor's degree in accounting or business administration, and must meet public-practice-experience requirements. A CPA candidate must pass years of schooling before he or she can even be considered for the exam.

In addition to the standard exam that grants the CPA license, many states require candidates to pass a special exam that pertains to ethics and accounting. This is not a one-time exam; to maintain their licenses, CPAs must successfully complete 120 hours of continuing professional education every three years. This ensures that CPAs can stay up to date with new tax laws and codes, which is essential for providing clients with accurate and timely accounting services.

A CPA must operate by the American Institute of Certified Public Accountants (AICPA) Code of Professional Conduct, which is emphasized in the ethics exam and throughout the duration of the CPA's career. This code is comprised of six principles of conduct, plus applicability of specific rules. According to the AICPA, the Code of Professional Conduct reads as follows:[13]

1. ***Article I: Responsibilities:*** *In carrying out their responsibilities as professionals, members should exercise sensitive professional and moral judgments in all their activities.*

2. ***Article II: The Public Interest:*** *Members should accept the obligation to act in a way that will serve the public interest, honor the public trust, and demonstrate commitment to professionalism.*

3. ***Article III: Integrity:*** *To maintain and broaden public confidence, members should perform all professional responsibilities with the highest sense of integrity.*

4. ***Article IV: Objectivity and Independence:*** *A member should maintain objectivity and be free of conflicts of interest in discharging professional responsibilities. A member in public practice should be independent in fact and appearance when providing auditing and other attention services.*

5. ***Article V: Due Care:*** *A member should observe the profession's technical*

---

[13] "AICPA Code of Professional Conduct," AICPA, accessed November 1, 2018, http://www.aicpa.org/Research/Standards/CodeofConduct/Pages/default.aspx.

and ethical standards, strive continuously to improve competence and the quality of services, and discharge professional responsibility to the best of the member's ability.

6. ***Article VI: Scope and Nature of Services:*** *A member in public practice should observe the Principles of the Code of Professional Conduct in determining the scope and nature of services to be provided.*

The last of the above six principles applies to those who are in public practice, which entrepreneurs are more likely to be working with. This principle speaks to the type of work engagements that CPAs may accept, as a CPA cannot take on work that he or she cannot do. It requires him or her to demonstrate objectivity and independence and to serve the best interests of the client, rather than those of the CPA. For example, if a successful business approaches a CPA with a lucrative contract—and the CPA believes he or she does not have the ability to provide the specific services described—he or she is ethically obligated to decline the job. Taking the job so would violate the Code of Professional Conduct quoted above.

A CPA can perform a myriad of services that are essential to the financial success of a start-up, which include the following:

- Assurance and attestation
- Corporate governance
- Estate planning
- Financial accounting
- Financial analysis
- Financial planning
- Forensic accounting
- Income tax
- Information-technology consulting
- Management consulting and performance
- Mergers and acquisitions
- Tax preparation and planning
- Venture capital

A CPA is also considered an accountant; however, an accountant is not always a CPA. This distinction is important, as hiring an accountant who is not a CPA entails working with a professional who may not be able to perform the services listed above and who is not bound to the Professional Code of Conduct. You will learn about some of the additional qualifications to look for in an accountant in a later section of this chapter.

The Business Attorney

While an attorney is a professional who practices law, a business attorney specializes in legal obligations that pertain to running, maintaining, and protecting a business organization.

Buggs realized she needed an attorney too late: when her business required protection for the first time. "There was a time when someone took advantage of my lack of knowledge, and I ended up paying. That's what led me to a business lawyer." Working in healthcare, her business takes on significant risk. As such, she relies on contracts and other agreements to keep her safe: "I do a lot of non-profit training, and I found out I have to use contracts. My business lawyer helped me to define what was a service agreement and what was a contract, helping me with the terminology, helping me with the paperwork, [reviewing] things that were said in the agreements and contracts." For these reasons and more, a business attorney may be necessary for your small business.

Business attorneys are only licensed to practice law in the states where they have taken the state's bar exam that is administered by the American Bar Association (ABA). Entrepreneurs should avoid hiring an attorney who does not practice in the state where their businesses are located. Each state has its own laws and regulations pertaining to businesses, so it is important to work with a business attorney who knows the specific laws that affect your business. Most states require that a candidate successfully complete the following four steps before taking the state's bar exam:

1. The Multistate Bar Examination

2. The Multistate Performance Test

3. The Multistate Essay

4. The Multistate Responsibility Examination

After successfully passing the state's bar exam, the business attorney takes an oath of office specific to each state. This oath forms a standard of professional conduct that attorneys will live by as they perform their roles.

People who obtain an advanced law degree, but do not take the bar exam, are lawyers but not attorneys. If you want to work with a professional who adheres to a higher standard of professional conduct and is approved by the state's ABA, search for a business attorney as opposed to a traditional lawyer.

Find the Best Professionals with Minimal Effort

As a business professional, you know that your time is best spent growing your business. You may also realize that finding the financial and legal help your business needs is vital to its stability and future success. You should not need to spend an excessive amount of time seeking the best professionals in these industries, especially if you use the techniques described in this section. Each of the following techniques will give you a firm understanding of what to search for in a high-quality accountant or business attorney. To find the best professionals with minimal effort, consider the following techniques:

Understand Your Business Needs

To find the best accountants and attorneys in your area, you need to understand precisely what you are seeking in a professional. If you do not understand the needs of your business—and how those needs relate to its financial and legal obligations—you will have difficulty finding the right accountant and business attorney for your start-up.

Buggs knew what tasks she wanted help with. When she set out to find an attorney and an accountant, sticking to her own needs helped her find a good fit: "[My attorney and I] consulted on what was beneficial for my business, and not what they have to offer. This particular person, she helped me with what I needed at the time. That's how I chose the accountant that I have, too. I picked that person because they said, 'What do you need now?' They helped me with that portion, and that's who I stuck with." Buggs did not allow her choice to be influenced by the variety of services these professionals could offer. She wanted someone willing to help her, a small business owner, with exactly her needs and nothing more.

To help determine your business needs, consider asking yourself the following questions:

- What is the purpose of my business?

- What type of business am I running? (For example, is your business in the service, distribution, or manufacturing industry?)

- What product or service am I selling?

- What resources are needed to perform the work (for example, equipment and supplies)?

- What kind of threats does my business face?

- Who are my customers?

- Where is the work being performed?

- How will the work be performed in my business?

- How will my business and customers interface with each other?

- How am I planning to grow my business?

- Am I planning to keep my business in one location, or do I plan on expanding to different locations?

- Am I planning to sell my business when it reaches a certain point (for example, it generates X amount of sales or has been in business for X amount of years)?

- Do I have plans to take my business public?

- Do I have plans to diversify my business?

Answering the above questions can help you realize what needs your business has now, and what needs your business might develop in the future. This knowledge can determine if you need to hire an accountant or attorney who can be flexible in meeting all the needs of your start-up both now and in the future.

Consider Recommendations Carefully

The advice and feedback of another business professional can provide significant help to you. For example, in this chapter's opening example, Matt was fortunate to find a great accountant and business attorney based on the recommendations of a friend in the industry. Like our fictional example, Buggs also found recommendations through other business owners: "I have a couple of friends that have big businesses, and I listened to a couple of webinars they have, and I just started asking questions." Those questions ensured that the recommendations she found were also a good fit for her.

Recommendations often indicate that a respected peer in the industry was satisfied by the services that he or she received. While this can be an excellent factor to consider, it should not be the single criterion in your search for financial and legal professionals. For example, if a peer who works at a Fortune 500 company recommends an attorney, this attorney might not be the best fit for a small local start-up.

While recommendations should not be the deciding factor in your search for financial and legal professionals, you should still make note of recommendations from peers and colleagues. Take the following steps to determine if these recommendations are worth acting upon:

☐ **Ask the recommender for more specific information about the accountant or attorney.** Ask why he or she thinks the professional would be a good fit for your organization. By asking for more specific information, you can determine if the accountant or attorney is worth a follow-up.

☐ **If the accountant or attorney seems like a good fit for your business, conduct online research to learn the services that he or she offers.** Your objective in this research is to find a professional who fits the business needs you identified in the beginning of this section.

☐ **Examine the accountant or attorney's Better Business Bureau rating.** This rating can give you an idea of the professional's customer-service history, which is a crucial component in finding the right person for your start-up organization.

Avoid Common Hiring Mistakes

Refrain from selecting an accountant or attorney based on an emotional reaction to that professional's advertisement. Also, never select a professional based on a telephone conversation. As busy as you might be, always schedule a face-to-face meeting with a potential candidate. This person is as crucial to the success of your start-up organization as you or your employees are. A face-to-face meeting will help you to determine if that accountant or attorney can give you the attention you deserve, as well as if you could work well together.

Price will undoubtedly play an important role in selecting an accountant or attorney; however, do not place too much emphasis on this factor, especially when in conversation with the accountant or attorney. Such emphasis may indicate to the professional that you have the wrong priorities. Instead, form a concrete idea of your budget for an accountant and attorney, then stick to it. Keep in mind you may not want the least expensive professional possible. These financial and legal professionals are worth investment, as a high-quality accountant or attorney can be a vital asset to a start-up organization.

Create Contracts for Your Business's Needs

Simply hiring an accountant or attorney does not automatically settle every instance in which you might need their particular services. You must define the scope of services for each professional, as this will help you understand the exact services you will receive for the fee that you are paying each professional. This section will cover the scope of representation for each professional and how you can determine what services you will receive based on your agreement with each professional.

The Accountant

When you approach an accountant to represent your business, the accountant will provide you with an engagement letter, akin to a preliminary contract, which spells out the following terms:

- The purpose of the engagement

- The exact services that will be performed by the accountant

- The services they will not perform (this is often beneficial for clarity purposes)

- The business that will benefit from the accountant's services

- Tasks that you as the business owner will be responsible for

- The period that the work will be applied (for example, from December 31, 2013 until December 31, 2014)

- How the service will be delivered

The engagement letter is a critical tool for finding the right accountant, as it clearly delineates what services you will and will not receive. This letter will explain what services you would receive in exchange for your money, which could sway your hiring decision if you are comparing more than one accountant.

The engagement letter is also important for defining your tasks as a business owner. Accountants rely upon financial documentation to perform their jobs. If you cannot supply these documents in a timely manner, the accountant cannot do his or her job.

A well-drafted engagement letter will include the approximate date that services will begin and the approximate end date of the engagement. This ensures that both the business owner and the accountant understand when services need to be renewed, if necessary. The engagement letter will include a schedule of fees to be charged per hour for services performed and an estimate of the total hours or fees. The engagement letter should also specify how the services should be paid, whether by check or through another payment method.

The engagement letter will address expenses—such as travel, copying, and delivery costs—and it may include an approximation of those expenses to help the entrepreneur understand how much he or she might spend. Remember this is an approximation, not a final estimate. The engagement letter will explain the basis on which billing will occur—whether it is by installment or upon completion of the engagement—in addition to payment terms and late-payment fees.

The engagement letter should also address how any financial records will be disposed of. For example, if you need to supply your accountant with budgets and expense reports during the tax season, be sure the accountant knows what to do with these sensitive documents after taxes have been filed.

You could request that the accountant shred the documents or send them back to your company within a certain timeframe.

If you, as an entrepreneur, want to make any changes to the engagement letter, be sure to do so in writing. Verbal agreements do not legally compare to a written contract, so have all requests and changes implemented in writing, as this avoids confusion between you and your accountant over changes in the future.

The Attorney

Entrepreneurs should take the same approach with business attorneys as they do with accountants. However, the entrepreneur should consider opting to receive a retainer letter instead of an engagement letter. The retainer letter simply provides the business owner with the details of the services that the attorney will supply in exchange for a monthly fee. This retainer agreement applies indefinitely unless the retainer fee is not paid or both the business owner and the attorney agree to terminate the contract.

While accountants typically work on a project-by-project basis (thus making it easier to discern what services to expect), projects are not as clearly delineated with business attorneys. For example, an entrepreneur may have routine questions of law that need to be quickly addressed by an attorney. Getting an engagement letter for these cases is not a valuable use of time, which is why some business owners might be tempted to opt for a retainer agreement instead. The retainer agreement simply changes the date and scope of services provided to be more generic.

An attorney engagement letter directed to the business owner should describe the services, dates, payments, and other associated terms of the contract. The engagement letter should disclose, in writing, the purpose of the engagement. If the entrepreneur opts to sign for a retainer agreement, the engagement letter will state the existence of a retainer agreement instead of outlining the purpose of the engagement. If the attorney is hired to represent the company for only a specific case or situation, these conditions should be noted in the agreement. Retainer agreements will not mention specific cases, as they are meant to be more generic. You may also want to ensure the engagement letter contains a section that notes that the business owner should retain the right to make decisions about the case after consulting with the attorney.

The engagement letter should clarify the kind of work the attorney will perform as a legal representative of your company. You may notice the engagement letter will state that by working for you, the attorney does not constitute an endorsement of your political, economic, social, or moral views or activities and behaviors. The attorney should also explain in the engagement letter that he or she is will not counsel your business in the event of criminal or fraudulent behavior. The attorney should reserve the right to terminate the contract if you as a business owner ask him or her to violate the legal profession's code of ethics.

The engagement letter will explain the responsibilities of the business owner and the limits of services provided by the attorney. This explicit boundary is essential so that the entrepreneur realizes that certain services are not included in the contract. The engagement letter should also describe the services that the attorney will provide, as this can help the business owner fully understand the scope of services offered.

Additionally, the engagement letter will include a schedule of fees to be charged per hour for services performed. The only exception to this rule is if you have the attorney on retainer. If this is the case, the retainer agreement should include how much the business owner should pay each month, the services that will be performed based on the retainer, and when the services should be paid for.

Regardless of whether you have an engagement letter or a retainer agreement, the document should address expenses, which can include travel, copies, and delivery costs. The document must explain the basis on which billing will occur. For example, an engagement letter could stipulate payment based on hours worked, while a retainer agreement could stipulate monthly payments. These documents should also outline any penalties that could occur over late payments, such as interest or additional fees.

The engagement letter will address disposal of any records that the attorney requires to perform his or her job. For example, you may want your attorney to dispose of records, or you could request that they be returned to you in a timely manner after a service has been completed. The engagement letter or retainer agreement should also outline provisions for termination of the agreement and other matters that may arise during the contractual timeframe. Any changes or provisions that you request should be made in writing and added to the contract.

Consider Intellectual Property Protection

If your company is developing a unique product or service, intellectual property protection is critical for helping your business become successful, as this right can protect your products, services, logos, slogans, and other business properties from being stolen by competitors. Potential investors will be interested in the steps you are taking to protect your business assets, as these protective measures can help you avoid being taken advantage of by a competing company. Intellectual property belonging to start-up entrepreneurs typically falls within one of the following three categories:

✔ **A trademark** is a word, phrase, symbol, or any other associated design that distinguishes one business from others. This trademark is typically protected by law, thus preventing other businesses from stealing the property and the relevant association that the trademark carries with it.

✔ **A patent** is a set of exclusive rights that the government issues to a person or business to protect a new product or service that the applicant invented. The patent gives the person or business the exclusive production rights, which prevents a competitor from creating and selling the same product or service.

✔ **A copyright** is a legal protection provided to authors, composers, website designers, programmers, and other professionals who create intellectual property. This protection prevents other individuals from copying and selling their original work. Copyrights last for the entire life of the author or owner, plus 70 years after his or her death.

Intellectual property protections reveal that your product or service is innovative and unique. This can be intriguing to potential investors who may consider investing their capital in an entirely new and potentially lucrative product or service. If intellectual property protections might be relevant to your business, be sure to discuss this topic with your business attorney.

Give the process of discovering the best accountant and business attorney as much time and attention as possible. Resist the temptation to procrastinate on this task until the last minute—or until a disaster occurs. As the opening example with Matt demonstrated, searching for an accountant or business attorney when you are in the midst of an audit or a lawsuit can be extremely stressful. Having an accountant and a business attorney on your team can help you grow your business with confidence and ease. When you know that your business is protected from a myriad of financial and legal troubles, you can focus more of your time, energy, and attention on creating an innovative and successful business.

Review Chapter 6

Now that you have completed Chapter 6, reflect on its content and how you will ensure protection for your business. As you review this chapter, consider the following questions:

☐ Do you understand the requirements of a certified public accountant (CPA)? Can you name the services they perform that would be beneficial to your business?

☐ Do you know what an engagement letter or retainer agreement should contain, and how it can help you select the best professionals for your business?

☐ Do you understand the requirements for a business attorney?

☐ Do you know the needs your business will have for an attorney, and what type of retainer agreement will work best for you?

☐ What are your business's specific financial and legal needs?

☐ Do you have a clear understanding of the hiring mistakes you must avoid when choosing the best accountant and attorney for your business team?

If you are satisfied with your understanding of how you will ensure protection for your business, resume reading with Chapter 7.

How to Manage the Finances of Your Business

"Financial freedom is a mental, emotional, and educational process."
-Robert Kiyosaki[14]

One of the most critical elements of sustaining a successful start-up involves managing your finances wisely. You must spend money to get your new business running. When you know how to spend and manage your finances in the beginning stages, you are much more likely to successfully grow your company.

For Justin Charnell, owner of Archareer.com, successful growth is his primary goal. He has started this mission by establishing a necessary service for prospective employees in the architecture and design industries: "The main goal was to be a middle ground between the general job boards, like Indeed and Monster, and the super expensive, niche job boards. What I found was, because [the latter] are so expensive, the only locations that had job postings were the major metropolitan areas like LA, New York, Phoenix. I wanted to be able to offer a lower cost."

Like many business owners, Charnell struggled at first with the new stressors of business financials. "One of the biggest challenges, especially with how I started, was: I was bootstrapping and trying to figure out the financial aspect, where to take profit and revenue. We put that back into the back end of the business. By trade I'm a marketer, so I want to try new things, but when you already have things that are working, you still want to experiment a little bit. Sometimes experiments work very well and sometimes they fail miserably. So definitely [one of our challenges was] where to allocate budget."

Successful growth might feel like an impossible task for entrepreneurs, especially in the beginning stages of a start-up, when you are spending money without seeing a single dollar in revenue returned. Rest assured, this phase is completely normal and likely to pass. Consider the following example of a business owner who found herself unable to properly budget her organization.

---

[14] "Robert Kiyosaki's Best Advice of All the Times," Profit Point EU, accessed November 1, 2018, http://profitpoint.eu/robert-kiyosakis-best-advice-of-all-the-times/.

***

Example: Jill

Jill is a small-business owner who recently started a local grocery store in an affluent neighborhood. The grocery store specializes in organic produce and meat products from local farms. As soon as the grocery store opens, Jill expects it to be a success. Many customers comment that they love going to a grocery store where they know the food is of the highest quality and free of pesticides and antibiotics.

In anticipation of the booming business, Jill decides to expand her grocery store immediately, even though she does not have the financing to do so. She does not worry about the needed capital; after all, many of her customers are happy with their services, and they seem to indicate that they will be loyal shoppers for years to come. Jill soon adds another section to the grocery store and invests in a greenhouse that features garden flowers and plants. Despite the hesitation of Jill's employees, she expands her meat offerings by searching for more unusual products. She has plans of becoming a high-end local grocer, and she reasons that spending money now can help solidify her company's reputation in the future.

However, Jill does not anticipate that a local recession will soon hit the town—and when it does, some of Jill's best customers be forced to reduce their spending. Some of her clientele begin avoiding high-end grocery stores in favor of less expensive national chains and supermarkets. Jill is alarmed to realize that her business finances are in disarray, due largely to the following causes:

×   **By expanding the grocery store and adding a greenhouse, Jill has not only exhausted the current month's profits—she has actually spent four months' worth of profits.** Jill is alarmed when she realizes that if she continues to earn the same amount of money each month (which, due to the recession, she will not) she will not see a dime in profits for at least another six months.

×   **Jill has not prepared a budget or any financial information regarding her liabilities.** When Jill calls a friend who is good with money, the friend asks to see her monthly budgets. When Jill informs her friend she does not have a budget, Jill's friend explains it is easy to spend excessively if she does not know what her liabilities are.

×   **Jill experiences difficulty finding investors.** In order to save the business, Jill needs to find investors who can financially support her grocery store while she remedies her spending problems. While investors are initially intrigued by the idea of a high-end organic grocery store, they are alarmed by how Jill has handled her finances during the first few months in business. They are more comfortable working with business owners who have a strong sense of their spending, and they are uncertain that Jill will change her behavior quickly enough to save the business.

Jill realizes that unless she changes her behavior with her business finances, her grocery store will be forced to close. She needs to find a way to revitalize her company's money quickly, or else her entrepreneurial dreams will certainly fail before they have even truly started.

***

The above example excellently demonstrates what can happen if a business owner is not savvy regarding his or her spending habits. As Jill's example highlights, out-of-control spending or the inability to keep a business budget is not just a mistake—it is in fact a disastrous error that can entirely undermine the success of your new business. This chapter will explore some of the techniques that Jill could use to improve her company's financials, including how to keep and track a budget, how to analyze financial information for risks and trends, and how to use more valuable financial tools. At the end of this chapter, we will apply these techniques to Jill's particular dilemma to see how they can help save her specialty grocery store.

This chapter will emphasize many financial techniques that can be applied to both business finance and personal finance. In order for business owners to be good with the company's money, they need to understand how to use money in general. Credit, loans, debt, and other money issues can be applied to both professional and personal finance. As this chapter progresses, we will explore financial techniques and tips that can be applicable to maintaining your company's finances as well as improving your own financial acumen.

Use Appropriate Financial Tools

As a business entrepreneur, you might feel like maintaining your business finances is a struggle. You might feel as if your brain cannot handle all the information required for managing your business's money. If so, do not worry: this is a completely normal experience—and fortunately, there is a myriad of financial tools and information that can help you improve how you maintain your business finances.

As you begin improving your business financing, consider networking with financial experts for additional assistance. Our previously mentioned financial authority, Joseph Molina, has extensive experience in the areas of business start-up and financing. Among other positions, Molina is principal partner of the business Alliance Funding Group, which provides assistance to small and micro businesses to help them connect to lenders and find financing.

131

Alliance Funding Group matches the request of the borrower to a list of lenders set up through a network. The company also purchases contracts internally in order to help small businesses with cash. There are no fees or charges, and all services have flat rates to make them easy and available for the client. Molina explains, "It is a nice niche, as there are two things that people in business always need. The first is financing, and the second is people."

The following section will explore some of the tools and methodologies that can help you improve how you maintain your business finances, including financial intelligence quotient (IQ) models, budgeting software, and other helpful financial techniques.

Understand Financial IQ

The ability to be smart with one's money, sometimes called financial IQ, seems to be a natural gift among many. Think about a friend or family member who always seems to be wise with spending and saving money. He or she may not have the highest paying job, but if there is a dollar in his or her pocket, he or she can turn it into five more. On the other hand, we all know a handful of people who cannot manage to keep their money, regardless of how great their paychecks may be.

Surprisingly, intellectual IQ and financial IQ are not one and the same. In fact, according to one study from the Center Human Resource Research at Ohio State University, conducted by research scientist Jay Zagorsky, intelligence quotient is not related to wealth or personal net worth.[15] This study, which surveyed several thousands of American baby boomers, concluded that being more intelligent does not grant any advantage in regard to financial success. Additionally, this study found that higher IQ is not consistently associated with experiencing less financial difficulty, as evidenced by individuals of above-average intelligence who still missed paying bills, went bankrupt, or reached credit card limits.

This study poses some interesting questions, especially in respect to business entrepreneurs who may have trouble maintaining their companies' finances. Consider the following inquiries:

- If intellectual IQ has no bearing on financial IQ, then what determines the kind of financial savviness that leads to a solvent business venture?

- Why are some entrepreneurs so good at saving money, while others seem to have so much trouble?

- If a business entrepreneur is not good with money in his or her personal

---

[15] Jay L. Zagorsky, "Do you have to be smart to be rich? The impact of IQ on wealth, income and financial distress," *Intelligence* 35, no. 5 (September-October 2007): 489-501, https://doi.org/10.1016/j.intell.2007.02.003.

life, is it possible to change his or her fundamental money behaviors and become financially smarter with his or her business?

The belief that smarter entrepreneurs make more money is a popular stereotype that economists have done little to dispute. However, Zagorsky's study finds that "people with above-average IQ scores are only 1.2 times as likely as individuals with below-average IQ scores to have a comparatively high net worth. Simply put, there are few individuals with below-average IQ scores who have high income but there are relatively large numbers who are wealthy." At the heart of this intriguing research lie the unspoken questions of financial IQ:

- Are some people just born with a natural ability to effectively handle their money?

- Is there something deep below the surface besides inherent abilities that can explain the results of this study?

Before exploring the implications of the study discussed above for business entrepreneurs, we will first define financial IQ. While financial aptitude does include a high level of financial education—understanding money, learning how to save and invest it, and knowing the difference between growing assets and growing liabilities—financial IQ, according to major studies, seems to extend deeper into the psyche than a simple financial education: it is the basic understanding of how money works, combined with the goal to adhere to good money practices.

The most financially successful entrepreneur is one who understands the importance of balancing the company's budgets, spending less than the company earns, making money work for the company. In fact, these rules also apply to maintaining your personal finances, and any entrepreneur can learn the basics of maintaining his or her company's money.

Business entrepreneurs who are better at maintaining their companies' money are so because they have a different attitude than those who have trouble with business finances. In order to improve your attitude toward money—and thus improve your ability to handle your business finances—consider the following ideas:

☐ **Place your values outside of material wealth.** Our values largely shape what we do with our money. For example, if you value material things such as a nice house, flashy car, and a designer wardrobe, it is likely you are spending in excess of your personal income. As an entrepreneur, you might see this attitude spread from your personal life into your business life.

If you want to improve your attitude toward money, consider spending more time with loved ones, such as your family members and friends. This shift in activities may immediately fix for your business finances, but it can temper the spending habits that damage your company.

☐ **Continue to demonstrate a willingness to learn.** According to investor, industrialist, and philanthropist, Warren Buffett, financial IQ is not inherent; rather, it is indicative of how much you, as an entrepreneur, are willing to learn about money. Buffett indicates that the problem with the financial industry is that investors are not willing to learn about how to make their money work—and this lesson can extend to business entrepreneurs as well.

Buffet convincingly argues that consumers with the highest financial IQs have an essential mistrust of the sales world, and rightfully so; Buffett indicates that little comes from a sales pitch that is not entirely motivated by making more money. In Buffet's eyes, the business entrepreneurs who are the most willing to buy into sales pitches—including those from credit-card companies, lenders, and vendors offering unneeded products—are setting themselves up for the biggest money mistakes.

☐ **Understand the difference between an asset and a liability.** Many business owners tend to buy into schemes and purchases that are labeled as assets, like monthly subscriptions to unnecessary software and expensive high-end office technologies. However, those entrepreneurs with a high financial IQ know a liability when they see one, and they stay far away from it.

When purchasing something for your company, be sure you are not buying into a sales pitch about how the product is an "asset" for your company. If the pitch is coming from a salesperson or someone who can directly benefit from the purchase, treat this pitch with caution. Ask yourself if the purchase will truly benefit your start-up business in the immediate future. In the example that opened this chapter, Jill decided to purchase a greenhouse because she believed she could earn more money from this venture. While this could have been true over time, the greenhouse was nonetheless a liability: it was not ready to bring in profits, and it cost Jill's company more than it could afford. Approach your business purchases with objectivity and determine what "assets" are actually liabilities in disguise.

☐ **Demonstrate the following three financial IQ factors:**

1. **The habits of thrift and moderation**

2. **The diligent pursuance of a plan of action**

3. **Good luck**

While very little can be done about the third factor, typically a combination of the first two determine financial IQ and why people do what they do with their money. Diligence may be the most important of the above character traits, as building a company's wealth involves little more than repeating successful procedures. Business owners who want to disrupt their routine procedures by making extravagant purchases and expecting to make the money back in the future are putting their start-ups at serious risk.

This spontaneous spending is a bad money habit that is often rooted in the world of personal finance as well. Making a big purchase with confidence that your business will make the money back later can earn you a great load of debt. This kind of spender likely has the mindset of, "Why bother acting cautiously with money now, when one day, my business will more than make up for my purchase?" However, this invalid reasoning can prevent a business entrepreneur from building up savings. As demonstrated in Jill's example, having a savings can support a start-up through an economic recession or provide capital for necessary expenses. If you find yourself tempted to make a purchase based on the belief that your company will make up for it later (and it is not a critical purchase, such as structuring your business or hiring an accountant), it is in your best interest to delay the purchase until your company is making enough money to support it.

Now that you understand more about financial IQs and how they relate to building better businesses, let us summarize this section with the following main points:

- Those with high financial IQ are often more persistent. Balancing a budget, saving money, and building wealth all require a large degree of diligence—and entrepreneurs who are the most tenacious in their pursuit of financial solvency are most likely to be successful.

- While science cannot yet determine the influences of nature and nurture, those individuals with high levels of financial IQ are generally more educated about their finances and less trusting of sales pitches from credit-card companies, lenders, and other financial institutions. Additionally, individuals with high financial IQ are more fastidious about research and will often compare financial products before making any decision. Financial research is critical for business entrepreneurs who want to know everything about a potential purchase's impact on their companies before actually making it.

- Some evidence suggests financial IQ is largely determined by the entrepreneur's values. Entrepreneurs with more material-oriented values tend to have lower financial IQ scores than those who are deeply invested in family and friends.

- Of course, financial IQ is determined by a willingness to take educated risks with money. Knowing the key differences between assets and liabilities can play a major role in financial IQ, as well as demonstrating a basic understanding of how to use money to make even more money.

While changing your financial personality can be challenging—especially when your spending habits have been ingrained in you since you first began making money—it is possible. Improving your money habits requires understanding what makes it difficult for you to maintain your company's finances.

Manage Your Business Budget Intelligently

Your business budget will play a key role in maintaining the success of your business. Your business budget can alert you to whether you are spending too much money or whether you have too many liabilities to make considerable profits. Your business budget can also forecast financial risks or payoffs, which can guide you to make smarter and more confident business decisions. A budget is especially helpful during the normal ebbs and flows of a new business' income. Justin Charnell explains: "The consistency isn't there, as far as a paycheck. Some months it's great and some months we have to cut back on some things." During the great months, it is important to save for the months you might have to cut back.

Learning to manage a business budget involves knowing how to spend smarter, save more, and carefully track your expenses so that you avoid unpleasant surprises with your company's finances. With this in mind, the following section will explore techniques you can use to better manage your business budget.

Make a Personal Business Budget

The reasoning behind the personal business budget is simple: while your accountants work with a more complex business budget, you need a brief document that can help you make a business decision without searching through complex numbers that are more appropriate for tax reasons. Think of the personal business budget as a "cheat sheet" for understanding the financial health of your business. You can look to this budget when you need answers regarding how much income your business is taking in and how much is being expended.

While the personal business budget acts as a quick guide, it is not necessarily a rapidly produced document. The following techniques can allow you to construct a personal business budget that is reasonable and flexible and that, above all things, actually aids your financial decision-making:

☐ **Track income and expenditures.** This is the most basic start to the budget; however, this first step can be daunting. Income includes any liquid cash that enters the business, including invoices paid by customers, capital from investors, money in savings, and so on. Common expenditure categories include the purchase of office technologies, recurring bills (utilities, insurance, employee paychecks, and business credit-card minimums), and payments to vendors.

You cannot simply guess the amount of money flowing in and out of your budget; instead, you must corroborate all data by tracking your money. Gather as many receipts as possible to discover how much your business is actually making and spending. If you do not have receipts available, investigate your business bank account to learn what you have been making and spending throughout previous months. If you have not yet created a business bank account and the money is coming from your own account, examine this account. Sort your business expenses from your personal expenses to gather this information.

☐ **Cut unnecessary expenses.** Keeping a successful budget means cutting unnecessary expenses and "whittling down" the budget to its most basic form. Whatever money can be cut, should be cut. The only exception to this rule is if cutting a specific expense have a detrimental impact on your business. For example, if you run an IT business and you are determining whether to opt for cheaper office technologies, you might consider investigating whether the high-end brands will actually help your company perform faster. To determine other ways to cut spending from your business budget, consider asking yourself the following questions:

- Are you spending too much on your office location? If so, is there a way you could move your business to a less expensive place?

- If you are spending excessively on office technologies, can you find another supplier who can meet your needs at a lower price?

- Are you opting for the most expensive employee benefits package? Can you offer the same benefits to your employees with a less expensive insurance company?

- Can you save money by bundling your business internet and phone services—or could bundling actually be costing you more? You may want to inspect how much you could save by getting these services from different vendors, as bundling your utilities is not always the best option.

Searching for all the ways you can save money might be a significant expenditure of your valuable time, but this process is a necessary step toward maintaining the finances of your business.

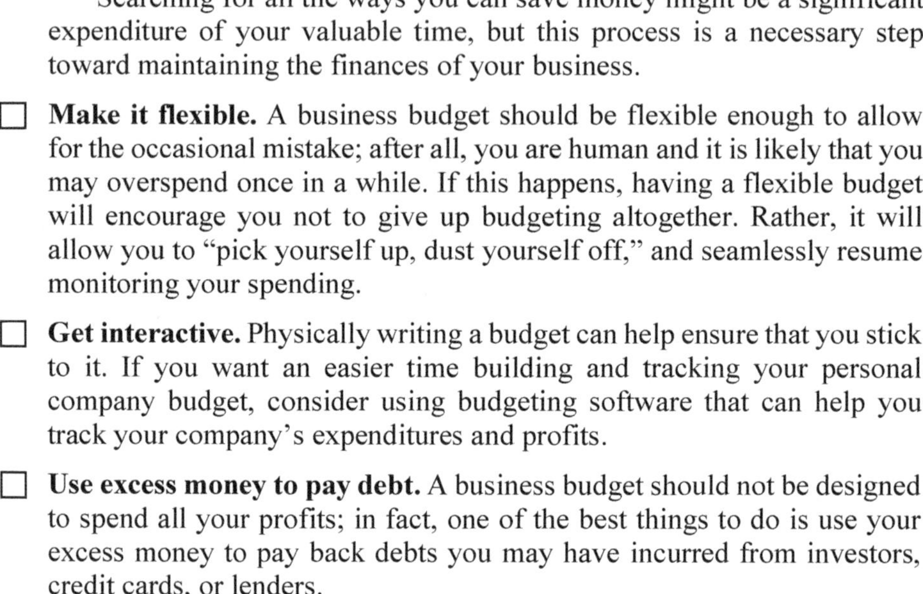

☐ **Make it flexible.** A business budget should be flexible enough to allow for the occasional mistake; after all, you are human and it is likely that you may overspend once in a while. If this happens, having a flexible budget will encourage you not to give up budgeting altogether. Rather, it will allow you to "pick yourself up, dust yourself off," and seamlessly resume monitoring your spending.

☐ **Get interactive.** Physically writing a budget can help ensure that you stick to it. If you want an easier time building and tracking your personal company budget, consider using budgeting software that can help you track your company's expenditures and profits.

☐ **Use excess money to pay debt.** A business budget should not be designed to spend all your profits; in fact, one of the best things to do is use your excess money to pay back debts you may have incurred from investors, credit cards, or lenders.

Creating a personal business budget does not need to be a complicated endeavor. In fact, a personal business budget can be a simple spreadsheet you keep on your desktop at work. The personal business budget should provide you with a quick snapshot of your company's financial solvency when you need it. This can help you make business decisions with confidence and speed, as you will not need to visit your accountant for critical financial information. For additional assistance in creating your personal business budget, see the following template:

	Jan	Feb	Mar	Apr	May	Jun	Jul	Aug	Sep	Oct	Nov	Dec
Income												
Cash Sales												
Accounts Receivable												
Investments												
Loans												
Savings Withdrawals												
Etc.												
Expenditures												
Raw Material Costs												
Manufacturing Costs												
Inventory												
Packaging												
Shipping												
Supplies												
Rent												
Utilities												
Loan Payments												
Insurance												
Licenses and Permits												
Dues and Subscriptions												
Advertising												
Travel Expenses												
Maintenance and Repairs												
Accounting Expenses												

Legal Expenses	Payroll	Sales Commissions	Employee Benefits	Etc.	Loan Payment #1	Loan Payment #2	Loan Payment #3 Etc.		Net Income

Pay Business Debts Strategically

Paying business debts is a critical component of running a successful business. When you first make profits, you may be tempted to reinvest that money into your business. However, start-up businesses that first clear their obligations to lenders and investors are typically more successful. As with personal debt: when you owe a lot of money, it can be very difficult to build savings and a great credit history. Owing money may even make lenders and investors hesitant to work with you in the future, as your business's unpaid debts might lead them to believe you do not prioritize repaying what you owe.

Making minimum payments to lenders and credit cards is not a viable option. Minimum payments are designed by lenders to get as much money as possible from you as the loan or credit card is fully paid back. Erasing business debt entails learning the payment techniques that can put you steps ahead of lenders. Use the following techniques to gain motivation, build momentum, and achieve the results you need to completely repay your debts.

- ☐ **Find extra money allocated in your personal business budget.** Be sure that your business budget already includes repayments to lenders and creditors. This extra money is "free" money that you can contribute in addition to minimum payments to lenders.

- ☐ **Address the debt with the shortest payoff period first.** Collect all your debts and sequence them according to the length of time required to pay them off while making only minimum payments. Next, add the minimum payment of the debt with the shortest payoff period to the start-up expenses notated in your budget. By first addressing the debt with the shortest payoff period, you will pay off this debt faster. You will give yourself an incredible boost of self-confidence and assurance that debt will not to plague your start-up forever.

- ☐ **Keep consistent payments.** The minimum payment on your debt will decrease as the debt shrinks, but continue paying the original minimum payment plus the starter-money amount to speed the repayment process.

- ☐ **After you have paid the debt with the shortest payoff period, combine the original minimum payment of the first debt, the starter money, and the minimum payment of the debt with the second shortest payoff period.** This can exponentially decrease the amount of time required to pay off the second debt, which means your business will not have to pay as much in interest to lenders and creditors.

Business entrepreneurs should approach debt consolidation "solutions" with caution. When your business has a significant amount of debt from lenders, creditors, and other providers of capital, you may be tempted to seek out a debt-consolidation strategy to make the debt more manageable. However, plenty of unethical lenders are willing to reap personal benefits by capitalizing on start-up entrepreneurs' desires to pay off debts as quickly as possible. Before using any debt-consolidation strategies, be sure you understand the following:

✗ **Debt consolidation could be trouble if you have bad money habits.** For example, if you choose to move a majority of your start-up debts under one loan, you could be tempted to charge purchases on the newly cleared business credit cards. This could cause a new debt load in addition to the debt you are already dealing with.

✗ **Debt consolidation is not a "magic wand" for effortlessly removing all your business debts.** You still need to pay the total amount that you were paying on various bills; however, consolidating under one monthly payment can make the paying process easier.

✗ **Debt consolidation may result in paying debt over a longer period of time.** You might be interested in the lowered monthly payments offered through debt consolidation, but realize that you could be paying that loan for years longer if you agree to a payment-plan amount identical to the original bills.

Now that you understand these important notes about debt consolidation, we will next explore the best consolidation strategies that can help lighten the debt load your business may have accumulated:

☐ **Consider taking a debt-consolidation loan.** Paying off one loan instead of what seems like hundreds of debts could be the perfect option for the entrepreneur whose start-up is hindered by extensive debt. A debt-consolidation loan can consolidate business credit-card debts, personal loans from investors, and even business loans from banks, thus making the debt easier to manage. A debt-consolidation loan can even reduce the amount of interest that you pay over time, which is ideal for entrepreneurs who find a large portion of their business income devoted to high interest rates.

☐ **Consider consolidating your debts on a low interest credit card.** Consolidating your business debts on a credit card via a balance transfer can give you much-needed support. However, misuse of credit-card consolidation can severely backfire, which may leave you under a massive debt load that can hinder the growth of your company. If you have a business card with a low interest rate, consider transferring any other business card debts to that one. Before you use this method, however, be aware of the following risks:

✗ **The interest rate is likely to change.** Although advertisements might suggest otherwise, balance-transfer cards do not have a fixed interest rate. Interest rates can change within fifteen days' notice. Additionally, you should be wary of introductory rates, as the initial interest rate can increase dramatically after the introductory period.

✗ **Additional purchases on the balance-transfer card may be charged at exorbitant interest rates.** Furthermore, your monthly payments might not pay these off until the balance-transfer debt is entirely paid.

✗ **Making only minimum payments on a balance-transfer credit card is not a financially viable option.** These cards usually carry large debt burdens, therefore you must be dedicated and disciplined enough to regularly pay off large portions of the debt load. Use the methods explored earlier in this section to learn how to pay down this type of business debt faster.

✗ **Your credit score may be ruined.** In regard to your credit score, it is better to have smaller amounts of debt across several credit cards rather than one large debt on one credit card. Weigh your options; your business might receive a better credit rating if you transfer the balance and pay the single credit card faster. Choose the method that will lead to your business becoming debt-free faster.

Reducing your start-up's debt burden as soon as possible is one of the best ways to successfully manage your company's finances, as debt can significantly hinder the growth of your company. Start using the methods explained above to pay down your debts so that your business becomes debt-free in a short time span.

Know How to Spend

Businesses need to spend money, especially in their start-up stages. Entrepreneurs must know how to spend their company's money wisely in order to help protect business profits as well as put more money into the company's savings.

Build Your Business Budget

A written business budget is one of the most essential financial documents your start-up can have. Business budgeting can give you a better understanding of what money is coming in, what money is being spent, and how much revenue you need to make in order to achieve organizational goals and objectives. Building a business budget can be a relatively straightforward process, provided you have enough documentation to track your income, your expenditures, and your needs for growing your start-up organization. To help guide your efforts in building a business budget, consider tracking the following items:

- **Your assets:** Assets include any property that your company owns. This property can be divided into two categories: liquid assets and intangible assets. Liquid assets are defined as assets in the form of cash on hand or tangible objects like manufacturing equipment that have physical value and can be converted into cash. Intangible assets, on the other hand, are defined as the assets that cannot be physically touched or traded for cash. These intangible assets include patents, product research, licenses, and other items that have value but cannot be touched. The combination of these two types of assets represents how much money your company has under its name. Assets may include the following:

  - Accounts receivable (money customers owe the business)

  - Inventory

  - Land

  - Buildings

  - Equipment

  - Furniture

  - Other valuable property

  Determining your assets can also help determine your company's net worth, which will be defined in a later section.

- **Your liabilities:** Liabilities can be defined as every amount of money that the company owes. This can include payments owed to creditors, lenders, suppliers (or accounts payable), employees, as well as any other costs— even those payments that are made over the course of several years. Business entrepreneurs should also consider pending lawsuits or other potential costs as liabilities, as they may take money away from the organization.

- **Your net worth:** To determine your company's net worth, subtract your total liabilities from your total assets. This formula is as follows:

  Net worth (also called equity)
  = Total assets – Total liabilities

This record of how your organization's value can help you to determine whether to cut down your company's liabilities or increase your company's assets. Net worth, when it refers specifically to your business (as opposed to personal worth), is also known as owner's equity.

After you have identified the above three values, you should have a more solid understanding of the financial health of your business. The initial numbers might be discouraging, especially when you are in the beginning stages of a start-up and owe more money than you are making. However, creating a statement of your company's financial value can provide you the knowledge you need to make smarter decisions that lead to more equity and an increasingly greater net worth.

Remember that your business budget should be flexible enough that you can make changes as they become necessary. For example, the cost of operating your business may change, or you may start making more money as your business begins to settle. No matter what changes occur, ensure that your business budget is able to reflect them. If revisions to your liabilities or assets requires a great deal of effort, you may not be as vigilant in tracking your business finances.

Another necessary component of a business budget is the income statement, otherwise known as the profit-and-loss statement. This can be a critical document for your lenders and investors, as it provides them with a record of the financial stability of your organization. To build the income statement, you will need the following information:

- **The cost of goods sold:** This value is simple to discover, as you will simply need to obtain the price of the products or services your organization offers.

- **Gross profit:** This vital piece of information can be determined by subtracting the cost of sales, or the total amount of money spent creating a product (including employee wages, manufacturing costs, and raw-materials costs), from your company's revenue, which is its total income. If you want to determine which products are more profitable than others, subtract a specific product's cost of sales from your revenue. This can establish which products are making your company more money and which ones might be worth removing.

- **Operating expenses:** This value can be determined by identifying the fixed and variable expenses that exist within your business. Fixed expenses are expenses that are incurred no matter how many products or services your company sells (for example, rent, utilities, etc.). Variable expenses are determined by the level of sales your company has. To keep your sales more consistent, you may consider taking measures such as hiring seasonal workers during the holiday season, or increasing the marketing budget for your store's most popular time of the year.

By subtracting your operating expenses from the total gross profit, you can achieve a clear understanding of the net profit or loss for your business. When reviewing this statement, you and your investors can gain a better understanding of your company's financial health, which products are more likely to increase revenue, and whether or not your organization is spending an excessive amount of money on operating costs. Additional information on creating your income statement is available in Chapter 10.

Your business budget should also include a cash-flow statement, which can clearly display whether your organization has enough cash on hand to pursue a particular goal or objective. A cash-flow statement can also come in handy if you need to determine whether or not you have the necessary assets to pay bills during a slow sales season, or if you have ample monetary resources to purchase manufacturing equipment for a new product. To build a cash-flow statement, you will need to identify the following information:

- **Operational activities:** These are the activities your business engages in for the purpose of making money. Operational activities can include the costs of marketing, buying, manufacturing, processing inventory, or other costs. These costs should be subtracted from your initial cash balance, then added to the income generated from your operating activities.

- **Investing activities:** This section of the cash-flow statement pertains to the money used to make long-term investments, as well as money being earned from these investments. Here, make note of activities including stock purchases, securities, and investment strategies which last more than one year.

- **Financing activities:** These items include reports of cash flowing out, in relation to long-term liabilities (such as debts to creditors and lenders), as well as cash flowing in from the issuing of stock. In this section you should record all payments made in order to reduce debt. For example, any loan payment your company makes falls under this category. Any incoming capital from the sale of stock should also be included here.

After you have identified the above three activities, subtract the total cash outflows from the total amount of money coming in. To simplify this process, you may want to identify a specific period of time in which you will track the flow of cash in your company. This calculation will reveal if you have enough cash to achieve a specific objective or if your company is operating at a deficit.

Additional information on creating your cash-flow statement is available in Chapter 10.

All of the documents discussed in this section are critical for understanding the financial stability and well-being of your business. Without these documents, you may not have the information you need to make smart and financially sound decisions. This could, in turn, lead to the ruin of your start-up.

Be sure to continually update these documents, as your assets, liabilities, cash, and other items will most likely change over time. Consider hiring an employee to conduct these assessments, as they can be particularly time-consuming calculations for business leaders after the start-up has become more stable.

Analyze Your Financial Trends and Risks

Compiling financial documentation for your business should include ensuring you have the necessary information to identify financial trends and potential risks. From seasonal sales to economic slumps, this financial information can help you make decisions which protect your business in times of crisis, and take advantage in times of plentiful sales.

On their own, the numbers in your financial documentation might not mean anything. But with careful analysis, you can identify the trends and risks that could have a considerable impact on your business. To identify these trends and risks, consider the following steps:

1. **Understand the key financial ratios that can be applied to your start-up.** These financial ratios can show the relationship between how your business is performing and your industry is performing in general. This can provide you with the quick information you need to determine whether your business is performing well or is experiencing significant trouble. Two important ratios that you may benefit from using in your business are the current ratio and the acid-test ratio:

   - **The current ratio** indicates a business's liquidity and ability to repay debts. This ratio can be determined by dividing your current assets by your current liabilities. This formula is as follows:

     Current ratio
     = Current assets / Current liabilities

     For example, let us suppose your business has $45,000 in current assets and $15,000 in current liabilities. The current ratio would solve as follows:

Current ratio
= $45,000 / $15,000
= 3:1

This is considered a healthy number for businesses. Acceptable ranges vary between different industries, though financially healthy businesses generally have a current ratio of 1.5:1, or greater. A current ratio less than 1:1 indicates the business in question may encounter financial difficulty.

- **The acid-test ratio** reveals a business's ability to use its assets to quickly eliminate its current liabilities. This ratio can be determined by subtracting your inventory from your current assets, then dividing this difference by your current liabilities. This formula is as follows:

  Acid-test ratio
  = (Current assets – Inventory) / Current liabilities

  This value can determine your company's financial strength apart from inventory, as inventory is not a liquid asset. For example, if your company has $40,000 of current assets, $10,000 of inventory, and $15,000 in liabilities, the formula would solve as follows:

  Acid-test ratio
  = ($40,000 – $10,000) / $15,000
  = ($30,000) / $15,000
  = 2:1

  This is considered a heathy ratio for a business. An acid-test ratio of 1:1 or greater indicates that a company's financial health is in great condition, while a ratio less than 1:1 demonstrates that a company lacks necessary cash and assets.

Remember that these two ratios are designed to demonstrate that you and your company have the assets on hand, should your organization encounter financial hardships. This is especially critical for avoiding bankruptcy, as you could use these assets to pay any debts or loans.

2. **Determine your debt-to-asset ratio.** This value can provide you with quick evidence as to whether or not your company is at risk for bankruptcy. Bankruptcy risk happens when your debts are more than your assets, which makes it almost impossible to pay back loans or debts your business might have. To determine your debt-to-asset ratio, simply divide

your total assets by your total liabilities as the following formula indicates:

Debt-to-asset ratio
= Total assets / Total liabilities

This value demonstrates what percentage of your assets is being paid for with borrowed money. For example, if you have a 60 percent debt-to-asset ratio, this means that your lenders have supplied about sixty cents of every dollar of your company's assets. While this may be a reality for some start-ups in their beginning stages, do not allow this number to persist for a long period of time. High debt-to-assets ratios give lenders reason to hesitate and may cause some investors reject the investing opportunity. Companies with high debt-to-asset ratios may not be able to acquire loans or investments because they do not demonstrate they have money-making potential.

3. **Determine your company's return on investment (or ROI).** This value can demonstrate whether your company is making enough money to justify your marketing and production costs, or if your organization is not making enough money to support its operations. To determine your company's ROI, divide your net profits before tax by your shareholder equity. This formula is as follows:

Return on investment
= Net profits before tax / Shareholder equity

If you have a low return on your investments, you may consider analyzing your company's financials to determine what can be done to improve this number.

Financial analysis involves making comparisons between the values generated on your company's financial reports and standard numbers in your industry or among your competitors. When you make these comparisons, you will better know your company's overall financial health. You can also use these numbers to determine if your financial estimates are close to your actual organizational finances. If you find a wide disparity between your estimates and your company's actual finances, you may consider to reassessing how you are reaching your conclusions.

These ratios can be crucial to determining the potential risks and trends that can impact your organization. If your calculated ratios indicate your business is in critical condition, take immediate action to support your organization. If, however, your ratios show that your start-up is financially healthy and well performing, use your financial analysis to determine what goals and objectives you can start working toward.

Improve Your Budget Management

While the above financial ratios and documents can provide you with a greater understanding of your company's overall financial health, you must know how to utilize these values in effectively managing your business budget and making smart financial moves. To help ensure your start-up is continually progressing toward success, and not struggling to make and keep its money, consider employing the following techniques:

☐ **Find a business record-keeping system that works.** Not only is record keeping a requirement by federal law, but it also can help you track your company's finances. Do not settle for any record-keeping system; find the one that you are most likely to use and will work best for your business. For example, if your filing cabinets are constantly unorganized, avoid using this record-keeping system. If you lose track of documents that you have uploaded onto your computer, forgo this option in favor of another system that works. At a later stage of your business, you can purchase a better record-keeping system, but initially, it is critical to find a system that fits your needs and organizational style.

☐ **Set a threshold for your debt-to-asset ratio.** As a start-up entrepreneur, you may find that it easy for your debt-to-asset ratio to slip out of control. In order to maintain a successful business, you need to set a threshold for how much debt you are willing to incur. Keep track of this threshold, as you will need to reduce your debt if you find yourself getting close to this predetermined number.

☐ **Reduce your operational expenses.** One of the biggest expenses that businesses can incur is the cost of producing a product or service. If you find that you are spending a great deal of money to make your product or service, search for ways to reduce this expense. Review the production process to discover where savings could be made. For example, you may find that you can substitute one resource for a less expensive version without impacting the output's functionality and minimum quality standards. If you use this option, be sure to test the resulting products and services to test whether or not they have been impacted by the changes. Selling an inferior product or service to your clients certainly is not a solution to expensive operational costs, as it could end up undermining your business altogether. Instead, find less expensive ways to continue producing a high-quality product.

☐ **Estimate the cost of your business goals and objectives.** To help maintain your business finances, know how much it will cost to achieve your biggest goals and strategies. For example, if you want to open a second location within the first three years of operating your business, consider analyzing how much profit you will need to make to reach this goal. This can help you set financial milestones and action plans to reach this financial threshold.

☐ **Ensure you have some cash available.** Always have some kind of liquid asset on hand in case of emergency. Having these assets available allows you to make emergency purchases and cover anything in your business that might require a quick payment. Although the number does not need to be specific, give your business enough on-hand cash to ensure that you will be covered in the event of a financial emergency.

☐ **Maintain your company's credit score.** Maintaining a business budget is similar to maintaining your personal finances. Ensure your company has a perfect credit rating, as this can make it easier to acquire loans and work with suppliers in your company's name. Ensure that your company's debts are paid on time. Schedule automatic credit-card payments, make note of when your company's loan payments are due, and ensure that any other debts are paid in a timely manner. By keeping your company's credit score healthy, you increase the possibility of gaining access to funding you might need in the future.

☐ **Take care of your personal assets.** One of the biggest missteps that start-up entrepreneurs make with regards to business finances is failing to care for their personal financial health. If you do not have enough money in savings to support you through the first few months of your start-up (the months where you may not yet be making money), you increase your likelihood of making rash financial decisions that could negatively impact your organization. Your personal finances and business budget are linked. A poor personal credit score, savings shortage, or other personal-finance missteps could make it difficult to build a financially healthy organization.

☐ **Hire the right people for the job.** There will be a time when you no longer need to be the point person in charge of your company's finances. Eventually, you will be able to hire accountants, record keepers, and other employees who can regularly track your organization's financial health. Hire the right people for these tasks, as these employees will provide you with the information you need to make critical business decisions. Hire people with a considerable amount of experience and knowledge, and ensure they report to you on a regular basis.

☐ **Learn more about your industry.** One of the best ways to protect the financial health of your business is to understand what is considered normal for your industry. You might not be able to identify risks to your company if you do not understand how other organizations in your industry are operating. By learning more about the financials of your industry, you could improve your ability to identify when your company is performing well or when emergency financial decisions must be made.

Maintain your company's financial health in the same way you would manage your personal finances. Financial uncertainty is one of the biggest stressors a business owner might encounter. Charnell's military experience has helped him to push through his uncertainty. "Be comfortable with being uncomfortable," he advises. "Just start! Unless you have a big budget to spend, just try to make the bare minimum you need to make or create or start." Keeping your finances simple and straightforward will help you stay on top of them. Make your company's payments on time, ensure that you are tracking financial trends within your industry, and keep liquid assets on hand should you need to make an emergency purchase.

As a start-up entrepreneur, you must maintain the financial health of your business without putting it at risk. By managing your financial health, tracking your financial documentation, and maintaining your business budget, you can ensure you are able to pursue new business objectives and goals without struggling to find necessary funding.

Review Chapter 7

Now that you have completed Chapter 7, reflect on its content and how you will manage the finances of your business. As you review this chapter, consider the following questions:

- ☐ Have you examined your financial IQ, including the values, willingness to learn, and understanding of assets and liabilities that have shaped your use of money?

- ☐ Have you completed both a personal budget and a business budget?

- ☐ Have you implemented a monthly debt repayment plan in your budget?

- ☐ Are the monthly expenses of your business maintainable?

Use the tools discussed in this chapter to manage your business's financial health and maintain your business's cash flow. After an initial start-up period, your business should be capable of paying off all debts and beginning to profit. If you are satisfied with your understanding of how you will manage the finances of your business, resume reading with Chapter 8.

How to Wisely Utilize Your Capital and Loans

"What makes small business develop into big business is not spending, but saving and capital accumulation."

-Ludwig von Mises[16]

In the previous chapter, you learned the importance of ensuring your company's financial health. You also discovered that keeping a start-up business running involves carefully tracking your debts to lenders and investors. Using capital and loans wisely is another vital part of financial management. A smart business owner is able to handle every aspect of capital and loan usage effectively and efficiently, from finding the best loans for his or her business to understanding how much capital is truly needed to achieve business goals and objectives.

In this chapter, you will discover how to use capital and loans to start and run a business venture. This chapter contains techniques for determining the amount of capital needed and identifying the lenders who can provide you with the best loans possible for your business.

Understand Business Capital

Capital can be defined as the funding required to start running your business until it begins making enough money to become sustainable. Having enough capital is critical for a successful start-up, as depleting your funding before you have turned a profit could financially undermine your organization. On the other hand, gathering too much capital may increase your obligations to creditors and lenders, which can have a similarly disastrous impact on your business finances. In this situation, your long-term repayments could impair your business growth, which could impede the long-term objectives you might have had for your organization.

Business expert Michelle Keshel has extensive experience in securing

---

[16] "7 wallpapers," QuoteFancy, accessed November 1, 2018, https://quotefancy.com/quote/855520/Ludwig-von-Mises-What-makes-small-business-develop-into-big-business-is-not-spending-but.

income for businesses. Keshel's company, SAS-GPS, has two main functions: proposal management and proposal writing. Her company offers technology developed as the Internet was emerging that automates communications for easier marketing—to high-level contacts.

Having already acquired some clients before she went full-time with her business, Keshel was in a good position to support her start-up from the beginning. Several large projects acquired soon after going full-time helped as well, and she and her business partner quickly progressed with the software they were developing as early adopters of the Internet—software that led to the development of her current products. To stabilize finances, she brought on additional shareholders. Keshel explains, "Money is always an obstacle." She knows well that all businesses must overcome the obstacle of financing, either through obtaining revenue or borrowing money. Keshel elaborates, "As a small business, you will always be signing away your life, your property, your home—that is a difficult position to be in. It adds extra weight to your investment decisions. You need experience to make it work out."

To ensure you have identified the right amount of capital for your business, determine your start-up-capital needs. This process can range from finding funding for one-time costs to backing long-term obligations, such as rent or utilities for an office. No matter which type of cost you might have, carefully analyze how much capital you will need to fulfill these financial obligations. Let us analyze the difference between one-time costs and ongoing costs so that you can identify your own capital needs:

- **One-time costs:** One-time costs can be defined as expenses that your business will incur only one time. These will typically include your company assets, such as manufacturing equipment, computers, and other items that can help your start-up become successful. One-time costs can also include start-up legal fees, company logo designs, website design, and security deposits on an office. These costs cannot be leveraged for any future loans or capital, unlike the assets defined in Chapter 7.

  To ensure you find the best capital for your business, separate your one-time costs between assets and expenses. This categorization help you determine whether you are able to cover the cost of one-time expenses or whether you need capital to purchase assets as well as to cover these necessary business expenses.

- **Ongoing costs:** As a business entrepreneur, you may already know that you may need several months before your company starts making enough money to cover operational costs on its own. Due to this starting-up period, you must identify the running costs of operating your business, as this can keep your organization afloat until you can support it with the money you earn from your sales.

You must have a precise understanding of how much money you will need to keep the business operational. Despite expecting that your sales will not support your business for a certain amount of time, exhausting your capital reserved during this phase could deplete any money and assets that your organization might have. Running out of cash at the start would end your business altogether.

In order to avoid this problem, ensure that you have what is known as working capital. You must have all necessary cash on hand to make payments for your ongoing costs until you have enough money from your organization's sales to support the business.

When estimating these one-time and ongoing costs, you might assume it is safer to make generous estimates. However, it is also important to avoid unnecessarily obligating yourself to lenders and creditors, as this could stunt your business growth. Making accurate yet conservative estimates can be critical to the success of your company. Prepare a higher estimate for running costs and ensure that you have realistic expectations about your sales revenues. While it would be great to make a profit within your first six months of operation, this would be atypical. Realistically estimating your start-up costs as well as your expected sales revenue can aid in identifying the precise amount of capital your business needs.

To determine the amount of working capital you will need to support your business, multiply the total estimated monthly running costs by the number of months you estimate your business will require before sales revenue reaches profitable levels, then add your one-time costs. This formula can be expressed as follows:

Working capital needed
= (Total monthly running costs * Number of months before revenue becomes profitable) + One-time costs

The number of months before your company turns a profit will depend on your industry and the economic conditions in your local area. Ensure you conduct the necessary research to determine whether your working-capital estimate is realistic and achievable.

Identify Your Best Funding Sources

You have just estimated how much capital you will need to keep your business operational until you start making sales revenue. Now that you have this number available, you are ready to request funding—but how do you identify your best funding sources?

Jeanette Dempsey has built her business on her solid entrepreneurial skills and her passion for making people smile. She is the owner of Carolina Donut Diva, a custom donut operation located in South Carolina. Her business model and low startup capital required her to make many difficult funding decisions before she could start.

In particular, she recalls financing her equipment—not a bad choice in itself, but made hastily: "I contacted Lil' Orbits, who I wanted to buy my equipment from. They listed people that would offer financing for it. I had to sign an agreement to make payments every month, until it was paid off." In her eagerness to get her business running, she selected the first lender on the list. "I was trying to get the first option and do it as quickly as possible, because I wanted to go ahead and start," she explains. "There was another [lender] that was probably a better option for me, but it took too much time for me to get in contact with him. In hindsight, I would have taken more time, and found the absolute best resource for me."

Fortunately, there are many funding sources that can be utilized to acquire the start-up capital you need. Each funding source has its own advantages and disadvantages, all of which are important for business entrepreneurs to consider before pursuing funding. When searching for start-up capital, consider the following funding sources:

Equity Financing

Equity financing can be defined as the process of accruing funds by accepting money from other individuals or firms in exchange for partial ownership. This resembles a traditional investment: in exchange for providing money for your start-up organization, the individual or company has a partial stake in your company. The ownership share can change based on the amount of money that the person or company provides to you. Additionally, this person or firm can make a considerable amount of money when the company goes public or is purchased, depending on the amount of ownership that he or she has in your organization.

Equity financing can help you start your organization without embracing considerable debt; however, you agree to share the profits of your company should your business go public or be purchased. Equity financing also prevents you from making 100 percent of the company's decisions, as you will be obligated to make decisions in collaboration with the other owners of your organization.

If you are interested in equity financing and want to use this as a means to raise capital and avoid debt, consider the following two equity-financing methods:

- **Use your personal funds.** This is perhaps the most common form of equity financing, as it provides you with the funds you need to start your business without losing a considerable amount of ownership stake. Many business entrepreneurs are also willing to put up their homes, cars, and other assets as collateral to secure business loans.

While an advantage to this method is that you can keep making all major decisions for your business, a considerable disadvantage is that you could risk losing your personal assets if your business fails. If your assets include your home, car, and other essentials, you could be placing yourself or your family in financial risk. Carefully consider the benefits and costs of this equity financing option before using personal assets for a start-up. Realize you cannot recover your money if your business fails.

- **Use funds from investors.** This is a more complex equity financing option, as investors will want control over the operation of the business before releasing funding. There are also considerable legal and regulatory requirements when working with investors. Accredited investors, persons having a net worth of over $1 million, are deemed to have sufficient knowledge of investment decisions, and they require fewer protections than non-accredited investors. Non-accredited investors are protected by strict laws and regulations.

  Investors often gather to create venture capital groups, which minimizes the risks these investors encounter when providing funding to start-up organizations. Angel investors, or individuals who provide funding to start-up businesses, can also help, but they may not want as much return on their investments as venture capital groups.

  If you are interested in working with an investor, consult a legal advisor who can guide you through this complicated process. Ensure your interests are protected and that you have secure compliance with all legal and regulatory requirements.

Debt Financing

Debt financing, the most common type of funding in the start-up world, involves you taking out a loan from a lender or similar creditor, then paying off the debt over time. One of the advantages of debt financing is that you maintain 100 percent control over your financial decisions; however, one of the disadvantages of debt financing is that it can negatively affect your company's equity and financial health. Debt financing is often associated with interest rates and other financial penalties and can negatively impact your organization's credit rating if you miss a payment. If you are interested in using debt financing to fund your start-up business, consider the following options:

- **Fund your start-up business with personal credit.** Many business owners use their own savings and credit cards to start businesses. While this may not always the safest option, as you would be provided little protection if your business fails, using your own savings and credit cards can be one of the fastest solutions for obtaining funding. Additionally, using your own money means you can avoid answering to investors or paying interest rates on any business loans.

- **Ask friends and family members to loan the capital you need.** This can be the quickest way to fund your start-up without going through a credit check or being charged exorbitant interest rates.

  However, approach this method carefully. Many personal relationships can be negatively impacted when one person borrows money from another. If you want to protect your relationships while still getting the funding your business needs, create a written agreement that contains the repayment terms, the date of the loan, the purpose of the loan, and when you expect the final payment to be made. For accuracy, have a lawyer draft these documents, as this will ensure legal terms are correct and the agreement is beneficial to both parties. Understand if you break this contract, your family member or friend can legally request that all of his or her money be repaid. If you do not want your relationship to be potentially impacted by money, consider opting for a more traditional method of debt financing.

- **Obtain personal loans from banks and other lenders.** These loans can provide you with low-interest financing, provided you have an excellent credit score. Many start-up businesses have trouble securing loans in the company's name, as they have not yet established credit and are considered a risk to finance. If you take out a loan in your name, you can get the start-up funding you need at a lower interest rate.

  However, one of the major disadvantages to this method is that you are personally responsible if your business fails, as you will still be required to repay the borrowed money. Since personal loans are taken out in your name, not being able to pay back the loan could drastically affect your personal credit score (as well as your spouse's credit score). If your business fails and you have no alternative method for making money, you may be forced to file for bankruptcy in order to be released from this financial obligation. Carefully consider whether you want to take out a loan in your name, as a failed business will not excuse you from your repayment obligations.

- **Pursue a loan through development agencies and small-business investment companies:** These agencies, sometimes called certified development corporations, are funded by state and local governments to support businesses in the creation of employment opportunities. A small business investment company (SBIC) is connected to the Small Business

Administration. Some SBICs will lend you money if you have a convincing business plan, or if you are part of an ethnic minority group, a woman, a military member, or belong to some other specialized group.

- **Pursue a loan through the Small Business Administration's (SBA) loan-guarantee programs.** These loan-guarantee programs reduce the risk that lenders face when they loan funding to a start-up business. The SBA guarantees that a lender will only take on part of the risk, as the SBA will pay back the lender should the small business fail to be profitable. Business leaders must understand that traditional lenders like banks are still providing you the loan; however, the SBA is offering the lender more favorable conditions to incentivize providing your start-up with working capital.

  Each SBA loan-guarantee program is designed for certain uses and has an attached set of guidelines for approved lenders to follow. These guidelines define each loan program's maximum loan size, the maximum interest rate that can be charged, the minimum amount of collateral required, and other terms of the loan agreement. SBA maintains a list of approved lenders, an excellent resource for small-business owners to locate potential lenders in their areas. This list can greatly reduce the research you need to conduct in order to find a lender willing to loan to you.

  While the SBA loan-guarantee programs can help small businesses find the capital they need, there are several drawbacks to this source of funding. Interest rates are much higher with SBA-guaranteed loans, as lenders are still taking on a considerable risk in financing you. Additionally, the SBA sets a limit on how much money a lender can loan you, which might present a problem if you need more money than the maximum allowance.

  Business leaders should understand where they can go to apply for loans through SBA loan-guaranteed programs. These loan programs are as follows:

  - ✔ **Proceeds from a Basic 7(a) Loan Program type of loan can be used to start a new business, acquire an existing business, or assist with the operation or expansion of an existing business.** This can be a great option for business entrepreneurs, as it gives you considerable control over what you can spend your money on. The maximum loan amount is $5 million to any one business, and loan funds can be used to purchase land, buildings, equipment, and inventory. Loan funds can also be used to provide working capital to pay operating expenses. To learn more about the Basic 7(a) Loan Program, visit the SBA website to determine your eligibility.

✔ **Military or veteran business entrepreneurs who have at least 51 percent ownership of their businesses can utilize the SBA loan program.** This program was designed to provide quicker loan processes for active-duty military personnel, veterans, service-disabled veterans, reservists, National Guard members, and the spouses or widows of any of these individuals.

The maximum loan amount under this program is $500,000 at the lowest interest rates available for SBA loan programs. Loan interest rates will range from 2.25 percent to 4.75 percent over prime, depending upon the size and maturity of the loan. The loan can be used for start-up costs, equipment purchases, business-occupied real-estate purchases, inventory, and other business-related expenses. You can find more information about the SBA loan program via the SBA website.

✔ **The Microloan program provides smaller loans (up to $50,000) to business entrepreneurs.** One of the advantages of this loan is that lenders are required to provide borrowers with business training and assistance. One of the disadvantages to this loan, however, is that the funds cannot be used to purchase real estate or pay off existing debts. You can learn more about the Microloan program on the SBA website.

▪ **Accumulate capital from private investors.** A number of investors might want to invest their capital in your business. These investors can range from venture capitalists to private individuals who have liquid capital available to them. Be sure that your investors are comfortable investing capital in your business. Detail how their money will be used during this process and how investors will be rewarded should your business become successful.

Take Out Loans Responsibly

Now that you know the different types of capital that are available to you as a small-business entrepreneur, you will need to ensure you can take out loans without harming the success of your business. Taking out loans can provide you with the funds you need to keep your business running before you achieve sales, and it is important to do this responsibly.

Business loans are like personal loans: you do not need to take out a large loan amount simply because you qualify for one. Taking a greater loan than you need can negatively affect your credit score, your ability to grow your finances, and the amount of money that is available to you after you pay back your loans. The more loans you take out, the more of your organizational profits must go back to the lender—and this can seriously inhibit your company's growth if done improperly. To ensure you take out business loans responsibly, take the following steps:

1. **Have a firm idea of how much you need to take out before applying for a business loan.** You will find it detrimental to apply for more money than you need, as the large repayments could impede your ability to achieve organizational objectives and strategies. Carefully assess how much money you will need to fulfill your one-time and ongoing costs, then apply for a loan in that amount. Resist the temptation to take out extra funds for "just in case" emergencies, as this will lead you to pay back more money over the lifetime of the loan.

2. **Understand your obligations to your lender or creditor.** For example, if you take out a small-business loan from your local bank, understand your personal risk if your business fails. Your bank may have a forgiveness clause, or you and your family could be personally liable to pay back the loan, even if your organization goes out of business. By understanding your personal obligations, you will be able to make a stronger decision.

3. **Compare small business loans for the best interest rate.** You may be a start-up, but you do not have to accept the first loan that is offered to you. Dempsey cautions against this practice: "I just went with what [the equipment company] had on their website. But I could have used my bank and I would have had a lower interest rate," she explains. Shop around for better interest rates, gain a better understanding of your credit score, and search for alternative lenders, like a credit union, to find the best loan for your start-up organization.

4. **Pay back your loans as soon as possible.** While you do not want to exhaust your business in an effort to pay back your loans, make an attempt to repay more than the minimum payment each month. Check with your lender to ensure there is no penalty for paying a loan back early.

5. **Set up automatic repayments for your loan if possible.** This can ensure you will never miss a payment date, which could drastically affect your organization's credit score and ability to gain loans and capital in the future.

Taking out a business loan and using it responsibly is a similar process to that of taking out a personal loan. Shop around for the best loan, take out only what you can afford, and maintain regular repayments.

Finding capital for your start-up organization can play an important role in becoming a successful business entrepreneur. By understanding the different types of funding available to you and your business—as well as any personal obligations that might be associated with these options—you can make smarter financial choices toward securing the success of your start-up.

Naturally, all businesses will need some form of capital as they start up, but Keshel emphasizes the need for income to keep a business running for any length of time. She explains, "Getting a business with a steady stream of revenue involves you selling, often before you have the personnel to do so. You, as a seller, represent the product. You have to get that going as soon as possible, because revenue money can be reinvested in your business, whereas all other sources of money are definite liabilities."

This focus on making sales is especially important because the first few years of a start-up will require all of the owner's energy. Keshel confirms, "The agonies and ecstasies of starting a business are the same thing. At the end of the year, you look back and see that you were paid exactly what you were worth. Not every year is the best year—some are great and some aren't. But the best part is not working for someone else, ever again. You control your destiny, for good or bad, and you have the opportunity to shape your business to match your own skills and surround yourself with similar talent." Having an organization weakened by loan repayments, investment obligations, and other financial consequences could prevent you from achieving the kind of entrepreneurial success you have been searching for. Choose your funding carefully, and carefully consider all advantages and disadvantages before signing any dotted line.

Review Chapter 8

Now that you have completed Chapter 8, reflect on its content and how you will wisely utilize your capital and loans. As you review this chapter, consider the following questions:

☐ What is business capital? What one-time costs and ongoing obligations will your business have?

☐ What funding will your business require? What funding sources best fit your business? Will you use personal funds, equity financing, or debt financing to fund your business?

Consider making a chart of your financing options and decisions. Most businesses will start with debt, and will need to find ways to repay this debt. By creating and adhering to a detailed financial plan, you will enable yourself to focus on other aspects of growing your business. If you are satisfied with your understanding of how you will wisely utilize your capital and loans, resume reading with Chapter 9.

How to Implement Basic Human Resources in Your Business

"Never doubt that a small group of thoughtful, committed people can change the world. Indeed, it is the only thing that ever has."

-Margaret Mead[17]

When running a successful start-up business, do not underestimate the importance of implementing basic human resources within your company, especially as the number of your employees starts to grow. Instating human-resources processes can provide your employees with the safe and healthy workplace they need, and it can ensure your business is protected from legal vulnerabilities and potential lawsuits.

Human resources (HR) can be one of the most difficult departments to manage properly within a business. However, help is available—especially from experts like Jody Friend. Friend started her business, JLM HR Consulting, in April 2011. JLM HR Consulting provides outsourced human resource services and support to customers and clients of all sizes, from businesses as small as seven employees to as large as six hundred, both in the United States and internationally. Friend explains, "We offer customized HR solutions for our clients. This can be as simple as developing an employee handbook or company policy, or we can provide complete outsourced HR support." Primarily, JLM HR Consulting works with employers; however, they also offer services in recruiting and direct placement, as well as staff optimization.

Friend spent her career in human resources. She has twenty-five years in corporate HR experience and has worked in HR-leadership roles in companies of varying sizes throughout a variety of industries. She says, "Working with people and solving their problems is my passion. What I've found over the years is that employees who can get their questions answered are the most successful employees. That makes a happier employer." She sees challenges as opportunities to use her skills, declaring, "Really, I love the people, working

---

[17] "BookBrowse's Favorite Quotes," BookBrowse, accessed November 1, 2018, https://www.bookbrowse.com/quotes/detail/index.cfm/quote_number/379/never-doubt-that-a-small-group-of-thoughtful-committed-people-can-change-the-world.

with the people and helping folks solve whatever challenges they might have, big or small." JLM HR Consulting was started when Friend decided to do something different in her career. In a stroke of inspiration, she combined her long-standing desire to start her own business with her experience in HR.

One crucial workplace skill taught and encouraged by her company is the ability to communicate properly. Friend says, "Communication is completely necessary, because no one works in a vacuum. Typically, you're going to be on a team; but if you're not, you'll likely have to communicate with external or internal customers." JLM helps companies and individuals strengthen every type of business communication: "We use e-mail for so many things that we do today. It's even more important to be able to write well so that whatever information you're relaying is clear and understandable. Nonverbal communication is also important; we help people understand what body language means." These skills are crucial to good human resources, as are the other types of training Friend's company provides, including HR-specific compliance training, online sexual-harassment training, and more. Anything relating to interaction within the workplace is considered human resources.

In this chapter, you will discover the antidiscrimination and anti-harassment laws that you must follow in order to maintain a productive and positive workplace for employees. This chapter will also provide one example of an entrepreneur who nearly lost his business when he violated federal employment law. Read this chapter carefully, as you may discover crucial laws and employer requirements that could save your organization from potential lawsuits and other debilitating consequences.

Understand the Value of Human Resources

When starting your business, building a human resources department might be one of the lowest priorities on your list of duties. However, when you hire employees, you will benefit from having some form of HR department operating to protect the interests of your organization. In addition to protecting your organization, human resources are also critical for achieving strategic goals and improving your clients' perceptions of your company.

One entrepreneur who quickly realized the importance of human resources is Raul Lopez III, owner of Faraday Electric Motors. Electric motors can be found in machines of all sizes—even something so small as an electric toothbrush—but Faraday Electric Motors' customers are on a different scale. "The machines we work on are big. They move rock crushers, conveyor belts, anything that rotates," explains Lopez. Many of the machines they repair are too old to be replaced with anything comparable yet must be in perfect working condition. As a result, about 90% of their work is onsite and requires immediate attention, with customers such as ships stuck at port without working fire suppression systems, and hospitals unable to perform surgeries without air conditioning. "When we get called it's pretty much an emergency," says Lopez, "They need to be up and running or they're losing money. Lives are at stake." With such critical tasks, is technical knowledge the key to Lopez' success? According to him, it is not. Instead, his employees are the most important factor of his business' success.

At the time of writing, Faraday Electric Motors employs five excellent, trusted employees, whom they know they can rely on to uphold their hard-earned reputation. As a new business, it can be difficult to establish a name for yourself. Proving his company to be prompt, honest, and reliable has made them profitable: "The biggest obstacle we had was getting customers to give us a shot," Lopez explains. He upholds these values himself, among others: "You have to lead by example, never making your guys do anything you wouldn't do yourself. [My employees] see me down in the mud, getting dirty, in the cold [...] it's a morale thing."

Once your organization has found employees who uphold its mission and values, Lopez stresses the importance of keeping those employees safe. "It's still a really small operation," he says of his business, "but we do training, making sure they're up to date. You've got to check the boxes of safety and safety inspections."

Let us explore the benefits of prioritizing human resources in your start-up organization:

- ✔ **A human resources department can improve your start-up organization's bottom line by connecting the safety of your employees with their productivity.** Happy and motivated employees are usually found in organizations that prioritize their safety and rights, and implementing human resources within your company can do that.

- ✔ **A human resources department can provide you with an accurate pay scale for your employees.** Without human resources, you might not provide your employees with the compensation or benefits that are necessary for attracting top talent.

- ✔ **Human resources can help create a safe and secure workplace for your employees.** Workplace safety is a legal obligation, which means you will need to take critical steps to ensure that your organization is safe for your employees. Human resource specialists are well-trained and knowledgeable regarding United States occupational safety and health laws, which means that you can take critical steps to verifying your start-up's compliance with federal and state regulations.

- ✔ **Human resources can enable you to design successful training**

programs for your employees. As a business owner, your valuable time is best spent growing and developing your company. While you work on tasks that grow your business, your human resources department can focus on providing your employees with the training they might need to fit into the company and adapt to their job roles and responsibilities.

✔ **Human resources can present an excellent company image to your customers and vendors.** When you demonstrate that you take your employees' care and rights seriously, your customers and vendors are likely to assume you will treat them in the same manner. "If you're not safe," says Lopez, "nobody wants to do business with you." Customers and vendors are nowadays more conscious than ever about how corporations treat their employees.

✔ **Human resources can manage the entire recruitment and hiring processes.** This ensures that your organization is attracting top talent and prospective candidates without taking a great deal of your time. For example, a human resources department can prequalify applicants for a job position, which means that you will only interview top candidates who are ideal for a particular role or responsibility.

Once you have set up a human resources department in your organization, learn about the antidiscrimination and anti-harassment laws that pertain to your business. These federal and state laws are designed to protect your employees' rights and outline your responsibilities as an employer. By learning more about these laws, you can take the critical steps to ensure that you are in compliance with all federal regulations. Being found guilty of breaking a critical employment law can halt your company's growth entirely. In the next section, you will learn about the antidiscrimination and anti-harassment laws you need to implement within a start-up to avoid breaching federal and state employment regulations.

Learn About Antidiscrimination and Anti-harassment Laws

As a business leader, your actions may have considerable legal consequences, regardless of how benign or innocent they might appear to you. For example, an explicit joke made to an employee could make another colleague uncomfortable and lead to a harassment claim, or hiring only men to work within your company could lead to discrimination lawsuits. To highlight the necessity for business leaders to be aware of their actions, let us explore one example of an entrepreneur who became subject to a devastating harassment claim:

***

Example: Tom

Tom is a small-business owner whose organization specializes in creating software that business leaders can use to accurately predict seasonal sales. Tom's workforce is a fair mix of men and women from various cultural backgrounds, and his organization benefits from each of these unique perspectives.

Tom is good friends with Ben, a male employee who first joined the company when Tom started it almost ten years ago. Because of their long-term working relationship, Tom and Ben often make jokes with each other in the same way friends would if they were outside the workplace. Many of these jokes are not appropriate for the workplace.

However, Tom and Ben fail to realize several of their colleagues are uncomfortable with these jokes. Many of Tom's employees consider the jokes to be in bad taste, while a handful of employees are outright offended by the jokes, particularly when they pertain to women and sexuality. After Martha overhears Tom share an inappropriate joke with Ben, she takes her complaint to human resources to report Tom.

The human resources department handles Martha's claim as expediently as possible. The director of HR speaks with Tom privately to inform him that the complaint will need to be dealt with in a satisfactory manner. Tom is issued a disciplinary warning based on his actions and is sternly told not to repeat these inappropriate jokes. If Martha or any other employee reports that Tom has been discussing inappropriate jokes in the workplace again, Tom could lose his job and be reported to the Equal Employment Opportunity Commission. Tom's organization could also be sued by any victims of the harassment, which means Tom could lose everything that he worked hard to build.

***

In the above example, Tom did not intend to cause Martha to feel uncomfortable; however, harassment does not need to be intentionally malicious in nature to be considered discriminatory. If an action causes another employee or colleague to feel victimized, discriminated against, uncomfortable, or persecuted, it could be considered harassment and/or discrimination, depending on the nature of the offense.

Business leaders do not need to be overly cautious of their every action to avoid accidentally discriminating or harassing against another employee. Federal and state laws outline what is legally considered discrimination and harassment. For example, an employee cannot claim that you harassed him or her as a retaliatory action for a poor performance review. Antidiscrimination and anti-harassment laws were implemented for the benefit of both employees and business owners.

You must have a clear understanding of federal antidiscrimination and anti-harassment laws that may apply to your organizations. You will need this information to protect your interests as a business owner. You are also required to share this information with any employees within your organization via employee handbooks, posters, or shared documents on company servers.

Let us explore an overview of antidiscrimination and anti-harassment laws. The Equal Employment Opportunity Commission (EEOC) handles cases of discrimination and harassment. This federal organization is designed to protect employees and promote awareness of anti-harassment laws that pertain to all organizations, regardless of what industry they fall within.

The EEOC takes a strong stance against discrimination and harassment within a workplace setting, so business entrepreneurs must have a grounded knowledge of equal employment opportunity (EEO) laws. These laws are designed to protect your employees from all types of harassment, whether intentional and malicious or unintentional, as in the above example of Tom. These laws protect employees from discrimination and harassment ranging from unwanted sexual advances to cyberbullying by colleagues. The EEOC defines harassment as follows:[18]

> *"Harassment is a form of employment discrimination that violates Title VII of the Civil Rights Act of 1964, the Age Discrimination in Employment Act of 1967 (ADEA), and the Americans with Disabilities Act of 1990 (ADA)."*

For a brief overview of antidiscrimination laws, let us examine the following four EEO guidelines:

✔ **Title VII of the Civil Rights Act of 1964,** which is interpreted by the EEOC as follows:[19]

> *"This law makes it illegal to discriminate against someone on the basis of race, color, religion, national origin, or sex. The law also makes it illegal to retaliate against a person because the person complained about discrimination, filed a charge of discrimination, or participated in an employment discrimination investigation or lawsuit. The law also requires that employers reasonably*

---

[18] "Harassment," U.S. Equal Employment Opportunity Commission, accessed November 1, 2018, https://www.eeoc.gov/laws/types/harassment.cfm.

[19] "Laws Enforced by EEOC," U.S. Equal Employment Opportunity Commission, accessed November 1, 2018, https://www.eeoc.gov/laws/statutes/.

accommodate applicants' and employees' sincerely held religious practices, unless doing so would impose an undue hardship on the operation of the employer's business."

The above excerpt may be one of the most well-known EEO principles, and is considered an umbrella law that can be used in many cases of discrimination and harassment. This law was also one of the first to declare that employers cannot discriminate or retaliate against their employees for filing a discrimination or harassment claim against them.

Business leaders may struggle with treating an employee in a professional manner when they know that their employee has filed a complaint against them. However, as an employer you must offer the employee the same protection and respect that you would give any other colleague. Resist the urge to engage in retaliatory actions, which could ruin your legal and professional identities.

- **The Age Discrimination in Employment Act of 1967 (ADEA),** which is interpreted by the EEOC as follows:[20]

  "This law protects people who are 40 or older from discrimination because of age. The law also makes it illegal to retaliate against a person because the person complained about discrimination, filed a charge of discrimination, or participated in an employment discrimination investigation or lawsuit."

The Age Discrimination in Employment Act enables elderly people to seek employment without worrying they will not be hired because of their age. This law was initially implemented for the following reasons:

- Employers often did not want to provide benefits to an elderly employee who would likely need them more than a younger employee would.

- Employers often felt that hiring an elderly employee was a poor decision, as the employee would likely retire soon.

- Employers often favored younger employees more because they could be paid less than senior workers with decades of experience in the industry.

While the ADEA is important for protecting the elderly, it cannot be used by a young employee who claims that he or she was discriminated

---

[20] "Laws Enforced by EEOC," U.S. Equal Employment Opportunity Commission, accessed November 1, 2018, https://www.eeoc.gov/laws/statutes/.

against because of his or her age. Regardless of the age of your employees, ensure they feel welcomed and safe in your workplace environment. Unless the work you are hiring for is extremely physical in nature, resist assigning more active roles to younger employees. Ignore your employees' ages during work and throughout the recruitment and hiring processes. If you place emphasis on the age of a prospective employee, you might violate this EEO guideline.

✔ **Title I of the Americans with Disabilities Act of 1990 (ADA),** which is interpreted by the EEOC as follows:[21]

> *"This law makes it illegal to discriminate against a qualified person with a disability in the private sector, and in state and local governments. The law also makes it illegal to retaliate against a person because the person complained about discrimination, filed a charge of discrimination, or participated in an employment discrimination investigation or lawsuit. The law also requires that employers reasonably accommodate the known physical or mental limitations of an otherwise qualified individual with a disability who is an applicant or employee, unless doing so would impose an undue hardship on the operation of an employer's business."*

The EEOC vigilantly protects employees with disabilities, particularly with regards to ensuring that workplaces are able to support disabled employees. To ensure you are in compliance with ADA laws, consider hiring an ADA consultant who can confirm that your organization's building is up to code. This will ensure you have not unintentionally created a workplace that discriminates against a disabled employee. For example, if you do not have at least one handicap accessible restroom, you may be determined noncompliant with this EEO law.

✔ **The Genetic Information Nondiscrimination Act of 2008 (GINA),** which is interpreted by the EEOC as follows:[22]

> *"This law makes it illegal to discriminate against employees or applicants because of genetic information. Genetic information includes information about an individual's genetic tests and the genetic tests of an individual's family members, as well as information about any disease, disorder, or condition of an individual's family members (i.e., an individual's family medical history). The law also*

---

[21] "Laws Enforced by EEOC," U.S. Equal Employment Opportunity Commission, accessed November 1, 2018, https://www.eeoc.gov/laws/statutes/.

[22] "Laws Enforced by EEOC," U.S. Equal Employment Opportunity Commission, accessed November 1, 2018, https://www.eeoc.gov/laws/statutes/.

makes it illegal to retaliate against a person because the person complained about discrimination, filed a charge of discrimination, or participated in an employment discrimination investigation or lawsuit. This law came into effect in November 21, 2009."

This relatively new nondiscrimination law mandates that employers cannot utilize genetic information to discriminate against employees. This act is important for employees and business owners in today's technology-laden workplace, where a range of background searches, medical records, drug tests, and other information could expose a person's potential for having a disease based on his or her family members' health.

This law ensures that employers cannot terminate or refuse to hire someone who could develop a disease that may prevent him or her from fully participating in the workplace. For example, if a background check of an employee reveals that her mother developed breast cancer, federal law prohibits you from refusing to hire the prospective employee because you believe that she may develop breast cancer and thus be a considerable expense to the workplace. The Genetic Information Non-Discrimination Act of 2008 takes a critical step toward ensuring that this personal information is not used for making hiring, promoting, or disciplinary decisions.

The EEOC website further states:[23]

"Harassment is unwelcome conduct that is based on race, color, religion, sex (including pregnancy), national origin, age (40 or older), disability or genetic information. Harassment becomes unlawful where 1) enduring the offensive conduct becomes a condition of continued employment, or 2) the conduct is severe or pervasive enough to create a work environment that a reasonable person would consider intimidating, hostile, or abusive. Anti-discrimination laws also prohibit harassment against individuals in retaliation for filing a discrimination charge, testifying, or participating in any way in an investigation, proceeding, or lawsuit under these laws; or opposing employment practices that they reasonably believe discriminate against individuals, in violation of these laws.

"Petty slights, annoyances, and isolated incidents (unless extremely serious) will not rise to the level of illegality. To be unlawful, the conduct must create a work environment that would be intimidating, hostile, or offensive to reasonable people.

"Offensive conduct may include, but is not limited to, offensive jokes,

---

[23] "Harassment," U.S. Equal Employment Opportunity Commission, accessed November 1, 2018, https://www.eeoc.gov/laws/types/harassment.cfm.

slurs, epithets, or name calling, physical assaults or threats, intimidation, ridicule or mockery, insults or put-downs, offensive objects or pictures, and interference with work performance. Harassment can occur in a variety of circumstances, including, but not limited to, the following:

- *The harasser can be the victim's supervisor, a supervisor in another area, an agent of the employer, a co-worker, or a non-employee.*

- *The victim does not have to be the person harassed but can be anyone affected by the offensive conduct.*

- *Unlawful harassment may occur without economic injury to, or discharge of, the victim.*

"Prevention is the best tool to eliminate harassment in the workplace. Employers are encouraged to take appropriate steps to prevent and correct unlawful harassment. They should clearly communicate to employees that unwelcome harassing conduct will not be tolerated. They can do this by establishing an effective complaint or grievance process, providing anti-harassment training to their managers and employees, and taking immediate and appropriate action when an employee complains. Employers should strive to create an environment in which employees feel free to raise concerns and are confident that those concerns will be addressed.

"Employees are encouraged to inform the harasser directly that the conduct is unwelcome and must stop. Employees should also report harassment to management at an early stage to prevent its escalation."

The EEOC has carefully defined harassment to protect employers from lawsuits for petty disputes or slights. The EEOC specifically outlines its terms to avoid being used as a retaliatory tool for employees who may be upset about an employer's decision. As with other EEO laws, post this information somewhere that is easily accessible to your employees. This can ensure your employees understand the difference between harassment and non-harassment. This can also ensure your HR department is not subjected to claims of harassment when employees are simply complaining about petty disputes or seeking revenge for a perceived slight.

If a charge is placed within an HR department and the employee seeks assistance from the EEOC, this group is legally obligated to conduct an investigation into the complaint. If the EEOC finds that the business is not in violation of federal EEOC laws, the case will be dropped. If, however, the EEOC finds that discrimination has indeed occurred, they have the right to file a lawsuit on behalf of the employee who brought the original charges. Business entrepreneurs must be quick to settle any discrimination or harassment claims, as even an unwarranted EEOC investigation could damage your workplace's reputation.

Business entrepreneurs are advised to seek additional information that could be fundamental for building a knowledgeable HR department. If you have any questions about your rights and responsibilities with regards to antidiscrimination laws, use online searches to explore the following topics:

- Equal Employment Opportunity laws

- U.S. Equal Employment Opportunity Commission

- Leadership Conference on Civil Rights, Equal Opportunity

- Small Employers on Employer Liability for Harassment by Supervisors

- Understanding Workplace Harassment

- "Sexual Harassment: Developments in Federal Law"

- "Age Discrimination in Employment Act (ADEA): A Legal Overview"

If you have any additional questions about your rights and responsibilities as a small business owner or manager in creating a harassment-free workplace, contact your local EEOC office, which may be found via the EEOC website.

Before we discuss how to create fair business policies within your workplace, it is important to note the discrimination laws that are not enforced by the Equal Employment Opportunity Commission. While the EEOC does not conduct independent investigations into businesses that break these federal laws, these laws are nonetheless protected and legislated by the federal government. Businesses found in violation of the following laws could accrue considerable financial and legal damage:

- **The Civil Service Reform Act of 1978 (CSRA),** which makes it illegal for employers to discriminate based on marital status, political association, and sexual orientation

- **Executive Order 11246,** which makes it illegal for federal contractors and certain subcontractors to discriminate on the basis of race, color, religion, sex, or national origin

- **The Fair Labor Standards Act,** which regulates workplace practices related to minimum wage, overtime pay, and child labor

- **The Family and Medical Leave Act (FMLA),** which requires that certain employers grant up to twelve weeks of leave during a twelve-month period to eligible employees who need time off because of a serious health condition that they or someone in their families is experiencing

- **The Immigration Reform and Control Act of 1986 (IRCA),** which makes it illegal for certain employers to fire or refuse to hire a person on the basis of that person's national origin or citizenship

- **National Labor Relations Act,** which protects workers who wish to form, join, or support unions or who are already represented by unions, and workers who join together as a group (two or more employees) without a union seeking to modify their wages or working conditions

- **The Occupational Safety and Health Act of 1970 (OSHA),** which defines safety requirements for workplaces

- **Section 503 of the Rehabilitation Act,** which prohibits certain federal contractors and subcontractors from discriminating against qualified employees and job applicants with disabilities

- **Section 504 of the Rehabilitation Act,** which prohibits disability discrimination in programs and activities that receive federal financial assistance

- **Section 508 of the Rehabilitation Act,** which requires federal agencies to ensure that electronic and information technology used by the government can be accessed and used by people with disabilities

- **Section 1981 of the Civil Rights Act of 1866,** which protects the equal rights of all persons within the jurisdiction of the United States to make and enforce contracts without respect to race (this includes hiring, discharge, and the terms and conditions)

- **The Social Security Act,** which provides Social Security Disability Insurance (SSDI) to certain individuals with severe disabilities who can no longer work

- **Title I of the Genetic Information Nondiscrimination Act,** which addresses the use of genetic information in health insurance

- **Title II of the Americans with Disabilities Act (ADA),** which makes it illegal to discriminate against peoples with disabilities in all programs, activities, and services offered by state and local government agencies

- **Title III of the ADA,** which prohibits disability discrimination by private entities that provide services to the public (also known as public accommodations)

- **Title VI of the Civil Rights Act of 1964,** which makes it illegal to discriminate on the basis of race, color, or national origin in programs and activities receiving federal financial assistance

- **Workers Compensation Law,** which provides compensation for on-the-job injuries and illnesses

For more information about the specifics of the individual laws listed above, please visit the EEOC website.

Encourage Fair Business Practices

Now that you know more about the antidiscrimination and anti-harassment laws that are bound to your business, let us examine four ways you can communicate fair business practices. Communicating fair business practices ensures that your employees are protected by federal and state laws, and that they can work in an enjoyable, fair, and tolerant organizational environment. As a business entrepreneur, you must demonstrate that you are committed to remaining fair and open with your employees. These attitudes can create the kind of cohesive and productive workplace that leads a start-up business to success. To communicate fair business practices in your start-up, implement the following actions:

Create a Fair Business Policy

Your business policy can be critical for outlining what you and your employees should expect with regards to how discrimination and harassment are treated within the workplace. Your employees can look to your business policy to understand what behaviors are expected from them as well as what behaviors they can expect from you. In regard to your legal obligations, the business policy can provide you with another opportunity to outline how your employees are protected under state and federal law. To ensure that you are creating a fair and accurate business policy, consider the following process:

1. **Outline all antidiscrimination policies as listed in the previous section of this chapter.** Preface all discrimination laws by stating that you are required to uphold them within the workplace. Explain specifically how your business will handle cases of discrimination. Also provide information to your employees on how to file a charge or make a complaint if they are subjected to discrimination and/or harassment.

    Be sure these antidiscrimination and anti-harassment laws form the foundation of behaviors you expect from your employees. Inform your employees, in straightforward terms, that everyone is expected to uphold the law as outlined by the EEOC. Use your business policy to explicitly outline the consequences should any employee fail to uphold an EEO laws. Once you have expressed your disciplinary policy, be sure to adhere to it. Your employees will notice if you allow certain colleagues persist in discriminating or harassing behaviors.

2. **Outline compensation requirements as determined by the EEOC.** Many EEO laws are designed to ensure companies are paying men and women the same wage for the same work. Advance beyond this minimal requirement by outlining specifically how compensation will be scaled within your business. When you explain how compensation will be determined, your employees will know how and why they are paid in a certain manner.

   Also ensure your business policy outlines your legal requirements regarding additional compensation, including overtime pay, salary increases, bonuses, and more. If you do not know your legal obligations regarding compensation, or if you would like more information on the subject, visit the United States Small Business Administration website.

   You may also consider including a breakdown of compensation deductions within your business policy or employee handbook. We recommend you disclose how much pay will be deducted for state and federal taxes and also any voluntary deductions for company-related benefits. Visit the United States Small Business Administration website for more information on this topic.

3. **Include information about employee work schedules.** Detail your expectations regarding work hours, employee attendance, absence reporting, and other information pertaining to your company's schedule standards. Consider consolidating these details with information on compensation pay.

4. **Outline Your Standards of Conduct.** Though your employees should already have the necessary information to comply with EEOC requirements and federal law, ensure this compliance by creating a standard of conduct within your business policy or employee handbook. The standard of conduct typically pertains to your organization's dress code, ethics, conduct, and other behaviors that can have an influence on your workplace. Having a standard of conduct can also protect you from harassment or discrimination claims, as many lawsuits are based on dress codes or a relaxed attitude toward employee misconduct.

   This component of your business policy also deserves special attention, as it must be written according to EEO laws. For example, you cannot instill a dress code that prohibits skirts (unless, of course, the main function of the job prohibits it), nor can you insist on observing certain religious holidays within the workplace. These behaviors can be seen as discriminatory; therefore, it is in your best interest to compose a standards of conduct that follows all EEO obligations.

Your clearly communicated business policy can ensure your employees are in compliance with EEOC requirements and other federal discrimination laws.

Detail Your Harassment Policy

An important aspect of maintaining a fair and productive workplace is ensuring you have an unwavering anti-harassment policy in place. Harassment can take many forms in the workplace. It can resemble traditional harassment, in which one employee bullies another, or it can be a more atypical or modern type of harassment, such as cyberbullying. Regardless, your employees must know you will not tolerate any form of harassment in the workplace. To detail a zero-tolerance harassment policy, to consider taking the following steps:

1. **Understand that harassment may manifest differently than you expect.** For example, in cases of sexual harassment, many people assume a man is responsible for harassing a woman. However, sexual harassment can be experienced and perpetuated by either gender. Ensure you are not approaching your company's anti-harassment policy with a fixed conception of how it might appear within your workplace.

2. **Inform your employees that harassment of any kind will not be tolerated within your workplace.** Provide your employees with examples of how harassment could take place, from the obvious (unwanted physical contact, sexual comments about another employee, etc.), to the more subtle (jokes of a sexual nature, inappropriate pictures within the workplace, sexual compliments, etc.). The more specific your examples, the greater the likelihood your employees will understanding what behaviors are considered harassment.

3. **Collaborate with other managers and leaders within your business to create an anti-harassment policy.** The different perspectives brought to your collaborative group may ensure you are in compliance with all EEO laws.

   Provide your employees with a precise definition of what behaviors are considered harassment. We recommend you use the definition provided by the EEOC, as using this definition ensures you are in compliance with EEO laws and that your employees understand their obligations under your zero-tolerance harassment policy. Consider using the following definition, found on the EEOC website:[24]

   "Harassment is a form of employment discrimination that violates Title VII of the Civil Rights Act of 1964, the Age Discrimination in

---

[24] "Harassment," U.S. Equal Employment Opportunity Commission, accessed November 1, 2018, https://www.eeoc.gov/laws/types/harassment.cfm.

Employment Act of 1967 (ADEA), and the Americans with Disabilities Act of 1990 (ADA).

"Harassment is unwelcome conduct that is based on race, color, religion, sex (including pregnancy), national origin, age (40 or older), disability, or genetic information. Harassment becomes unlawful where 1) enduring the offensive conduct becomes a condition of continued employment, or 2) the conduct is severe or pervasive enough to create a work environment that a reasonable person would consider intimidating, hostile, or abusive. Anti-discrimination laws also prohibit harassment against individuals in retaliation for filing a discrimination charge, testifying, or participating in any way in an investigation, proceeding, or lawsuit under these laws; or opposing employment practices that they reasonably believe discriminate against individuals, in violation of these laws.

"Petty slights, annoyances, and isolated incidents (unless extremely serious) will not rise to the level of illegality. To be unlawful, the conduct must create a work environment that would be intimidating, hostile, or offensive to reasonable people."

4. **Follow up on your anti-harassment policy with quick and decisive action.** If an employee reports harassment to you, keep all information confidential (unless you require the assistance of another manager or business leader). Do not take retaliatory actions against the employee who reported the claim, as doing so would be incredibly damaging to your business reputation, and may lead to serious legal consequences with the federal government.

Your anti-harassment policy should provide your employees with the necessary information to ensure that their workplace behaviors are positive and productive. Additionally, this policy can create an atmosphere of acceptance in a diverse workplace, as your employees should have a clear and definitive understanding of how you will protect their rights according to the law.

Remember, laws constantly evolve and change. As a business owner, it is your responsibility to ensure you are well-informed about current workplace policies. You must continuously ensure your business's compliance by finding resources, whether online or in print, that keep you updated with EEO laws. The Department of Labor website is a good place to start. Some newsletters and other sources that can keep you informed as well. As you work through your start-up, find the resources you will use and check regularly for any changes.

Provide Clear Definitions of EEO Laws

Your employees can greatly benefit from having clear and concise definitions of EEO laws at their disposal. Providing clear definitions of EEO laws ensures that your employees understand their legal rights and responsibilities. Having clear definitions of these laws also enables you to recruit, hire, and discipline employees without worrying about accidentally violating your legal obligations.

Clear definitions of harassment and discrimination laws can also build a workplace of mutual respect and honesty. If your employees understand they are protected in the workplace—and that you are committed to providing their protection—they will be more likely to engage in enthusiastic and productive behaviors that contribute to a start-up's success.

One of the greatest benefits of providing clear definitions of EEO laws to your employees is that you will understand your rights and responsibilities as an employer. If you are ever in the unfortunate position of facing an EEOC investigation, you will better understand what actions you must take to legally protect your business.

To ensure your employees clearly understand the definitions of EEO laws, consider placing the definitions in a location your employees will have regular access to. For example, you might opt to put EEO laws and other federal discrimination laws in an employee handbook or on a poster in the employee break room.

The EEOC has specific rules about posting information regarding your employees' rights against discrimination and harassment. The EEOC website states the following:[25]

"The law requires an employer to post a notice describing the Federal laws prohibiting job discrimination based on race, color, sex, national origin, religion, age, equal pay, disability or genetic information. The 'EEO is the Law' poster, prepared by the Equal Employment Opportunity Commission (EEOC), summarizes these laws and explains how an employee or applicant can file a complaint if s/he believes that s/he has been the victim of discrimination. EEOC's poster is available in English, Arabic, Chinese and Spanish."

Some of the posters are also available online, for free, to be printed. Check the Department of Labor website for more information. If you need more than five copies of the poster, contact the U.S. Equal Employment Opportunity Commission Clearinghouse.

---

[25] "'EEO is the Law' Poster," U.S. Equal Employment Opportunity Commission, accessed November 1, 2018, https://www1.eeoc.gov/employers/poster.cfm

To comply with the EEOC law regarding the poster, make sure you have all current, relevant required posters and supplements posted in a visible, well-trafficked area in your workplace. As a business owner, you have a serious responsibility to display all current, compliant, and relevant information as provided by the Department of Labor. You must be well informed and educated on all laws pertaining to human resources and post all information in a place where your employees can easily access it.

In your proactive information mission, you should know that many of the resources you will need are free. Visit the Department of Labor website to find current editions of EEOC posters and supplements, available for you to print. Check the website frequently or sign up for a newsletter to ensure that you stay informed and up to date.

Refer Your Employees to Additional Resources

While you may do your best to uphold a fair environment within your workplace, your employees may have additional questions about their rights under federal and state laws. If you or your employees need more information about the EEOC and other antidiscrimination laws, be sure to explore the following aids, available online:

- Small Business Administration

- US Business Advisor

- Department of Commerce

- Department of Justice

- Department of Labor

In addition to these government websites, you can also explore EEO-specific resources, including the following:

- The Computer/Electronic Accommodations Program (CAP)

- US Merit Systems Protection Board

- Federal government disability information

- Resource Allocation Plan Model for Special Emphasis for Program Managers, www.deomi.org/

Should you have additional questions about your EEO rights and responsibilities as a small-business owner or manager, you can contact your local EEOC office or the main headquarters at its physical address, both of which may be found online via web search.

Protecting the rights of your employees is a vital function of both a successful human resources department and a successful business leader. Your employees are the essence of your organization, as Raul Lopez knows from experience. "Once you get a good team in place, then you can take a backseat and intervene when you need to," he says. However, if you cannot provide your team with the protections they are guaranteed by law, you will be solely responsible. You may even find yourself facing serious legal and professional ramifications. No business leader can be successful if he or she leads a workplace that tolerates offensive and illegal employee behaviors.

By providing your employees with an outlet in instances of harassment, discrimination, or other offensive behaviors, you demonstrate to your employees that you are wholly dedicated to their happiness, safety, and productivity in the workplace.

Review Chapter 9

Now that you have completed Chapter 9, reflect on its content and how you will implement basic human resources in your business. As you review this chapter, consider the following questions:

- ☐ Why is implementing human resources vital to your specific business?

- ☐ What constitutes discrimination and harassment? What do antidiscrimination and anti-harassment laws mean, in practice?

- ☐ What are your rights and responsibilities, as a business owner, in regard to antidiscrimination and anti-harassment laws?

- ☐ How will you encourage and enforce fair business practices in your business? How will you encourage and enforce EEO laws?

Be sure you understand the Civil Rights, Age Discrimination, Americans with Disabilities, and Genetic Information Nondiscrimination Acts, as well as the outside resources listed earlier in this chapter. Ensure these foundational policies are applied in your business to create a safe and happy workplace environment for your employees. If you are satisfied with your understanding of how you will implement basic human resources in your business, resume reading with Chapter 10.

How to Create Your Formal Business Plan

"He who fails to plan is planning to fail."
-Winston Churchill[26]

In order for your start-up business to be successful, you will need to prepare and create a formal business plan. Unfortunately, simply owning a marketable product and possessing practical business ownership skills will not guarantee success. Regardless of your previous experience, failing to create a business plan can ruin your start-up aspirations. Let us explore one example that illustrates the importance of creating a formal business plan.

***

Example: Keith

Keith is interested in starting his own business. He has worked in the software start-up industry before, and he has recently stumbled across a fantastic idea for a new type of software. The program helps customers identify the amount of money they need to save for retirement. Keith imagines that this software could be marketable, as many customers will need to determine if they are saving enough for retirement. Keith also plans on creating an entire line of new products that build on the original software. For example, Keith believes he could partner with accountants and other investment firms to help customers make better financial decisions if they find that they are currently not saving enough to retire.

After researching his market, Keith discovers there are indeed enough potential customers for him to start his own business. Despite spending months developing the software product, numerous obstacles set him back:

---

[26] "Winston Churchill Quotes," AZQuotes, accessed November 1, 2018, https://www.azquotes.com/quote/855229

✕ **He runs out of money at almost every turn.** It seems like no matter what he does, he cannot find the necessary funds to spend on his new business venture. Because Keith is pressing for a certain release date, he decides to put the bills on numerous credit cards and hopes to pay them off when his software becomes a success.

✕ **He lacks the necessary support to get his software launched on time.** He finds that his personal technology is not nearly as effective as it needs to be. He needs to invest in high-quality equipment and a space where he can work without disturbing his family. However, after viewing local leasing spaces, Keith realizes he does not have enough money to rent an office space.

✕ **He encounters a number of personal obstacles because he cannot foresee when this product will be successful.** The entire design-and-implementation stage is being done on a whim. His only structure is the one ultimate release date he is working toward, and even then he is unsure what to do afterward. He hopes the ideas will come to him as he gets closer to launching his software.

By the time Keith is finished designing the software, he realizes that he does not have enough capital to start a website that advertises the product. His dream of selling his software in local stores is also now unrealistic, as he no longer has enough money to package the product. He decides to approach a group of venture capitalists with the hopes of getting the funding he needs. However, his credit card bill is getting higher with every day that passes. When he realizes that his potential investors will not be prepared to make a decision for another three months, Keith realizes that his poor preparation and planning have run him out of options. Keith's software sales are not enough to make up for his bills, and he is forced to shut down his operations to stop his debt from accruing.

***

In the above example, Keith's product did not fail because it was a poor idea. Rather, Keith's business crashed precisely because he failed to plan before he took the first step. This could have been avoided if, prior to launch, Keith had spent the necessary time working on a formal business plan.

Think of a business plan as you would a map. If you are about to go on a long journey into entrepreneurship, you need to carefully map out your route to avoid getting lost along the way. A business plan functions in the same manner: it can provide a business with the steps to take to endure through those first few rocky years.

Anita Williams is the owner of Asherone Group, a recruitment and staffing agency. The company is still in its startup phase, and as such is mapping out its business plan. "Before Asherone Group can achieve our mission," says Williams, "we have to have a business and long-term plan. I am currently working on the company's business plan." Williams knows that her business plan is a critical first step to sharing her vision: "As an entrepreneur, I am the only one that knows my business idea to the core. Right now, I am the only one that can envision the story of the future of Asherone Group."

There are more benefits to a business plan besides sharing your vision. "Creating a formal business plan has benefited me in several ways," explains Williams. "My business plan tells the story of what I plan to do and how I plan to do it." A new business is prone to numerous obstacles, challenges, and setbacks. Without the guidance of a business plan, these setbacks can slow or even halt a new company's momentum. A business plan should outline steps that increase the likelihood of a business being successful, prior to the aspiring owner taking those steps. It should also help an aspiring entrepreneur look practically and holistically at a business's future assets and liabilities to determine what financial outcomes are realistically possible.

A business plan can be defined as a written document that allows businesses to plan ahead. Ultimately, this document will make it easier for business leaders to overcome challenges, obtain funding, and anticipate risks prior to their happening. Creating a solid business plan has many advantages, including the following:

- ✔ **It helps entrepreneurs get vital funding.** Your start-up should not cause you to take on a load of personal debt. Many business owners use business plans to gain funding from investors who foresee the product or service as a likely success. But before investors get involved with the business, they will probably have a great deal of questions, like who the market is composed of and what the products will accomplish. A business plan can answer all of these questions in a neat and convenient document.

  A business plan also demonstrates to investors that you are organized and responsible, and that you have "mapped out" your business strategy for success. This is perhaps even more critical for investors to see, as they want to place their capital with a business owner who understands what is needed to become successful. Therefore, a business plan can greatly increase your chances of gaining funding without fronting the entire cost of the business yourself.

- ✔ **It aids in obtaining advice.** When it comes to starting your own business, it pays to have industry experts provide you with as much advice and feedback as possible. These are the people who have stood where you are standing now and have come through the start-up process successful and knowledgeable. You may increase your chances of gaining this helpful advice if you can provide these resources with objective numbers and descriptions within the business plan. When these experts are able to analyze objective information related to your business, they may be better equipped to offer you valuable and personalized expertise.

- ✔ **It helps you identify potential risks.** New business face encountering insurmountable problems and risks. In order to keep a new business afloat, business owners must create a plan that can help them overcome these challenges should they arise. When researching the business plan, you may discover that some of your ideas regarding legal obligations, licensing, marketing, and the like, might not be accurate. Learning this before your new business is launched can help you make any necessary adjustments and revisions before contracts are signed.

- ✔ **It outlines how much funding your business will have for its first year of operation.** As anyone who has created a personal budget knows, tracking your incoming and outgoing expenses can help you make smarter decisions. You do not want to learn that your business has run out of money a few months into operations.

- ✔ **It objectively measures successful outcomes.** The business plan helps entrepreneurs think critically about a measurable and achievable benchmark for success. Once this benchmark has been achieved, a business plan can outline what steps a business leader should take with regards to selling the company, growing the company, franchising the concept, opening new units or locations, increasing sales, becoming publicly traded, or otherwise increasing one's personal and business success.

- ✔ **It provides an exit strategy.** The business plan also provides business leaders with an exit strategy should the company turn out to be a failure. Owning a failed business can be an emotionally troubling experience, and may cause business owners to make critical mistakes when shutting down the business. Solid numbers and exit options can provide you with the steps to shut down the business and protect your investors, even when emotions prevent you from being objective.

- ✔ **It minimizes potential legal problems.** Your business plan gives you the opportunity to research if you need local, state, or federal licensing to operate your business. Your business plan can also help you identify the proper legal structure for your company, obtain a federal employer identification number, and complete any other outstanding responsibilities that might be required by the Internal Revenue Service.

The business plan is perhaps one of the most important strategic tools to use during the beginning stages of a start-up. Without the business plan, it is usually difficult for business owners to identify the challenges and obstacles they might face on the journey to entrepreneurial success. Additionally, a business plan gives entrepreneurs the opportunity to find valuable funding and feedback that can be pivotal to the new company's success.

Before we examine how to structure the business plan, let us briefly discuss the issue of standardized "boilerplate" business plans. Any online query will reveal thousands of web pages devoted to helping entrepreneurs create standard business plans with just a few keystrokes. While these templates can provide you with an introduction to business plans, be warned: these are not nearly as complex and detailed as you need them to be.

A large part of gaining trust and capital from an investor involves projecting a professional image. If your business plan has been downloaded from Google and pasted into Word, you will not be displaying your business skills in a positive light. In addition to this drawback, you may discover that a business-plan template does not provide you with the guidance you need in the event you encounter any obstacles. Therefore, it may be in your best interest to avoid using templates; they may save you time initially, but they may seriously damage your entrepreneurial efforts in the future.

The process of creating your business plan may involve a great deal of research and data collection, so prepare to learn everything there is to know about your business and its potential. Williams found research and data collection to be one of the most intimidating—and also the most helpful— aspects of writing her business plan: "One of my main challenges that I've encountered while writing my business plan was getting started. I overcame this obstacle by just diving right in. While I do not love excessive research, I love learning new things especially if it's for the good of Asherone Group. Also, I simply must have solid and the best information for my business. I must have clear, concise and understandable goals, these goals must also be realistic. When people can't see the vision of the plan, they won't take action to pursue the plan. In addition, by having set goals that align with my plan, I had measurable targets to track my progress."

Now that we have defined a business plan its advantages to a start-up entrepreneur, let us explore each of the necessary sections of a successful business plan.

Cover Page

The cover page of your business plan should include accurate contact information, as your readers and potential investors may wish to connect with you to learn more about your proposed business. The cover page should include the following information:

☐ The business's name (and legal name, if different)

☐ The business's primary address

☐ The business owner's name

☐ The business owner's mailing address

☐ The business owner's phone number

Table of Contents

Like with a book, the business plan should start with a table of contents that outlines what readers can expect to find. The table of contents should contain headings, subsections, and page numbers that accurately correspond with the content contained within the actual business plan. Although this section appears first in the business plan, you will most likely formulate this section last, after the page numbers for the following sections are determined.

Executive Summary

The executive summary is a brief description of the key points that will be discussed throughout your business plan. The executive summary provides your readers with a snapshot of what they can expect to learn about. It is important not to treat the executive summary as merely a brief restatement of facts. Rather, this section of the business plan must be compelling and enticing, as you want to encourage your readers to continue through the remainder of your business plan.

Business plans may be used for a variety of purposes. While the main structure of your company's information and projections should remain similar throughout different iterations of your business plan, consider creating different versions of your executive summary to match your specific audiences. For example, if you are using the business plan to draw potential investors, your executive summary should focus on how any invested capital will be used. If you are not using your business plan to seek investments, you may opt to focus your executive summary on how your business will be different from your competitors, potentially convincing readers that your company will attract and retain more customers.

Keep the length of your executive summary between one and one and a half pages typed. This summary should include all critical information for readers, yet also be as concise as possible. To determine whether you have the right length for your executive summary, ask yourself the following questions:

■ Have I communicated the main points about my business?

- Does this highlight how my business is different from my competition?

- Is this executive summary properly addressing its intended audience (for example, an investor versus a marketing strategist)?

- Is there any information in this executive summary that could be removed without damaging its overall integrity?

Although the executive summary section will appear second in the business plan, after the table of contents, consider creating this section after completing the following content portions. Writing the executive summary after completing the body of your business plan allows you to better introduce and summarize the content to follow, which will result in a stronger and more readable business plan. The executive summary portion of your business plan should include the following subsections: business overview, market overview, financial overview, business objectives, and mission statement.

Business Overview

The business overview subsection of your executive summary section should introduce your company and why it will be successful. This subsection should summarize your business description, products and services, and organization and management sections (described later in this chapter).

Market Overview

The market overview subsection of your executive summary section should introduce your target market and how our business intends to capture it. This subsection should summarize your market analysis section (described later in this chapter) and focus especially on your target market size and your sales and marketing strategies.

Financial Overview

The financial overview subsection of your executive summary section should include introduce your company's financial health and projections. This subsection should summarize your financial management section (described later in this chapter) and focus especially on any equipment, loans, or capital you are seeking, any proposed terms of repayment for your loans, and your expected sales and profits.

Business Objectives

The business objectives subsection of your executive summary should detail how your business will work to achieve major goals, milestones, and accomplishments, which might include growing the brand, opening new locations, and increasing sales by quantifiable measures. These objectives express to readers of your business plan the hopes you have for your company, and what actions you plan to take to achieve these objectives.

Mission Statement

Your mission statement should be concise, no more than two to four sentences in length, and should answer the following questions:

☐ What does your business do?

☐ What is your business's goal in relation to its customers?

☐ What impression should your business's customers leave with?

If you need assistance editing and revising your executive summary, contact a business colleague or professional writer who can help you create a concise and accurate opening. Reviewing your executive summary with another writer can help you determine if your business plan is compelling and engaging, or whether you need to make changes to the document to enhance the message.

Now that we have outlined what you should include in the executive summary of your business plan, let us analyze one example executive summary.

***

Example: Executive Summary

Neverhill Advertising is an advertising agency that will offer marketing services to clients who seek to integrate traditional commercial advertising with text-message marketing techniques. Neverhill Advertising represents a novel approach to effective marketing techniques, as it allows clients to reach out to new customers using emerging technologies while enhancing their current commercial presence via commercials, print ads, and other traditional forms of marketing and advertising. Text-message marketing is quickly becoming the most popular cost-effective form of marketing to a target audience, as it has a higher conversion rate than e-mail and direct-marketing methods. According to recent research, anywhere from 95 to 98 percent of text messages are read within minutes of when they are received. This means that clients are in a great position to take advantage of the conversion rates that are afforded with SMS marketing.

One of the greatest challenges of text-message marketing is ensuring that the texts are compelling enough to warrant client action. Text-message marketers often discover that it is difficult to communicate an advertisement campaign with a limited character allowance. Additionally, many businesses find it challenging to integrate text-message marketing with current advertising cornerstones. SMS marketing is a science; there are effective strategies that can ensure that businesses successfully integrate text-message marketing with their current forms of advertising.

Neverhill Advertising specializes in successful text-message marketing campaigns that are seamlessly integrated with traditional direct-marketing methods. Founder and CEO Martin Twinning has over five years of experience in the SMS-marketing field, making him one of the most experienced professionals in the industry. Twinning has led successful SMS marketing campaigns for major brands, including RJK Clothing, Smartphones 4 U, and Young and Fab Retailers.

Neverhill Advertising is committed to building text-message marketing campaigns from the ground up. Neverhill Advertising will design, build, test, and implement a text-message marketing campaign in alliance with a client's current direct-marketing methods. Neverhill Advertising will also record and report the real-time progress of a text-message marketing campaign for a client's review and approval. At the end of an SMS campaign, Neverhill Advertising will analyze conversion rates to determine how to make future campaigns increasingly successful.

***

As demonstrated by the example above, an executive summary should contain as much detail as possible about your business purpose, your marketing strategies, your customers, and how your business fits within its industry and marketplace. In addition to these details, your executive summary should be as exciting as possible.

Business Description

The business description section will be the foundation of your business plan. This part of your plan you will introduce your company vision to readers considering financial contributions. In the business description section, you will outline your business's premise, structure, and strategic goals for achieving success. Williams points out that the business description section of her business plan forced her to detail her basic business concept: "I had to discuss the industry, my business structure, my particular service, who is my market, and how I plan to be successful in this area of the market."

Your business plan's opening business description section is comparable to the first chapter of any book. This opening section plays a critical role in outlining what investors and other readers can expect to learn about your business. With this in mind, ensure that the opening "chapter" of your business plan is well written, interesting, and designed to keep readers interested in the fundamentals of your start-up business. The business description portion of your business plan should include the following subsections, outlined in greater detail below: general information, legal structure, location, financing, assets, and company objectives.

General Information

The general information subsection of your business description section should answer the following questions:

- ☐ What is your business's name?

- ☐ What industry category does your business belong within?

- ☐ What products or services will you provide? What is the value of these products or services?

- ☐ What is your business's significance—to you, to the market, to the industry, or to the customer?

- ☐ What are your business' strengths and core competencies?

- ☐ What is your business' mission statement, or business philosophy?

- ☐ Why is this business needed? How is your business's purpose not currently accomplished by existing businesses?

- ☐ If your business is already operational, what are its age, history, past successes, and past problem resolutions?

Legal Structure

The legal structure subsection of your business description section should answer the following questions:

- ☐ What is your business's legal structure?

- ☐ Why have you chosen this form over others?

Location

The location subsection of your business description section should answer the following questions:

- ☐ Does your business operate at a conventional "brick-and-mortar" physical location, as a mobile site, or online via the internet?

- ☐ If you will need a physical location from which you operate your business, have you selected one? If so, list your business address.

  - ☐ What will this location cost?

  - ☐ What are the location's city, state, and immediate surroundings?

☐ What features did/will you examine while selecting your business's location?

Financing

The financing subsection of your business description section should answer the following questions:

☐ Will you be submitting your business plan to investors?

☐ How much funding are you requesting? How will funding be used?

Assets

The assets subsection of your business description section should answer the following questions:

☐ Do you already own any of the physical or financial assets you will need to start your business? If so, list your assets.

☐ If applicable, what additional assets will your business require to operate successfully?

Company Objectives

Your company objectives can relate to any aspect of your business operations. Common company objectives might include growing brands, opening new store locations, or increasing sales by specified quantities. Regardless of what your long-term goals may be, ensure they are specifically defined, measurable by predetermined criteria, realistically attainable, relevant to your business, and achievable within timely manner. This subsection can enhance your readers' understanding of your hopes for your company, and what actions you will take to achieve these objectives. The company objectives subsection of your business description section should answer the following questions:

☐ What are your business's precise goals or objectives?

☐ What are your plans to achieve these goals or objectives?

☐ What resources will you need to achieve these goals?

☐ Why did you set these specific goals?

☐ How will you measure these goals or objectives?

☐ When will your goals or objectives be achieved?

☐ What are the potential barriers to your success, and how will you overcome them?

You know your business better than anyone else. Your readers and potential investors, however, only know what you write in your business plan. Do not assume they will be able to fully understand and "fill in the gaps" based on existing industry standards. Instead, view your business description from an outsider's perspective. Ask yourself, "Have I answered all the questions my readers might have about this business?"

The business description offers you an opportunity to express your enthusiasm for your business concept. The more specific details you include in this section, the greater the likelihood that potential investors and other entrepreneurs will share in your optimism.

Products and Services

The products and services section is a critical part of your business plan. This section will provide investors with an overview of the goods your business plans on offering your customers. Your investors will want to know as much about your company's product as possible, as this information can help them determine if your business is a venture worth investing in. "While writing this business plan," says Williams, "I had to impress my readers with good, solid information about my company's services and why customers will want to purchase services from my company and not those of my competitors. I had to also lay out a marketing plan as part of this portion of the business plan. I had to answer the following questions: Who will my customers be? What are the demographics of my audience? How will I attract and retain enough customers to make a profit? What methods will I use to capture my audience? What sets Asherone Group apart from the competition? These are hard questions, but to answer them was even harder. I had to do research to get my best answers."

Thoroughly detail this section of your business plan, as your readers may be unaware of your products or services. Ensure all product or service components are completely defined, as this can minimize any misunderstandings your audience may have. Be sure to keep your language in this section as clear and concise as possible. Avoid using technical jargon, as this may cause readers to lose interest in your business plan. In order to accurately detail your business's offerings, the products and services portion of your business plan should include the following subsections, outlined in greater detail below: products and services description, product lifecycle, competitive advantage, business process, and future endeavors.

Products and Services Description

The products and services description subsection of your products and services section should answer the following questions:

- ☐ What products or services will your company market? Describe each product or service, then answer the following questions for each:

  - ☐ How will this product or service fill potential customers' needs? What features make this product or service desirable to potential customers? Include any functional and emotional benefits.

  - ☐ What are the capabilities and functions of this product or service?

  - ☐ What are the minimum functional requirements and quality attributes of this product or service?

  - ☐ What legal or technical considerations, such as patents, copyrights, or trademarks, will be associated with this product or service? Note any intellectual property plans. Include any documentation of intellectual property in the appendix section of your business plan.

  - ☐ What variations of this product or service will be available?

  - ☐ What will this product or service cost your customers? How was this price determined?

  - ☐ If you will be required to order supplies from other companies to provide your product or service, list the suppliers you will purchase from.

  - ☐ If applicable, how will this product be packaged?

  - ☐ If applicable, discuss this product's current stage of development. Is this product being manufactured, or already produced? Do you already have an inventory? Include a timeline of your estimated product development schedule.

  - ☐ If applicable, provide a description of the product's physical characteristics, as well as its components and interfaces. Include and clearly label a photograph, diagram, or brochure in the appendix section of your business plan.

Product Lifecycle

If applicable, detail every stage of the lifecycle of your product or service. All products have lifecycles, which can typically be summarized according to the following five stages:

1. **Development:** This stage occurs before sales, when the product is being created and tested for validation of its demand potential.

2. **Market introduction:** This stage occurs when the product or service is introduced into the market. This stage is characterized by higher

production costs, slower sales volume, and little revenue generation. During this stage, demand may be created as customers are educated and prompted to purchase the product or service.

3. **Growth:** This stage is characterized by decreased production costs, dramatic sales volume improvement, and recognized profitability. During this stage, threatened competition might result in lower prices, special promotions, and possible investment in your business.

4. **Maturity:** This stage occurs when your business reaches its peak sales volume and market saturation. This stage is characterized by reduced production costs as a byproduct of high sales volume. During this stage, other competitors may enter the market and reduce industry profits.

5. **Decline:** This stage occurs when sales volume declines, which results in diminished price and profitability. During this stage, profit is determined by production and distribution efficiency rather than sales effectiveness.

These product stages reveal the following truth about all products: they have limited lives, and a company must continually seek new ways to keep it relevant in the market. This impermanence explains why you may see so many "new and improved" markings on products, or companies rebranding themselves to appeal to new customers.

Competitive Advantage

The competitive advantage subsection of your products and services section gives you the opportunity to demonstrate how your product or service is superior to similar items offered by your competition. The competitive advantage subsection of your products and services section should answer the following questions:

☐ How are your products or services different from existing products or services?

☐ How will you convince customers to purchase from your business rather than from your competitors?

☐ Will your product or service save the customer time?

☐ Will your product or service offer your customers a price advantage?

☐ Does your company offer customers an easier purchasing experience compared to your competitors?

☐ Does your company offer customers greater product variety?

☐ Does your product last longer than other products that are currently on the market?

Business Process

Indicate that your business will utilize an efficient and productive organizational process to create consistently high-quality products or services. This process should describe all steps taken, from planning and implementation to delivering the product or service to the customer. The business process subsection of your products and services section should answer the following questions:

- [ ] What tools, technologies, resources, and other materials are necessary for fulfilling process needs and objectives?

- [ ] Will process resources originate from within the organization, or will you require external vendors?

- [ ] Which employees or team members will be involved in the business process?

Future Endeavors

The future endeavors subsection of your products and services section should answer the following questions:

- [ ] Will you market additional products or services in the future? If so, what will the new offerings be? Outline the proposed timeline for implementing the new products or services.

- [ ] Will your business serve as a subcontractor to larger organizations? Discuss this possibility.

- [ ] What advantages, challenges, and opportunities might your business encounter after the release of your product or service?

Your investors will pay careful attention to information regarding your product or service. Elaborating upon this section to ensure your investors will not be left with a single question about your business's product or service.

Market Analysis

The market analysis section of your business plan should contain a description and analysis of potential customers within your market. This section will explain to readers who your customers are, where they are located, what factors lead them to make purchases, and how your business will capitalize on these findings.

In addition to analyzing your customer base, you may also include additional information about your competition. Use the industry research performed when you read Chapter 2 to demonstrate to readers you have a firm understanding of your competition and how your business will differ from theirs. The marketplace evaluation portion of your business plan should include the following subsections, outlined in greater detail below: industry analysis, industry growth, target market, market share, marketing strategies, presentation and branding, selling tactics, pricing strategy, and distribution channel.

Industry Analysis

The industry analysis subsection of your market analysis section gives your readers the opportunity to understand the intricacies of your business's industry. The industry analysis subsection of your market analysis section should answer the following questions:

☐ What is your business industry's Standard Industrial Classification (SIC) code?

☐ What is your business's North American Industry Classification System (NAICS) code?

☐ What risks are inherent in start-up businesses in your industry? How do technologies, industry trends, government regulations, economic factors, raw materials, or labor availability affect your business?

☐ What is your business industry's history? Briefly describe this, using no more than one paragraph.

  ☐ When did your industry begin? What caused this development?

  ☐ How large is your industry today?

  ☐ How large is your industry projected to be within three years? How large is it projected to be within ten years?

☐ If applicable, what regulatory requirements, such as federal, state, or local laws, are associated with your industry?

  ☐ If applicable, what changes do you anticipate in these regulatory requirements? How will these changes affect your business?

Industry Growth

Provide an estimate of how your industry, and therefore your company, is expected to grow over the long term. As a new business, you have the advantage of access to historical data, which may be used to determine how your competitors have performed in your industry. This historical data, which may include current sales or projected industry growth, can convince potential investors and lenders of your business's likelihood of growth. Many informational resources are available at your local library or online. To gather information about your competitors' performances in your industry, refer to the following historical data resources:

- ✔ Standard & Poor's Industry Surveys

- ✔ US Industry & Trade Outlook

- ✔ Encyclopedia of Emerging Industries (Gale Research)

- ✔ Encyclopedia of American Industries (Gale Research)

- ✔ Hoover's Online (hoovers.com)

- ✔ Market Research (marketresearch.com)

- ✔ Industry Trade-Association websites

Target Market

Provide as much information as possible about your target market. The target market subsection of your market analysis section should answer the following questions:

- ☐ Who are your target customers? Describe each customer segment, then answer the following questions for each:

    - ☐ What ages, ethnicities, occupations, and other key demographic factors will you be targeting?

    - ☐ What are this customer segment's needs, and how will your company fill those requirements? Highlight concrete information that justifies the need for your business.

    - ☐ What are this customer segment's income and spending habits?

    - ☐ What are the attitudes and aspirations within this customer segment, and how will you market to them?

    - ☐ What influences this customer segment's purchasing decisions?

    - ☐ How much will this customer segment grow or decline in three years? How much will it grow or decline in ten years? What evidence leads you to this prediction?

- ☐ What percentage of your business revenue will come from each segment of your target market?

☐ What is your location in relation to the geographic distribution of your target market?

☐ What seasonal or cyclical trends will you consider?

☐ Why will your target market purchase products or services from you rather than from your competitors?

In addition to explaining your target market and customer segments, consider including a pie chart or similar diagram to visually display what percentages of your sales will originate from each segment of your target market.

Market Share

Your market share is the percentage of the target market that you expect will become your customers. If you are the only business of your kind, you can expect near a 100 percent market share, as no other businesses are competing for your target market. On the other hand, if you have many large competitors, you may only capture a small percentage of the market.

Remember to consider only the area in which your business will operate. If you are operating in a small local area, consider those numbers only in your market share estimates. However, if you are operating nationally or even globally, consider all the potential customers in those ranges. The market share subsection of your market analysis section should answer the following questions:

☐ How many potential customers are in your area of operation?

    ☐ What percentage of those potential customers are your competitors' market shares? If you have multiple direct competitors, include an estimate for each.

    ☐ What percentage of those potential customers do you expect will become your market share?

☐ What is your strategy for capturing customers from your competition?

☐ What businesses are your direct competitors? Name your top three to five competitors, then answer the following questions for each:

    ☐ What products or services does this competitor offer?

    ☐ What is this competitor's size and profitability?

    ☐ What is this competitor's market strategy?

    ☐ What are the strengths of this competitor, and how do they compare to your business's strengths?

☐ What are the weaknesses of this competitor, and how do they compare to your business's weaknesses?

☐ How does this competitor's pricing compare with yours?

In addition to explaining your market share, consider including a pie chart or similar diagram to visually display your market share in comparison to the market share of your competitors.

Marketing Strategies

Regarding her marketing strategy, Williams says, "I had to show strategies in my business plans for how Asherone Group will compete in the marketplace, through an analysis of what my competition lacks, and anticipate potential problems so I can solve them before they become disasters." This information was critical to her explanation of how her business would be successful.

The marketing strategies subsection of your market analysis section should answer the following questions:

☐ What strategies and tactics will you use to break into your industry?

☐ What tools or media will you use to advertise? Is this choice standard in your industry?

☐ What is your marketing budget? How will you fund marketing costs including fees, materials, travel, or other related costs?

☐ What will your advertising message be?

☐ When will you implement promotions or various marketing strategies? If applicable, include specific dates and scheduling goals.

☐ How will you generate publicity for your business and its products or services?

☐ If you are operating a physical store, what traffic patterns will bring customers to your site of operation?

☐ If you are operating an online store or business, what is your strategy for drawing online traffic to your website?

☐ If you are operating a mobile business, or if your business does not draw traffic in the ways listed above, explain how you will draw customers to your business.

Additionally, you should discuss your market dominance strategy and explain why this choice best fits your business. Market dominance strategies typically belong to one of the following four options:

- **Leader:** This strategy places you as a leader in the market, asserting your product or service.

- **Challenger:** This strategy places you as a challenger to the rest of the market's methods or products.

- **Follower:** This strategy places you as a follower of the successful methods or products of the competition.

- **Niche:** This strategy places you in pursuit of a niche market that has not yet had its wants or needs fulfilled.

Also, describe your generic marketing strategy and explain your rationale. Generic marketing strategies typically belong to one of the following three options:

- **Product differentiation:** This strategy implies that you will differentiate your product or service from the remainder of the market. If this is your strategy, how will you accomplish this?

- **Cost leadership:** This strategy implies you will lead the market in providing the best cost and pricing of your product or service.

- **Market segmentation:** This strategy implies you will divide the market into different customer segments, then use target marketing strategies to focus your sales attempts.

Presentation and Branding

The presentation and branding subsection of your market analysis section should answer the following questions:

☐ What is your company's name? If applicable, explain its meaning.

☐ Do you have a logo? If so, include this in the appendix section of your business plan.

☐ How will your customers obtain your products or services?

☐ Has your target market been introduced to your product or service? If so, what were your potential customers' reactions?

☐ Will you distinguish your product or service based on quality, price, customer service, or another factor?

Selling Tactics

Discuss your major sales emphasis, explain why you opted to focus on this aspect of your product or service, then explain how you will ensure your decision is implemented. Selling tactics belong to one of the following five options:

- **Customer service:** This tactic involves focusing on serving the customer to your best ability.

- **Customer philosophy:** This tactic involves offering a unique perspective on customer interactions.

- **Lowest price:** This tactic involves leading the market with competitively low pricing.

- **Convenience:** This tactic involves offering a product or service that is easier-to-use, or more readily available, compared to your competitors'.

- **Other:** If your selling tactic does not fit with the above for strategies, elaborate on your approach to selling.

Pricing Strategy

Discuss the pricing strategy you will employ and explain how this strategy fits your business. Pricing strategies belong to one of the following three options:

- **Cost Plus:** Pricing is determined by the costs of obtaining or producing your product or service, with an added value for profit.

- **Value Based:** Pricing is determined by your competitive advantage, brand, and perceived value.

- **Other:** If your pricing strategy does not fit with the above two pricing models, explain your alternative pricing strategy.

Additionally, the pricing strategy subsection of your market analysis section should answer the following questions:

☐ What discounts will you offer?

☐ What warrantees or guarantees will you offer?

☐ What is your return policy?

☐ Will you offer rebates?

☐ If you will allow customers to pay on credit, what are your credit terms?

Distribution Channel

Discuss all distribution channels you will operate, then explain how you made your selection. Discuss the advantages and disadvantages of each distribution channel in the context of your specific business. Also, describe how you will ensure your decisions are implemented. Distribution channels typically involve one or a combination of the following options:

- **Direct:** You will market and sell your products or services directly to the customer from a fixed location.

- **Executive selling:** You will sell products or services by marketing directly to executives of other companies.

- **Manufacturers' representatives:** You will employ sales agents who market your products to wholesale and retail customers.

- **Distributor:** You will be (or employ) an agent who supplies products to retail businesses.

- **National chain (retailers):** You will have several retail locations across the nation which all share a single central management and standardized methods.

- **Regional chain (retailers):** You will have several retail locations locally, which all have a single central management and standardized methods.

- **Independent (retailers):** You will own an independent store, hold yourself entirely responsible for it, and take care of the business' setup and needs independently.

- **Mail order (retailers):** You will sell products to customers via mail, marketing using tactics such as a catalogue.

- **Internet (retailers):** You will market and sell your products or services via the internet.

Organization and Management

Your employees are the foundation of your business. The organization and management section of your business plan will describe to your readers and potential investors your employees' relevant experience, credentials, and more. "Writing this business plan has forced me to determine the key personnel that I would need in order to run the company," Williams notes. "Since Asherone Group is a small start-up business, investors will scrutinize the people behind the business. Having information about key personnel is an important portion of a business plan. This part of the business plan is often misrepresented because it is not a long and detailed biography of each person involved but an accurate account of what they've done and what they bring to the table for this specific business opportunity."

The organization and management portion of your business plan should include the following subsections, outlined in greater detail below: employee roles and responsibilities, daily operations, and accommodations.

Employee Roles and Responsibilities

The employee roles and responsibilities subsection of your organization and management section should answer the following questions:

☐ Who are your company's primary decision makers? Introduce these individuals, then include the following information for each. If possible, include each employee's resume in the appendix section of your business plan.

    ☐ Name

    ☐ Position in new business

    ☐ Job description

    ☐ Primary duties

    ☐ Authority

    ☐ Educational Background

    ☐ Unique experience and skills relevant to the position

    ☐ Prior employment

    ☐ Industry recognition

    ☐ Community involvement

    ☐ Employee start date

    ☐ Compensation

    ☐ Ownership percentage

☐ Who will be involved in your business? Include a list of all your business's in-house employees (organized by position), key personnel, and support staff. Include the employees you listed above, as well as any external staff, such as an attorney, accountant, banker, or business advisor. Include the following information for each:

    ☐ Job responsibilities

    ☐ Relevant credentials and experience

    ☐ Employment status (full-time, part-time, or temporary)

    ☐ Pay rates (wages, salary, overtime, or commission)

    ☐ Benefits

    ☐ Total cost of this employee

☐ Will you need more employees in the future? If so, when will you need them, and what roles need to be filled?

☐ If applicable, how will you obtain workers with the specific skillsets your business requires?

☐ If applicable, what skills or knowledge will you or any of your employees require to successfully run your business? Describe the required training, its provider, dates, and costs.

Daily Operations

In the daily operations subsection of your organization and management section, discuss the daily considerations required for operating your business. Although every day may not be the same within your business, describe the typical process you will use for each customer. Include the entirety of your interaction with each customer, from first approach, to sale, to delivery of the product, to any follow-up or maintenance. The daily operation subsection of your organization and management section should answer the following questions:

☐ What is the standard operating procedure for the provision of each product or service you offer?

☐ What are the proposed daily and weekly schedules of operation?

☐ If applicable, what is the average production time from quote or estimate to the completion of the order?

☐ If applicable, what legal requirements must be met for your business's operation? Legal considerations might include licensing and bonding requirements, permits, health regulations, environmental regulations, industry-specific regulations, zoning or building code requirements, or insurance coverage. Consider these requirements on a federal, state, and local level.

Accommodations

The accommodations subsection of your organization and management section should answer the following question:

☐ Would your business likely, or likely not, qualify as "socially and economically disadvantaged" under the Small Business Act (15 USC 637)? Have you researched this certification, or contacted SBA regarding it?

Financial Management

The financial management section of the business plan will allow you to detail your financial information and funding needs, as well as your income statement, cash flow statement, and sales forecast. This section will be of keen interest to potential investors, as they will want to know about your company's financial health. In fact, you may find it extremely difficult to obtain loans or investments without first disclosing the information included in this section.

If your business is starting for the first time, your financial management section should project at least three years into the future from your intended start date. If your business has already started, your financial information should account for any existing balance sheets, income statements, and personal and business tax returns for up to the past three years. We recommend you divide your financial projections into monthly increments for the first year the business is operating, as this can ease the burden of research. You may then expand to reporting on quarterly increments for the second year of operation, then to one annual increment for the third year of operation.

Creating the financial management section of the business plan involves making educated estimates on how much capital your business will require to operate, and how much profit your business could realistically make. Formulating this section can be one of the most challenging aspects of creating a business plan because a great deal of in-depth research, realistic financial projections, and supporting data must be included. If you have trouble with this section, consider seeking the expertise of a professional accountant.

If you are starting your business and have not yet collected data on your sales, you may need to investigate your competition to generate estimates. Consider visiting your competitors' websites and utilizing their annual financial reports, or visiting your state's sales tax agency website for similar information. You might also generate estimates based upon measures relevant to your industry. For example, in the retail business, calculations are performed based on the square footage of the store area. These methods can provide you with accurate information that leads to a compelling financial management section.

Entrepreneurs should keep in mind that a business plan is a continually edited and updated "living" document. A business plan is likely to change over the course of the company's lifetime, so there is no need to pressure yourself to create a perfect business plan on your first draft. For example, you may discover that new industry research forces you to change your marketplace evaluations, or you may realize that you need more capital until your business becomes self-sustaining. Regardless of the edits you might need to make, your business plan will evolve and grow over time, just as your expertise and experience as a business owner will continuously improve.

Now that we have discussed what you can expect while assembling the financial management section of your business plan, let us continue by outlining the creation of this portion. The financial management portion of your business plan should include the following subsections, outlined in greater detail below: financial information, funding, income (profit-and-loss) statement, cash flow statement, sales forecast, balance sheet, and break-even analysis.

Financial Information

The financial information subsection of your financial projections section will include information regarding starting, owning, and running your business. This section should be as detailed as possible, as this section is vital to displaying your business's financial solvency. The financial information subsection of your financial projections section should answer the following questions:

☐ Who will your business bank with?

☐ How will customers pay for your products or services? If you will accept credit, how would you overcome the issue of bad debt?

☐ If your business is not successful immediately, how will you absorb financial losses in the first few years of operation?

☐ If applicable, discuss any financial highlights that your business or its market has experienced.

Funding

The funding subsection of your financial management section will explain how you will find the necessary capital for acquiring a workspace, investing in technologies and equipment, hiring employees, and otherwise starting your business. Finding and justifying start-up capital proves difficult for many new entrepreneurs, including Williams: "I had to provide an estimate of my start-up costs, and how much I would need to invest or finance. How is my credit? Can I get a loan for my business? What financial institution will I go to for loans or grants? What are the terms of the loan that I will get for my business?" These questions and more helped her shape the funding section of her business plan.

The funding subsection of your financial management section should answer the following questions:

☐ How will you be funding your start-up? Will you be using personal equity? Will you require loans from friends or family members, personal loans from banks, loans through development agencies, or capital from private investors?

☐ If you cannot obtain a business loan or capital investment, will you still be able to run your business? How will you work around this potential challenge?

☐ If you are taking out a loan, what is the loan amount and proposed terms of repayment?

☐ If you are accepting capital investment, who are your projected or current investors?

Additionally, consider including the following information in the funding subsection of your financial management section:

☐ Outline your capital opportunities in a sources and uses statement, which lists all the capital opportunities available to you and projects how this funding will be used in a detailed monthly analysis for the first year of operation, a quarterly analysis for the second year, and an annual outlook for the third year.

☐ If you are taking out loans, outline any repayment plans. Potential investors and lenders will avoid losing their money, so they will be curious about how you plan to pay back the capital you borrow. Regardless of the type of loan you take, outline precisely how you plan on paying back the loan and any interest that accrues. A lending institution can provide you with the legal paperwork you may need, while an attorney can help you work out a repayment plan for any complex loans.

☐ If you are taking loans from a friend or family member, create a promissory note, a legal contract that guarantees your agreement to the terms of the loan and repayment by a specific date. This promissory note must include the following information:

    ☐ The names of the lender and borrower

    ☐ The contact information for both the lender and borrower

    ☐ The amount of money loaned to the borrower

    ☐ The repayment terms, including any interest that must be repaid

    ☐ The start date of the loan

    ☐ The date by which the full loan should be repaid

☐ The amount of money that will be paid weekly, monthly, or yearly

☐ The legal penalties for defaulting on the loan

Have any verbal amendments to the contract implemented in writing and signed by both parties.

Income (Profit-and-Loss) Statement

Williams also recalls the importance of proving to potential investors that your organization will be successful. "I had to determine whether my business has a chance of making a good profit," she says. "We all have ideas that we think are profitable. Writing a business plan forced me to pull these ideas out of my head and write out every detail to determine if this company will be profitable." The income statement, also known as a profit-and-loss statement or P&L statement, represents the relationship between income and expenses during a specified period of time. Common time periods include monthly, quarterly, and annually. Where the balance sheet exhibits your business's financial condition at a single point in time, the income statement displays sales and expense activities across a duration of time. To create your income statement, take the following steps:

1. **Determine your total revenue during the time period being analyzed.**

2. **Determine your total cost of your business's products or services provided during the time period being analyzed.** This value might include the costs of raw materials, inventory, shipping expenses, and other expenses associated with the production and delivery of your product or service.

3. **Calculate your business's gross profit during the time period being analyzed by subtracting your total cost of products or services provided from your total revenue within this time period.** This formula is as follows:

   Gross profit
   = Total revenue – Total cost of products or services provided

4. **Determine your total fixed operating expenses.** This value might include the costs of rent, insurance, utilities, permits, licenses, and other expenses that occur regularly at the same rate.

5. **Determine your total variable operating expenses.** This value might include the costs you can control, or costs that vary according to your business's sales, such as wages, payroll, accounting services, legal

services, advertising, travel, and other miscellaneous expenses that you may determine.

6. **Calculate your business's total expenses during the time period being analyzed by adding your total fixed operating expenses to your total controllable operating expenses.** This formula is as follows:

> Total expenses
> = Total fixed expenses + Total controllable expenses

7. **Calculate your business's net profit/loss before taxes by subtracting your total expenses from your gross profit.** This formula is as follows:

> Net profit/loss before taxes
> = Gross profit – Total expenses

8. **Determine the taxes your business will pay during the time period being analyzed.**

9. **Calculate your business's net profit/loss after taxes by subtracting your taxes paid from your net profit/loss before taxes.** This formula is as follows:

> Net profit/loss after taxes
> = Net profit/loss before taxes – Taxes

For additional assistance in creating your income statement, see the following template:

	Jan	Feb	Mar	Apr	May	Jun	Jul	Aug	Sep	Oct	Nov	Dec
Total Revenue												
Cost of Products and Services												
Raw Material Costs												
Manufacturing Costs												
Inventory												
Packaging												
Shipping												
Wages (and Payroll Tax)												
Sales Commissions												
Etc.												
Gross Profit												
Fixed Operating Expenses												
Supplies												
Rent												
Utilities												
Loan Payments												
Insurance												
Licenses and Permits												
Dues and Subscriptions												
Depreciation												
Etc.												
Variable Operating Expenses												
Advertising												

Travel Expenses												
Maintenance and Repairs												
Accounting Expenses												
Legal Expenses												
Salaries (and Payroll Tax)												
Etc.												
Total Expenses												
Net Income (Before Taxes)												
Taxes												
Federal Taxes												
State Taxes												
Local Taxes												
Net Income (After Taxes)												

Cash Flow Statement

The cash flow statement highlights how much money is entering and exiting your business. This statement also serves as a projection of how much money you will require to cover your business's expenses. For start-ups, the cash flow statement should be divided into monthly increments for the first year of operation, quarterly increments for the second year, and annually for the third. The cash-flow statement can set potential investors' expectations for the realistic uptrends and downtrends in your industry sales. To create your cash flow statement, take the following steps:

1. **Determine your starting cash balance.**

2. **Determine your cash received (inflows).** This value might include the cash sales, accounts receivable, loans, investments, and other capital entering your business.

3. **Determine your cash disbursed (outflows).** This value might include equipment purchases, expenses paid, inventory, and other payments made by your business.

4. **Calculate your business's ending cash balance by adding your beginning cash balance to your cash inflows, then subtracting your cash outflows.** This formula is as follows:

   Ending cash balance
   = Starting cash balance + Cash inflows − Cash outflows

Having a high ending cash balance can allow an entrepreneur to pay for necessary and unexpected expenses. If your cash flow statement predicts your business will run at a deficit for several months of the year, you must find methods for compensating for this deficit. For example, you might decide to save surplus cash from prosperous months for less successful months.

For additional assistance in creating your cash flow statement, see the following template:

	Jan	Feb	Mar	Apr	May	Jun	Jul	Aug	Sep	Oct	Nov	Dec
Starting Cash Balance												
Cash Received (Inflows)												
Cash Sales												
Accounts Receivable												
Investments												
Loans												
Etc.												
Cash Disbursed (Outflows)												
Raw Material Costs												
Manufacturing Costs												
Inventory												
Packaging												
Shipping												
Supplies												
Rent												
Utilities												
Loan Payments												
Insurance												
Licenses and Permits												
Dues and Subscriptions												
Advertising												
Travel Expenses												
Maintenance and Repairs												

Accounting Expenses	Legal Expenses	Payroll (and Taxes)	Sales Commissions	Employee Benefits	Federal Taxes	State Taxes	Local Taxes	Etc.	Ending Cash Balance

Sales Forecast

This sales forecast aids readers of your business plan and potential investors in better expecting the success of your customer sales. Additionally, this subsection reveals your company's potential for expenses, profits, and growth. The sales forecast is a fundamental component of the financial plan, and it may aid business owners in tracking the success of their companies. Be sure to use develop your sales forecast with well-researched, educated, and realistic estimates, then revise this document as necessary. To create your sales forecast, take the following steps:

1. **Determine your products, services, or categories.** If possible, list each product or service your business provides. Depending on you business's catalog, you may find it more efficient to summarize products or services into logical categories, such as product lines, departments, customer groups, contract types, or any other natural divisions that make sense for your business. Consider designing these categories to correspond with your accounting records, as this similarity will enable you to easily compare forecasted and actual sales.

2. **For each product, service, or category, include the following information:**

   ☐ **Name of the product, service, or category**

   ☐ **Price at which you are selling this item**

   ☐ **Cost of production (cost of goods sold, or COGS)**

   ☐ **Quantity of units you expect to sell within the analyzed time period:** Depending on your business, your units might be defined as items, hours of services rendered, contracts, or trips.

   ☐ **Maximum number of units that can be provided**

3. **Calculate the total revenue for each product, service, or category, by subtracting each item's cost of production from its price, then multiplying the difference by the quantity of items you expect to sell.** This formula is as follows:

   Total revenue per item
   = (Price – Cost of production) * Quantity you expect to sell

4. **Calculate the total revenue during the period of interest by adding the total revenue or each of your business's products, services, or categories.**

5. **Regularly compare your sales forecast to your actual sales.** Consider scheduling a routine review of your forecasted and actual sales each month.

6. **Revise your sales forecast as necessary.** Note any beneficial and costly surprises, Make corrections to your sales forecast as necessary, then revise your sales and marketing programs to take advantage of what might be working well, and change what might be working poorly. Revise your sales forecast to match any changes in assumptions regarding your customers, market, or industry.

For additional assistance in creating your sales forecast, see the following template:

	Jan	Feb	Mar	Apr	May	Jun	Jul	Aug	Sep	Oct	Nov	Dec
Item #1 Name												
Sale Price												
Production Cost												
Quantity of Sales Expected												
Maximum Sales Possible												
Item #1 Revenue												
Item #2 Name												
Sale Price												
Production Cost												
Quantity of Sales Expected												
Maximum Sales Possible												
Item #2 Revenue												
Item #3 Name												
Sale Price												
Production Cost												
Quantity of Sales Expected												
Maximum Sales Possible												
Item #3 Revenue												
Item #4 Name												
Sale Price												
Production Cost												
Quantity of Sales Expected												
Maximum Sales Possible												

Item #4 Revenue											
Item #5 Name											
Sale Price											
Production Cost											
Quantity of Sales Expected											
Maximum Sales Possible											
Item #5 Revenue											
Item #6 Name											
Sale Price											
Production Cost											
Quantity of Sales Expected											
Maximum Sales Possible											
Item #6 Revenue											
Item #7 Etc.											
Total Revenue											

Balance Sheet

Consider including a balance sheet in the financial projections section of your business plan. Potential investors may be impressed by your preparation if they find this article included in your business plan. A balance sheet is a basic document that demonstrates what you own and what you owe. This can provide potential investors with a brief record of your company's finances. To create your balance sheet, take the following steps:

1. **Collect the monetary values of all your company's assets.** These assets may include cash, accounts receivable, inventory, equipment, or any other valuable property.

2. **Find the total sum of all your company's assets.**

3. **Collect the monetary values of all your company's liabilities.** These liabilities may include current liabilities, money due to lenders and vendors within the next year, as well as long-term liabilities, payments due over following years.

4. **Find the total sum of all your company's liabilities.**

5. **Calculate your business's net worth, also called equity, by subtracting your total liabilities from your total assets.** This formula is as follows:

> Net worth (also called equity)
> = Total assets – Total liabilities

Break-Even Analysis

Consider including a break-even analysis in the financial projections section of your business plan. This analysis is particularly relevant to small business involved in manufacturing physical goods. If your business has already been operating for over one year, you may have enough information available to generate this report. The break-even analysis reveals the duration of time required for your company's sales to become equal to the company's expenditures on bills, equipment, marketing, inventory, and other business expenses. To create your breakeven analysis, take the following steps:

1. **Determine your monthly operating expenses.** These expenses typically include rent, payroll, insurance, utilities, and other expenses that occur regularly at the same rate.

2. **Determine your average cost per product or service.** This value might include the costs of raw materials, inventory, shipping expenses, and other expenses associated with the production and delivery of your product or service.

3. **Determine your average price per product or service.**

4. **Calculate your business's break-even point by dividing your total monthly fixed costs by the difference of your average price and your average cost per product or service.** This formula is as follows:

> Break-even point
> = Total fixed costs / (Average price – Average cost)

The value of this break-even point represents the number of products or services that must be sold for the business to meet the expenses of operating, before profiting. If the break-even figure seems reasonable, this may be a signal for continuing with the small business in question. On the other hand, the break-even analysis may demonstrate that the required sales for the business to sustain itself are not feasible, and therefore the business will not succeed.

Throughout all the above information, explain how you developed your projections by providing a short narrative and listing your major assumptions with any relevant research. With each of the charts described above, include an explanation that elaborates on the material each chart reveals. Remember to include three years of financial projections, dividing data into monthly increments for the first year of operation, quarterly increments for the second year, and annually for the third.

Utilize any existing information about your business, if possible. Study your past sales in detail, noting any seasonal or periodic fluctuations, their causes, and when they are expected to recur. If your business is starting for the first time, use available research and well-educated estimates. Be sure to include as many details and projections as possible, even if you have not made a single sale yet. Have a financial expert or trusted colleague review your financial projections to ensure you have performed all calculations correctly. Finally, as your business expands, be sure to revise your business plan to reflect these changes.

Appendix

The appendix section of your business plan will provide readers with any accompanying documents relevant to your business plan. The information contained in this section should support suggestions of your business's efficacy. The appendix section of your business plan might include the following items:

- Credit histories

- Resumes

- Product pictures

- Letters of reference

- Certifications

- Licenses

- Permits

- Patents

- Legal documents

- Contracts

- Any other miscellaneous supporting documents

With regard to our previous example of Keith and his software company, you now realize many of his problems could have been avoided if he had created an in-depth business plan before launching his business. Instead of constantly depleting his funding sources, Keith could have used his business plan to identify how much money he would need for his first three years in operation. This detailed prediction may have prompted investors and lenders to provide him with liquid capital, which certainly would have helped him pay necessary start-up expenses. Creating a business plan would have also prompted Keith to conduct necessary industry research and predict exactly how potential customers would react to his business. By predicting and recording customer buying behaviors, he could have determined precisely when his business was likely to break-even and begin taking profits.

A business plan—especially a complex one—will be a long document. Be sure you carefully analyze each page for spelling mistakes, grammatical errors, and any missing information that could convince investors and lenders to participate in your start-up business. Have a trusted colleague or professional review your business plan to ensure your document is ready to be showcased to investors, marketers, lenders, and other relevant readers. Taking these careful steps can ensure your business plan establishes your start-up company as a business that is guaranteed to become successful.

A well-written business plan can convince lenders, investors, and other supporters that your business can achieve success. Writing her business plan helped Williams to define tangible results that Asherone Group would deliver and explain to potential investors how she planned to achieve those results. Additionally, this document can motivate lenders and investors to provide capital for your business. Use the tools included in your business plan to strategically design your operations, for your business, for yourself, and for all your potential supporters.

Review Chapter 10

Now that you have completed Chapter 10, reflect on its content and how you will create your formal business plan. As you review this chapter, consider the following questions:

☐ Do you have a business plan? Are you currently in the stage of planning, writing, or evaluating it?

☐ Does your business plan perfectly define your business concept?

☐ Does your business plan explain your products or services, as well as any trademarks or copyrights you might own?

☐ Does your business plan thoroughly explain your marketplace with an industry analysis, an explanation of marketing strategies, and a sales forecast?

☐ Does your business plan properly explain your business's financial health with an explanation of funding sources, an income statement, and a cash flow statement?

☐ Does your business plan fully explain all relevant details of your start-up? Is there any section that remains less strong?

Be sure your business plan is appropriately detailed in all its necessary elements. If you are satisfied with your understanding of how you will create your formal business plan, resume reading with this book's conclusion.

Conclusion

Founding and running a start-up business can be an exhilarating and thoroughly rewarding experience, especially when you have prepared appropriately and taken precautionary measures to ensure its success. By employing the instructions and advice included in this book, you will grant yourself the necessary techniques and confidence for setting the foundation of a successful start-up and fully realizing your entrepreneurial dreams.

Throughout the course of this book, you also learned the histories of several entrepreneurs who created successful business models. Every one of these men and women is also a service-disabled veteran of the United States military. Let us briefly revisit these successful start-up business owners to explore how their military experiences positively impacted their entrepreneurial journeys:

***

Real-world example #1: Victoria Buggs

Victoria Buggs started her career in Human Resources, then moved into nursing. Her experience includes a combat hospital, two deployments, and her own time moonlighting to improve her skills and work part-time. When she was able to retire, she quickly realized a slow-paced lifestyle was not for her. After some consideration, she identified her business opportunity, and began work on the Center for Health Educators and Safety Specialists, LLC.

CHESS is on its way to being recognized as a premier health and safety training center. Buggs says, "We are committed to providing competent health and safety education with integrity and compassion. We started achieving this mission by becoming eligible to train and certify our customers with curricula from four nationally recognized organizations." Obtaining their curricula from diverse certifying organizations allows CHESS to fulfill all types of customer training needs: Basic Life Support, ACLS, PALS, or CPR and AED training from the American Heart Association or American Red Cross curriculum for healthcare professionals; CPR and AED training for childcare professionals; and OSHA-approved certifications through the National Safety Council for construction, transportation, and wholesale companies.

What are the most important qualities for a new entrepreneur? "Integrity, drive, and will," says Buggs. She has months where she questions herself, but her drive and persistence have gained her new customers, partnerships with new organizations, and increased revenue. "You'll have slow times for a week, sometimes for a month. When you get continuous slowness, it's normal to doubt yourself." Buggs' advice for these times is to keep pushing forward. Continue to learn, ask for help when you need it, and grow your business even through the rough patches.

***

Real-world example #2: Joshua Earsley

Joshua Earsley of Semper Fi Catering knows that discipline is one of the most important qualities an entrepreneur can have. "Remember it's not just about doing what you love. You have to be willing to grind through all the red tape in order to have the opportunity to do what you love." Earsley exercises his discipline to accomplish thorough research. "Don't start spending money on a bunch of different things without a solid plan," he advises.

Discipline will also carry you through hard times, says Earsley. "We can all get to a place where we're really excited about accomplishing a certain goal. The problem is that we can't constantly be going a hundred miles per hour. And if we slow down before getting close to our goal, which happens most of the time for big goals, it's easy to lose focus, lose that excitement, because we think, 'I did all this work and nothing is happening.' This is what separates business owners and successful business owners. The successful business owner is probably not going 100 miles per hour the whole time. But they usually keep it above 70, I would say. They're determined to get it done, even if they can't see the finish line yet. This type of determination is something that I think is required to make any business happen. I don't think that I'd have that discipline required to stay focused—to stay determined—without building it up during my time as a United States Marine."

Earsley's determination pays off not only for himself and his customers. "Big picture, I want to be known for something great," he says. After each event, Semper Fi Catering gives back: "I always make extra. Whatever is leftover—there's a veterans' homeless shelter in Fullerton. I take brisket, macaroni and cheese, coleslaw, brownies, whatever I have. I'd like to [cater] an event once every two to three weeks. That means I could get over there at least once a month." Earsley's disciplined work creates an impact that radiates outward, into his business, his family, and his community.

***

Real-world example #3: Desma Brooks

Desma Brooks has always been devoted to her career, both during her eighteen years with the Indiana National Guard and in her latest venture, community-supported agriculture (CSA) 3rd Time's A Farm. Brooks offers weekly produce subscriptions and attends farmer's markets from Richmond to Indianapolis, Illinois. Her enthusiasm for farming, fresh produce, and a healthy lifestyle is mirrored by her happy customers.

Brooks finds her most valuable customers easy to recognize: "They're the repeat ones. The ones that want to know [what's happening each week], the ones that contact me back." She loves receiving positive customer feedback on any aspect of her business operations. "One guy was so tickled—he always loved my bags, my returnable bags that we would swap out every week," she laughs, "and he was leaving me notes in the bags. 'Hey, this is great. I'm so excited!' or 'I've lost so much weight!' I knew he would come back next year." She tailors her products and services to her customers from their first interaction with the CSA: "When they sign up, I ask them what are their wants? Needs? What do they want to get out of the service? Are they trying to change their life? A lot of people are trying to change their diet." Customers with specific dietary needs and unique taste are always accommodated.

Brooks' enthusiasm is contagious, and she's happy to share it. "Veterans who are interested in farming—to me, it's great," she says, "I'm excited to keep chugging at this. I really love what I do—it definitely keeps me busy and keeps me healthy!"

***

Real-world example #4: Jonathan Mart

In Lugoff, South Carolina, Jonathan Mart and his brother Bryan are providing homeowners and commercial clients with affordable, quality concrete work. Show Me Concrete, LLC, is working hard to increase their clients' trust in contractors—and trust is increasing. "Once you start to build the reputation that we've begun to build, the work [increases] so much that it's hard to manage," says Mart, who is in charge of the administrative side of the business. "Trying to maintain our mission of giving, providing all of our customers with the customer service that we want to provide—it's tough. You're constantly on the phone or sending out emails. It gets overwhelming and stressful at times."

To stay motivated, Mart also relies heavily on the discipline he developed during his service: "After serving in the military, you have a level of discipline and focus on things that are different than other people. In the military, you have a mission; you have a goal and you're going to accomplish it. There is no other option. If you take that same mindset that they instill in you and put it towards starting a business, owning a business, running it, then it'll help out tremendously."

Mart certainly has a unique level of discipline and focus. He is still working his nine-to-five job in addition to co-founding Show Me Concrete: "[Becoming a business owner] made my life extremely crazy at first. It's started to settle down a little bit to where I'm getting more in the rhythm of everything, but it makes life a little hectic. It also, to me, makes it a little bit more enjoyable. It gives you a sense of pride and satisfaction in yourself that you accomplished something. It definitely carries over into other aspects of your life and it'll change you to a good degree, it will change how you see things and how you react to other situations that come up."

Even as a fledgling business, Show Me Concrete is already expanding to offer curbing services to commercial clients, and Mart has begun brainstorming more future endeavors: "It's ever evolving at this point. There's so many [possibilities] out there that I could pursue, it's just a matter of taking the time and the effort to put it through, to make it happen."

***

Real-world example #5: Justin Charnell

Justin Charnell and Archareer.com provide job listings, resume services, and other resources for the architecture and design industries. Charnell had been recruiting for these industries for a few years before starting, providing him a foundation for his ideas: "I was working in the architecture industry and I wanted […] to move that either from finding the candidates or to finding companies hiring." He says, "It turned into 'I want to actually just do this.'"

Charnell found that a significant roadblock to starting a business was getting initial interest from customers. "I'd say the most difficult part was getting those initial companies posting […] I think it took about two or three months before the first paid listing came on site," he recalls. Through this difficulty, he relied on his friends for their support, whether they had their own entrepreneurial journeys or not. "They might not be able to offer any advice, but just being able to vent to them. If they can offer advice, I listen to it," he says. Talking through his ideas with others helped him sort his thoughts and make better decisions.

His advice for entrepreneurs is to do your due diligence, but do not let research take away your momentum. "There's only so much research and so much reading and analysis you can do. You need real world experience with real world data." He acknowledges that this will not be easy, however: "You're going in not knowing whether this will work or not, facing the unknown and the fear." Facing the unknown head-on, even with its new stressors, has worked well for Charnell. Archareer.com has seen steady growth since its start in 2019 and is looking forward to more.

***

Real-world example #6: Jeanette Dempsey

Jeanette Dempsey of Carolina Donut Diva has one mission: customer satisfaction. "I wanted to make sure that my product was the best that could be. I love getting feedback from the customers because they like it, and they come back to get doughnuts from me, some of them weekly." The response is loud and clear: her delighted customers leave happy reviews both in person and on Carolina Donut Diva's social media. They exclaim over every feature of her donuts, from their melt-in-your-mouth lightness to the delicious array of customization options. Dempsey's mini donuts are made-to-order and available at farmers' markets and more in the Midlands region of South Carolina.

Dempsey and her son, who works with her, recognize and greatly appreciate every return customer. She knows that, regardless of how personal they seem, her business decisions impact her customers directly. As such, she always makes choices with her customers in mind. "The greatest risk for me to me is being able to provide good quality products without causing residual effects to my clients," she says, "I didn't want to sell something that wasn't the best quality and cause somebody to get sick." Dempsey protects her customers by investing in her business, ensuring the quality of her products, and protecting her equipment.

Dempsey recommends researching all the potential implications of each option before making important business decisions. "I wasn't thinking about that in the moment, I just wanted my equipment," she says, "I was willing to take that risk to do what I wanted to do. I love what I do." Despite enjoying her current success, she looks back to learn from her early choices—a good practice for any business owner. Like Dempsey, learning from your mistakes and celebrating your successes will propel your business forward.

***

Real-world example #7: Raul Lopez

At eighteen years old, Raul Lopez joined the Army. After three years of active duty and one in the National Guard, he moved to Nevada to work for the Department of Energy. Fourteen years later, restless and unfulfilled, he moved to Corpus Christi to start Faraday Electric Motors with his father. "I felt a void," Lopez says, "I knew that wasn't what I was meant to do. My granddad was an entrepreneur, my dad was an entrepreneur. I felt that drive to be a problem-solver. I wanted to be my own boss, create something great, and leave my kids something special."

His father's years of experience have proved invaluable to Faraday Electric Motors. Like any family, they have had their disagreements, but ultimately their similarities win out. "When we started making decisions, we had differences in opinion," says Lopez, "We had to start being competitive, get a feel for the market. [...] In the long run, we know each other's jobs, and I get with him on everything." Their diverse knowledge, broad range of experience, and complementary strengths form a strong foundation for the company.

For their first few months, Lopez advises future entrepreneurs, "Don't give up. A lot of doors will be slammed in your face. You're going to be told no […] it's tough at first. If you break even, count yourself blessed." Establishing yourself as a contender will depend on the quality of your work, Lopez says. "Find something that separates you," he explains, "In my industry, not everyone cares about anything other than you getting that job done. What matters is you getting the product back to them as soon as possible. You've got to know your product—master it. People will really call you out. You have to be 100% committed in all aspects of it." In Lopez' experience, persistence is one of the greatest qualities a business owner can have: "Find something the market needs and wants, and don't accept 'no'. Keep calling: 'no' becomes 'maybe,' and 'maybe' becomes 'I need you now!' Be flexible, but be persistent, and give it 100%."

***

Real-world example #8: Anita Williams

Anita Williams and her company, Asherone Group, are working hard so others can, too. "We want to get America back to work," she says, "Not only do we want to do our part in putting America back to work, [but] we want to raise the level of job satisfaction for our clients and candidates." Asherone Group's recruitment and staffing efforts focus on three positions: Database Analyst, Administrative Assistants, and Medical Records Technicians. "We get to know our clients and customers," Williams says. "We are an employment matchmaker."

Selling your business idea is similar to selling yourself as an employee, and Williams is happy to share her experience. To start, she advises using your resources: "When I first started this entrepreneurial journey, I felt like no one understood, no one could help me and that I was all by yourself. The reality was I had an amazing support group right in my network. Once I swallowed my pride and began reaching out for help, I was overwhelmed by the support and encouragement. My advice is: Don't go it alone! Call on your trusted advisers and contacts to help work through your setback and get you back in the game. People in your support system will understand."

However, even when you use your resources well, things can go wrong. Williams also advises having a plan. "A back-up plan should tell you how to deal with a crisis, failure, or defeat," she explains. "Having that plan in place will give me a quicker response time and will allow my company to bounce back a lot sooner." Williams refuses to be discouraged by setbacks. "Entrepreneurship has also helped me to develop self-confidence and a great sense of courage," she says. "Deciding to take my career into my own hands by starting my own business took a very great amount of courage." Though starting your own business is difficult, it's worthwhile: "When I wake up every morning, remembering that families are able to feed themselves and live the lives of their dreams because of my company, [it] makes me feel fulfilled."

***

Aside from their experiences in the military, these men and women all share motivation and passion for their businesses. Along their own entrepreneurial journeys, these individuals have all learned how to manage the many tasks, activities, and responsibilities of owning their businesses.

Now that you have completed Chapters 1 through 10, let us summarize its content and how you will start your own business:

- ✔ You learned how to identify the ideal business opportunity among the three main opportunities for entrepreneurs: self-run businesses, franchising opportunities, and government contracting. You discovered that viable business opportunities exist for everyone, so long as you can determine your best fit.

- ✔ You learned how to conduct industry research to determine if a market opportunity exists for your start-up business. You also learned the incredible value of identifying your market *before* launching your business, which may save you expensive resources as even the greatest business concepts must be in high-demand for them to prove successful.

- ✔ You learned how to create wanted and needed products and services by conducting market research, identifying customer requirements, and employing customer segmentation methodologies. You also learned how to technically design your products or services, set benchmarks for their performances, and establish the business process for the creation of these products or services.

- ✔ You learned how to structure your business for taxation, ownership, and legal liability purposes. Additionally, you learned the most common forms of business entities in the United States: sole proprietorships, general partnerships, S corporations, and limited liability companies. You discovered the advantages and disadvantages of each of these entities, as well as how they can impact taxes, business and personal liabilities, and record-keeping requirements.

- ✔ You learned how to reduce the risk for your business with risk and business insurance. You also learned how to research the risks most relevant to your business and find a suitable insurance plan. You realized, regardless of how successful your entrepreneurial idea may be, your business will always need to manage and mitigate its risk.

✔ You learned how to protect your start-up business's interests with an accountant, for maintaining your finances for tax purposes, and a business attorney, for minimizing legal liabilities. You also learned how to find the best financial and legal professional, how to examine the qualifications of potential business team candidates, and how to determine the scope of services needed before making hiring decisions.

✔ You learned how to place your business in an advantageous position by paying off any debts strategically, noting financial trends and potential risks, and formulating a business budget to continuously update as your business grows and develops.

✔ You learned how to use a variety of funding sources to start your business with one-time start-up expenses and initial asset purchases. You realized capital and loans are often necessary to start a business venture, and so borrowing responsibly is critical to maintaining the financial health of your business.

✔ You learned how to ensure fair business practices and legal compliance with antidiscrimination and anti-harassment laws by implementing human resources in your business. You also learned how human resources can benefit your employee recruitment, hiring, integration, and evaluation processes. You discovered a key component of human resources entails knowing your employees' rights, as well as your own rights as a start-up business owner.

✔ Finally, you learned how to create a formal business plan that navigates your business through the tumultuous first years of operation and beyond. You discovered that creating a business plan is a prerequisite to founding a profitable business and attracting needed investors. You learned that a successful business plan includes detailed descriptions of your business mission, successes, structure, products and services, market analysis, sales strategies and forecasts, funding, financial plans, operating expenses, and the amount of capital needed for the business to reach a sustainable level of financial success.

Entrepreneurship is not a natural-born instinct that is limited to only a few lucky individuals; rather, it is a skill that can be learned by anyone willing to employ the techniques in this book and learn from his or her natural mistakes. Self-employment is a viable option for anyone, so long as they possess the determination and patience required to become well-informed and fully prepared for business ownership.

Remind yourself that many people of varying conditions have

accomplished this goal before you, and that you have every reason to continue pursuing your dreams. Give yourself a chance at achieving entrepreneurial success, clarify your purpose, and thoroughly prepare yourself for any challenges ahead. Believe in your own abilities, empower yourself the same way this book has empowered you, and use the tools presented in this book, as well any outside resources available to you, to take the first steps into your new journey of start-up entrepreneurship.

About the Author

Phillip Selleh has led organizations on both national and international scales by providing management to companies including AT&T, Inc., a world leader in communications, media, entertainment, and technology; META Group, a leading information technology research and consulting firm; Computer Sciences Corporation, a provider of information technology and professional services; and Ontempo eServices, a provider of business intelligence and marketing solutions. While hospitalized at Walter Reed National Military Medical Center during military service, Phillip Selleh interacted with service members who expressed interest in transitioning to careers in business and overcoming the obstacles to achieving their goals. These interactions inspired him to found and become a board member of About Giving, Inc. A 501(c)(3) Public Charity, About Giving, Inc., provides educational opportunities and high-quality resources to severely disabled Veterans in need of assistance. Phillip Selleh earned a Master of Business Administration in Entrepreneural and International Finance from George Washington University. He also gained education and training in leadership and operations from the United States Army before retiring as a Colonel.

Phillip Selleh now dedicates his unique skills and abilities toward aiding other severely disabled Veterans with professional career development at the Center for Business Acceleration (CenterForBusinessAcceleration.com/Veteran).

www.ingramcontent.com/pod-product-compliance
Lightning Source LLC
Chambersburg PA
CBHW050815050726
47601CB00017B/266/J